Sustainable Human Development

About the Author

Dr. Kamal Taori belongs to the UP cadre of the 1968 batch of the I.A.S. He had a short stint in the Army and has doctorate in Rural entrepreneurship.

He has been with the Khadi and Village Industries Sector for nearly 12 years. This was his opportunity for a deeper understanding of Gandhi, Vinoba, Lohia and Kumarappa and to sublimate his ambition into a mission with holistic action.

A short assignment with the UNDP, and subsequent study of the United Nations system were helpful in the convergence of his life-long studies, experience and understanding into a world-view and a global vision. He is always concerned about what could have been done, as against what has been done.

A Social Science Scientific researcher and author of a number of books and research papers, he has organized and led many a seminar and workshop on a whole range of socio-economic issues and topics.

Currently he is Director, Deen Dayal Upadhyay State Institute of Rural Development, Lucknow.

Sustainable Human Development
Issues and Challenges

DR. KAMAL TAORI, *IAS*

CONCEPT PUBLISHING COMPANY, NEW DELHI - 110059

ISBN-81-7022-818-2

First Published 2000

Published and Printed by
Ashok Kumar Mittal
Concept Publishing Company
A/15-16, Commercial Block, Mohan Garden
NEW DELHI-110 059

Phones: 5648039, 5649024
Fax: 091–11–5648053
E-mail: publishing@conceptpub.com

Preface

It is a great pleasure that Concept Publishing Company asked me to compile some issues in the over all development. I have been working around unorganised sector for the last 30 years. *Sustainable Human Development* has been brought to focus by UNDP annual report and concern expressed throughout the world.

While the definition part of many aspects is becoming increasingly clear, some important issues are still missing. To utilise this opportunity, I would like to quote in original from the First Five Year Plan document chapter I, page-12, para 13, titled '*Problem of Development*'. It says:

> "In the last four or five decades, there has been considerable industrial development in India, accompanied by urbanisation and expansion of commerce. Large towns and cities have grown and transport and communications have developed extensively. The isolation of the village has been broken and the average citizen lives in an environment significantly different from the one in which he lived and worked fifty or sixty years ago. Indian enterprise has made considerable headway, and the country has now considerable experience in the fields of modern business, industry and finance. New economic and social relations have emerged, given rise in turn to a general desire for more rapid change."
>
> "It continues, but the development that has taken place is partial and limited when judged in terms

> of the country's needs and potentialities. Industrialism and the use of modern techniques have affected only limited segments of the economy. Agriculture is still the mainstay of life for about 70 per cent of the population and productivity in this sector is exceedingly low. The size of agricultural holdings has progressively diminished; the old cottage and small-scale industries have been decaying, and the rural population which constitutes about 83 per cent of the total suffers from chronic underemployment and low incomes."

Population has increased by more than fifty per cent in the last fifty years, but the growth of alternative occupations either in the rural areas or in the towns has not been on a scale which could absorb this growing population. In the limited spheres which have registered expansion, the level of productivity and the level of incomes have naturally been higher. But, for the community as a whole, the economic development of the last few decades has brought no significant improvement in standards of living and opportunities for employment, and has perhaps accentuated to some extent inequalities of income and wealth.

The above statement of fact was provided to me by Dr. K.N. Kabra, a Professor of international fame at Indian Institute of Public Administration, New Delhi. IIPA has been working in the field of Public Administration training, research, codification, consultancies in diverse field for the last 40 years. When Dr. Kabra gave me this paper following were some of the questions which came in my mind :

1. It appears that above analysis pertains not to the situation of 1950 but of 1998 when we are

on the verge of arrival of 21st century.

2. What has been the role of National Institutions in bringing out at the right time and misdirection in the policies?
3. What were the missing links?
4. What are the challenges of our time and how do we learn from our mistake of our past?

As we approach 21st entury the socialism, capitalism, mixed economy become absolutely irrelevant if humanity and win-win for all led development model is not visible. It seems that economic development in terms of GDP concept becomes irrelevant.

The challenges of 21st century require total newness on all fronts. The holistic analysis, churning of knowledge, ruthless codification of lessons of past and total transparency, viability and replicability are some essentials for clear accelerated plan of action. This is the challenge of our time which we can neglect at our cost.

Before I close, I would like to mention for every ailment under the Sun.

There is remedy or there is none
If there is one, try to find it
If there is none, never mind it.

I am thankful to Mr. Ashok Kumar Mittal and his team of Concept Publishing Company for the excellent work done professionaly.

My special thanks to Mr. Navin Sinha who has done very well in helping in comprising these chapters.

Dr. Kamal Taori

CONTENTS

Part II — TRAINING ATTITUDE

PART III — SOME POLICY ISSUES

PART - I

MARKETING ISSUES

1

Sustainable Development Options and Marketing Concept

Regarding development options, Shri Nitish Sen Gupta has brought out some interesting, disturbing, probing difficult areas into open. One cannot deny that his assertion that most of India's anti-poverty programmes in past suffer from basic weaknesses of ignoring economics and a policy was considered good because it was announced in the name of the poor is correct. His other suggestion to develop supporting measures for agriculture industry, infrastructure and spreading literacy and basic education amongst masses along with his plea for integrating in developmental option with the on-going and in some respect irreversible process of globalisation of international trade and industry are also laudable. Based on my study of our development scenario specially related to rural development, rural industrialisation, non-farming sector development and taking the holistic approach of the problem, I have the following few points for consideration.

The time has come to become less ideological and more practical oriented. In other words we can call it tactical manoeuvrability of this programme has to be understood with reference to the studied objectives. Starting programmes in the name of the poor is not bad in itself provided adequate linkages are ruthlessly ensured. The classic case of infrastructural fund utilisation in integrated rural development programme will bring out the pathetic indifference to the monitoring of funds realised. Most of the decentralised sector have used them as easy money available from below poverty line grant. Direct attack on poverty does not mean total abdication, organised extension machinery, abdication of its responsibility. One may go ahead and also request for the income generating activities in rural areas through ruthlessly entrepreneurship development and initiating the process of percolation theory working at grass-roots. This calls for, apart from attitudinal changes, the development of rural and village industries on cluster basis so that their economic viability is ensured and demonstration, impact becomes clear. This failure has caused heavily and today in the name of village industries we only have some Khadi institutions and pockets of other ISB activities which are not replicable or self-supporting because they are not market oriented. The emphasis on training for the sake of training and giving above marketing activities to individual beneficiaries have caused total loss of confidence and clamour for organised wage employed job. The same can be said in terms of technology application. While scaling up of technology and skills should have been the main theme, we started first importing technology and then wanted to scale down under the garb of developing appropriate technology. Here the loss of confidence, funds, duplication of efforts made the entire exercise redundant and to day CSIR, KVIC, CAPART are struggling hard to come to some common understanding where appropriate technologies for rural industries can be extended on a self-supporting basis. Here again the linkages have been the missing factor and training centres, good institutions all could have been used for extension, follow-up, monitoring, marketing and feedback on a permanent basis but because of the easy availability of funds all these years, the organisations has developed a vested interest and culture of working in total isolation. The plethora of organisations both governmental and NGO and their mushroom expansion for the last few years makes this point abundantly clear and we must remember they are working on grants or subsidies and have hardly any internal resource generation worth the name. It is also not uncommon to find many R&D organisations spending majority of their funds on the staff and support services. Where are the resources, time and energies left for genuine R&D work and its extension?

It is in this scenario that the question of marketing as a concept, way of life and a continuous source for quality improvement and cost reduction become relevant. Whether it is passport office, Police Station, Extension work, R&D, servicing or any related aspect, are the systems attuned to marketing and internal resource generation? Most organised organisations have cornered the reputation of worst efficient and in turn usurps of the cream of the said resources. It is these unorganised groups, institutions and units which have paid the heavy price. While talking of choice of development option not only in our country but also on third world countries probably this lesson has to be borne in mind. In this connection one senior bureaucrat of U.P. had mentioned that the administrative system that we have are notorious for neglecting the most needy person. Our training, planning, monitoring, posting, system are all geared up to serve the better of the lot. The attitudinal changes and sensitising of bureaucracies will need linkages of *Adyatma, Vigyan, Viswas* and *Stri Sakti* as the four corner stone of any developmental processes. The integration cannot be only of those nearer but has to involve those beyond vision.

Adhyatmik inculcation of these routes will broaden vision and in turn help for self-supporting, replicable, well-knit models of development. It is a fact that tactical failures on all these fronts have to be first conceptually accepted. Rural entrepreneurship has to be developed and the fact of system that of those with capacity to risk taking moved away to politics or played middle-men or indulged in hoarding, law breaking and even fast buck making has to be understood. Funding of various developmental programmes has to be gradual output based and to that extent institutionalisation or democratisation (since privatisation may be a bad way) has to be accepted as a fact of life. All round attitudes, stringency of resources will make it happen. Government must get out of all service sectors. Wherever individuals, institutions groups, women groups etc. can take over those activities they must be handed over on adequate return basis. We have all these years neglected the self-employment out of the purview and liked lop-sided attention to various unorganised programmes. Self-employment has also been developed on totally western model of funding. The cost of funding has to be more and income generation enough to return. Social cost and quality have to be made integral part of our developmental processes by adopting holistic approach. While fully agreeing with Shri Nitish Sen Gupta that national economies are getting increasingly mutually reliant creating greater opportunity than before, we should not lose sight of the fact that if a free play of market is allowed to play it is again the unorganised which may be worst sufferer. It is here State must efficiently play regulatory role and ensure proper impartial, judicious umpiring. While third world countries will be our guiding force attitudinally we will also have to develop ourselves to compete with global market forces. Today we are not working in isolation but it also does not mean that we should be guided by those organised. Blending of various factors of national ethos will be called for and '*swadeshi*' too with a modification of products coming from rural areas will have to be accepted. Quality tests and codification of replicable models of development along with encouraging those who can provide difficult linkages must be made inseparable part of any development processes. Wage earner and privatisation or democratisation has to be linked up and all those with strength be made to optimally explore time tested activities which have sustained this vast country as a nation. Last but not the least, hard work, systematic efforts and output must be rewarded sufficiently to discourage those shirkers or short-cut takers. Here identity of the target group has to be suitably accepted as a national strength and not weaknesses.

2

Sustainable Development : Real Issues

Human Development Report 1991* brings out certain essential changes perceived in the Human Development analysis and evaluation. It has received universal recognition that the formula of development which at one time solely favoured G.D.P. now leans in favour of basic human qualities of development. In 1950s excessive emphasis was on increasing productivity, shift towards heavy machines and major modes of production and organised employment. This also followed automatically urbanisation and excessive swing towards urban sectors including urban transport, urban housing, urban drainage and water systems etc. It is only in 1990s that United Nations Development Programmes have come out with the need for broadening the parameters of this evaluation of human development. It has been felt that "human development requires economic growth — for without it, no sustained improvement in human well-being is possible. But while growth is necessary for human development, it is not enough. High growth rate does not automatically translate into higher levels of human development. Firm policy action is required to forge a closer link between economic growth and human development"*. It goes on further to say that just as

---

* *Human Development Report 1991* — published by UNDP Oxford University Press, p. 1.

economic growth is necessary for human development, human development is critical to economic growth. This two-way link must be at the heart of any enlightened policy action. While elaborating they have brought out the need for re-allocating funds so scarce to most of the countries today. They also bring out that the real problem is not of awareness of the problem, but the lack of political commitment and not the financial resources which is often the real cause of human angle. While accepting that the areas requiring attention are very clearly spelt out, there is a problem of translating the conceptual clarity into an action plan for sustainable development. Many authoritatively feel that much of the current planning is misdirected and resources inefficiently used. If the priorities are set right, more money will be available for accelerated HOPE generating human progress is possible.

The purpose of the article is to bring out some of the often neglected areas arising out of short-sighted approach to development. While reports do take man as a centre of development, there is need to widen

Broadening Vision — Understanding Components of Cosmos or Brahmand

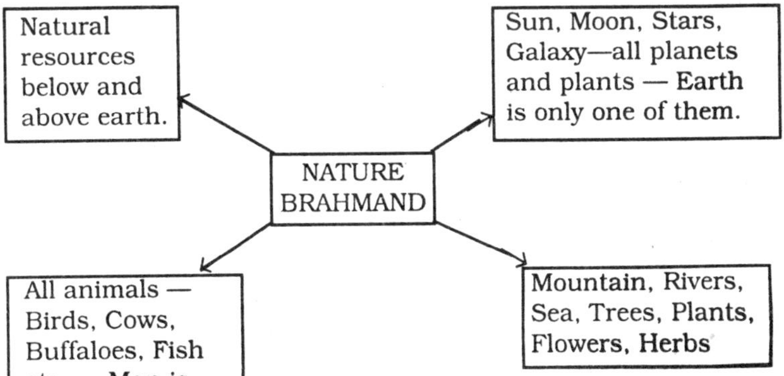

the horizon. The following chart below will illustrate the need for extending the field of vision from man to earth to cosmos:

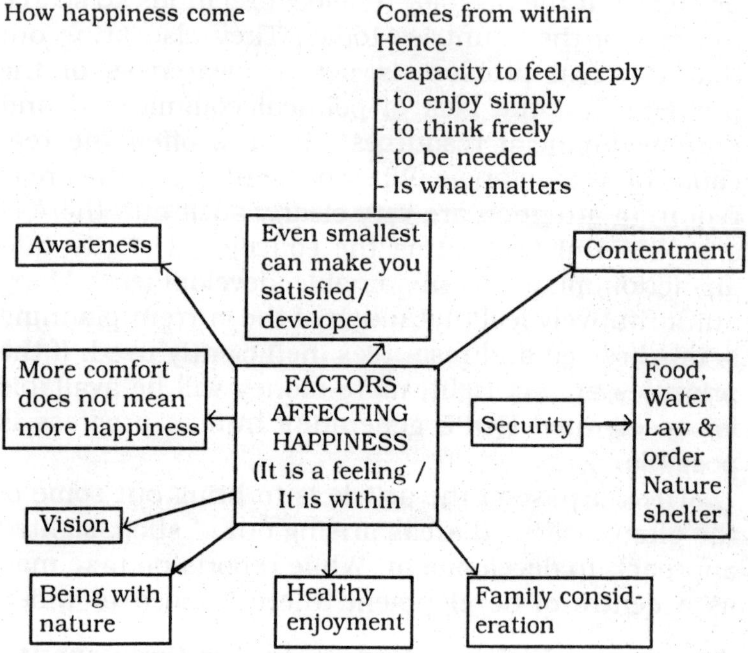

Since happiness has to come from within, hence there is need to develop capacity to feel deeply, to enjoy simply to think freely and be needed. Thus caring to sharing all that you have has to be the base of widening vision for everlasting happiness development.

Lessons of World History

Before we proceed to analyse the other aspects of development, which are excessively oriented towards material and consumeric society, it is necessary to understand clearly the well established codified lessons of the history. As per Will Durant* the following are some of the conclusions which are the result after indepth study of the History.

"Obviously historiography cannot be a science. It can only be an industry, an art, and a philosophy—an industry by narrating the facts, an art by establishing a meaningful order in the chaos of materials, a philosophy by seeking perspective and enlightenment. The present is the past rolled up for action, and the past is the present unrolled for understanding."

"Since man is a moment in astronomic time, a transient guest of the earth, a spore of his species, a scion of his race, a composite of body, character and mind, a member of a family and a community, a believer or doubter of a faith, a unit in an economy, perhaps a citizen in a state or a soldier in any army, we may ask under the corresponding heads — astronomy, geology, geography, biology, ethnology, psychology, morality, religion, economics, politics and war—what history has to say about the nature, conduct and prospects of man."

Over and above what has been said the lesson is that man never learn from history, but one has to be still positive, optimistic and HOPE for the best. "The heritage that we can now more fully transmit is richer than ever before. It is richer than that of Pericles for it includes all the Greek flowering that followed him, richer than Leonardo's for it includes him and the Italian Renaissance; richer than Voltaire's for it embraces all the French Enlightenment and its ecumenical dissemination. If progress is real despite our winning, it is not because we are born any healthier, better, or wiser than infants were in the past, but because we are born to a richer heritage,

---

* *Lessons of History* by Will Durant

born on a higher level of that pedestal which the accumulation of knowledge and art raises as the ground and support of our being. The heritage rises, and man rises in proportion as he receives it. "If a man is fortunate he will before he dies, gather up as much as he can of his civilised heritage and transmit it to his children. And to his final breath he will be grateful for this inexhaustible legacy, knowing that it is our nourishing mother and our lasting life."

Role of Planners and Attitudes

To become the right planner we have to identify certain priority bases of our attitude. Frustration, despondency, unhappiness, hopelessness do not come automatically. Confining our vision only to man is doing great harm. Glorious and living civilisation have lot to contribute for broadening of visions. There has to be a limit to exploitation of resources both of nature and man. There has to be an international consciousness control over the greed aspect. This control can be only by broadening the visions. Scientific temper, spiritual disposition will have to be understood in the context of 'VASUDEVA-KUDUMBAKAM' - world fraternity which only can be our saviour. Awakened social consciousness will be the guiding principle of future. This also means, indirectly attitudinal changes, value based management, application of inner economics and spirituality and faith. Staring faces which we see today are nothing but realisation of indication of beginning of a new era. Growing realisation that material prosperity can never be the only indicator of happiness. This leads us to invariable conclusion that it is only by broadening vision and adopting more human attitude through which sustainable development can take place.

Forming Attitudes

Human existence pre-supposes interaction among various species. The inescapable fact about a man is that he is a social being and finds it exceedingly difficult to live in isolation. This feeling though common to most living beings makes him a significant one among other socialising animals. This is the stage wherein the group concept is formed and affiliation, understanding and perception of persons are developed.

The perception of persons can be a two-way process as some studies have brought out. When a man looks at a table, the table does not look back at him. It depends on man's consciousness of himself and others that the perception may disturb or distort. The notions of other persons are influenced by the ideas which in turn are developed over experience, training, observation, treatment and teaching. In short, perception is an inference process.

Regarding attitudes, many feel that it is a mental status of readiness. More knowledgeable persons think that attitudes consist of three basic components of thinking, feeling and reacting. Indirectly it means belief which involves thoughts of persons about the topic in question. The value which relates to talking about where the person feels attracted, repelled and neutral regarding the topic in question and the third element is the pre-disposition of behaviour. This indirectly means reaction tendency.

Attitudes are formed by prejudices, experiences, learning and formation of belief, thinking or conditioning. The attitude has to play a very important role in the behaviour pattern of the individual and the society in general. The attitudes also lead to attraction, adaptation, hatred or development of certain approaches. The similarity, proximity and the nature of perceived personnel, characteristic do help in formation of attitudes. The competition and cooperation feeling developed over these concepts leading to either non-cooperative or cooperative attitudes. The leadership role also plays an important part in shaping of attitudes. This in turn leads to social value formations.

Making Best of Resources

In a traditional society trained by western concept of development, resources taken to be only economic strengths like raw material, reserves, building, training centres etc. Time has come to take a still bigger vision of the concept of resources and as Mao used to say every person who comes to birth brings with him hands, legs, eyes, ears, nose and the capacity to work. We should not consider that man comes only with mouth. The following would make this point very clear:

What all constitute : Resources?

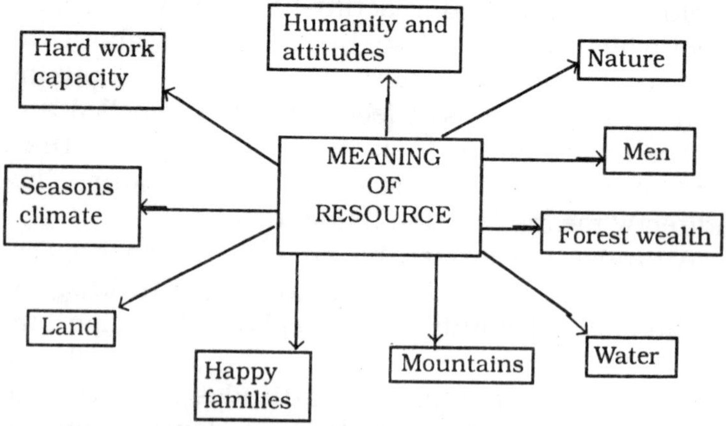

What is HOPE?

We may also take this opportunity to get conceptual clarity on the question of HOPE. While every effort must be made to bring back hope in every segment of population, it is common to hear the hopeless situation being prevalent all over. While concept of hope may differ from person to person and from time to time, there are certain common parameters by which we can judge the hope being perceived.

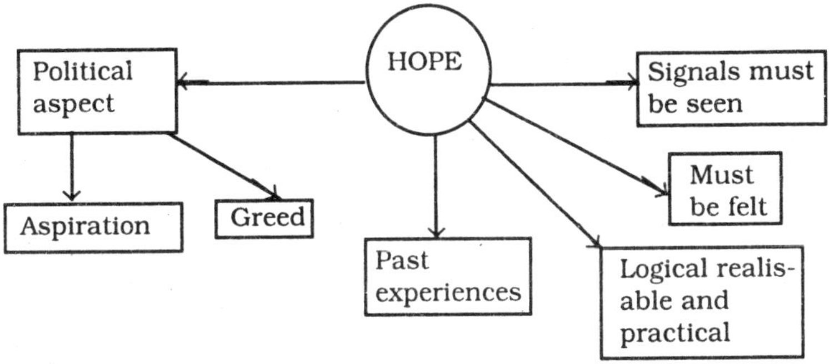

Once we are clear about HOPE, we may also like to see the impact of Hopelessness.

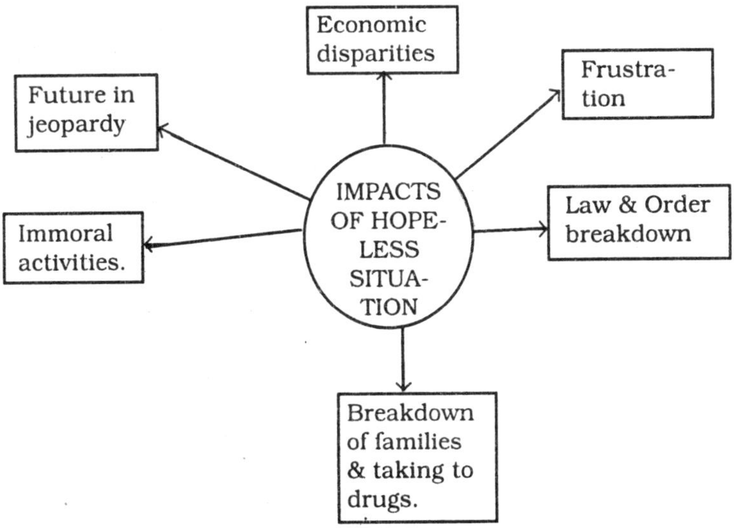

There may be other implications of HOPELESS situation, but we would like to say that for the survival of mankind it is not only that nature should remain vibrant but also that HOPELESS situation must always ruthlessly be switched over to HOPE signals.

Problem of Excessive Funds

All over the world the saints have been in favour of confining expenditure as per income. Sages all over the world in different times have brought out the wisdom living in their means. What applies to individual human beings equally applies to State management of resources and economy. After all, whatever is borrowed has ultimately to be paid. Indian ethos enjoins upon the children and grand-children to repay the loan of their fore-fathers without which they can never have the salvation. It is in this context one may try to understand the impact of excessive funds with reference to distributing, receiving and accounting maximisation. The following chart would make this partly clear:

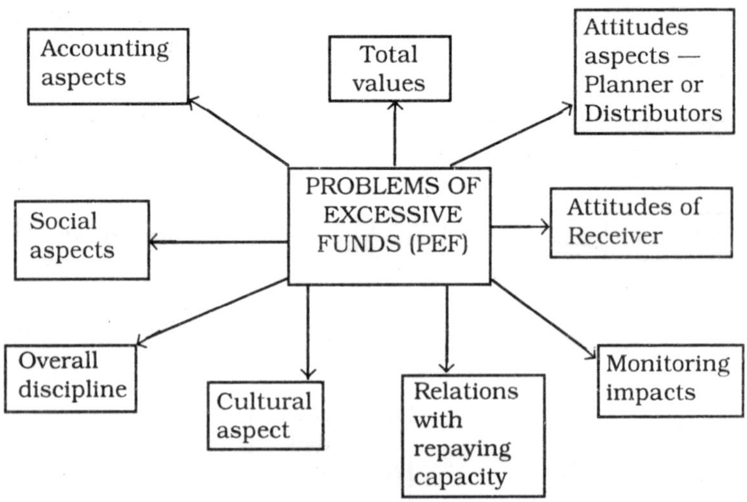

The time tested local recipe thus enjoins one and prods him towards savings and unless concerted efforts are made to generate savings and invest them fruitfully, no long term satisfaction and happiness can ever be gained.

Government Servants

Government Servants have always been in the History — a class to be watched. There are many stories and anecdotes bringing out their strength and weaknesses. They have been indispensable categories which have always been feared, admired, and equally caveated. The state has to depend on them for various regulatory, developmental, law enforcing, punishing and other duties. While they have been dreaded, they have also been liked. Many of them always over the times, served their masters faithfully. Human nature being what it is, it pre-supposes continuation of habits — both good and bad.

In a situation when funds become abundantly available and the traditional regulatory role is changed to developmental and commercial role, the following changes can be indirectly perceived:

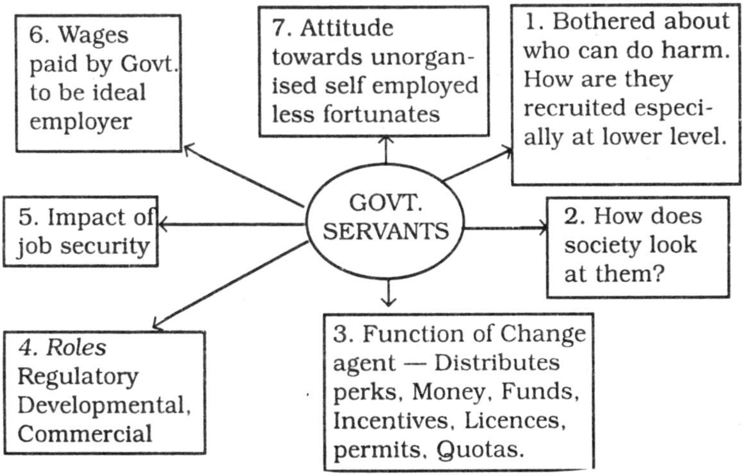

Public Finances

As the role of State developed from regulatory to developmental and more and more countries took up the work of commercialisation of field of activities through government and semi-government organisations, the question of managing public finance assumed importance. The limited role enjoined upon the Public Exchequer gave way to fantastic requirement. In a short period of years the machinery was required to bear the challenges not only to account but also in spending system with excessive emphasis on 31st March syndrome and change of value of judging performance of public servants, the attitudes switched from frugality to good and careless. The Planning Commission also has been distributing funds as per the spending capacity of the departments and no wonder that those who could not physically spend, created a number of autonomous and voluntary bodies to keep crores of rupees in this account to be utilised in the years to come. All these things are happening right under the nose of all the powers and they took it for granted that this is how the government runs. This concept of allocation, distribution, etc. gave further impetus to deterioration in the accounting and accountability of the fund manager. It has been a pity to see how it had affected the morality and attitudes of all those who matters. The impact of all these has been devastating in terms of morality, attention towards public funds, corruption and also overall deterioration in every possible aspect. The following would make some of these points clear: (see diagram on next page)

The objective to bring out the above in a chart form is to highlight how expansion in public activities affects the overall society's attitudes.

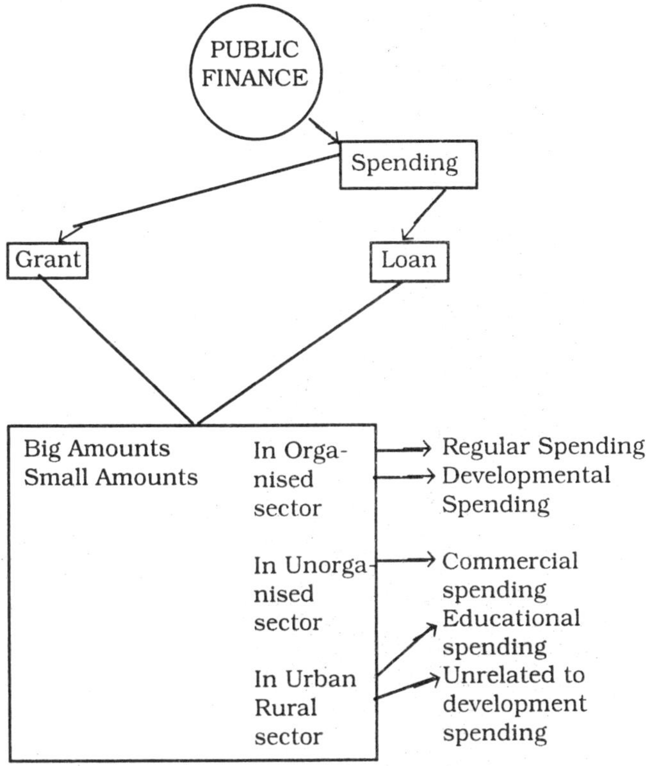

The traditional values of public finance have always hand-book brings out the policy dictum. It says that every public money should be spent as if it was one's own money. 'Do as you would like to be done unto you' — should be the underlying principle.

Some Open Secrets

To those who are familiar with Indian epics, the conversation between Yudhishtra and the Yaksha in *Mahabharat*, which speaks out the truths of life, should be a revealing one. Despite knowing very well that every one has to die one day and go back to nature from where one has come what a pity that we refuse to accept the harsh realities of life. We have come from nature and will be going back to be one with the *Panch Bhooth* — Air, Water, Earth, Fire and Sky. Needless to say the man basically is born through biological process and no different from animal. Over a period of time he improves and becomes more civilised and discrete and positive and proves himself different from other animals.

The third stage is of enlightenment which stage could only be reached by the great Rishis. But as the *Sanatana Dharma* confirms again and again any commoner can reach to that enlightened stage which ultimately results in *Nirvana* through intense "*Sadhana*". What is basically required is realisation that man cannot be the only centre of development, he has to be viewed from the cosmos angle. Man can never be happy by making other creations of God unhappy. The input of spirituality, moderation, holistic approach and economics broaden this vision render to his thoughts positiveness with harsh realities of life and help him reach glorious heights. This will be the real salvation. Only when this development growth of everybody is sustainable development will become a reality. Till such a time when the aspect of development is understood, any effort in this direction will remain only an imaginary and futile attempt.

Conclusion

The question of sustainability of development has to be understood from different angles. Whether it is the question of happiness, lessons of history, role and attitudes of planners, optimisation of resources and impact of hopeless or hopeful situation have to be understood in totality. The sustainability question has to be understood with all these backward and forward linkages. The situation do not deteriorate on their own as they cannot improve of their own. The policy planners have to have a broad vision to understand the intricacies of the policies they enunciate with reference to the target group time-frame. It is only by proper appreciation that the holistic situation that better policy with practical implementation and pragmatic appreciation would solve the long term problem of the development. The issues are much wider and need the visionary approach in today's world. Needless to say appropriate technologies, right blend of policies, active involvement of women force, right definition of economics and blending of faith and spirituality can only generate long term hope. The role of the above 5 forces have to be understood with reference to sustainable development.

3

Religion and Development

A religious man surrenders himself to a higher power may be God or Universal soul. When he surrenders himself completely to the higher power, he understands that there is nothing which works within him. Whatever he does and achieves is attributed to the higher power. Such being the case, he becomes perfect and consequently he identifies himself with one and all. He does not find any difference between him and any other creature on the earth. He, therefore, works for the benefit of the entire beings on the earth. Nobody need tell him to work. Nobody need tell him to be sincere and honest. Nobody needs to tell him to put his utmost to achieve the end results in his work. He goes on working according to his capacity and he does not take pride in the end results. He eats, drinks, sleeps and works only for the maintenance of his body which belongs to the society and the entire universe. He knows that he performs the actions with the means of his body and hence one of his duties is to keep the body in good stead by giving it the required right food and exercise, so as to make it more and more useful to the society. He has no selfish ends to be achieved either by keeping his body or by the actions it performs.

Imagine for a minute that such a person undertakes the work of producing useful goods to the society. Can he cheat the customer? Can he adulterate in his goods? Can he exploit the labourers? Can he accumulate black money? Can he sell the goods at very high rates? Can he go on advertising in the advertising media for his goods attributing far higher values in them than what they are? These are all the questions for which the answer will be 'NO'. Why? Because the person having attained such a high state of mind cannot have any selfish motive in him. It is only the persons at lower levels who can entertain selfish ends and to achieve the selfish ends, they begin all sorts of manipulations and cheating.

Let us again imagine a person of the same state of mind working as a worker in a factory. Can he come late to the factory? Can he sit idle when his boss is not present? Can he steal something from the Factory? Can he boast too much of the work he did than what he exactly did? Can he stop working because his boss did not reward him with increments or promotions? Can he instigate other employees to go on strike and put an end to the production work? Can he try to exploit the boss or the factory manager or the factory owner with blackmail? No, he cannot do. He cannot stop the work. He cannot cheat the organisation. He will always put the best out of him for the betterment of the factory.

The above two examples are very clear that if we want to turn out a better production we should have the personnel of this state of mind both at the managerial level and lower level. Again we should have persons of integrity and religious values at entrepreneur level as well. All these things are possible when the religious values are really understood and practised by the people. In such a society where such people exist, there will be no fear of thefts and terrorism. There will be harmony and happiness in the entire society. There will be no jealousy and no scope for terrorism. People will be speaking the truth and become straightforward. Cannot human society achieve such a standard or life? Yes, it can. The only condition is that the people should follow the principles and values of religion.

In all the above cases, we many times talk of religious values. Some people may ask what is this religion and what are its values. Whether all the religions are one and the same or different. If different how we define their religious values as one. For this, the answer is that the essence of all the religions in the world is one and the same and there is no difference. No religion teaches its people to rob others, kill the fellow beings, exploit the weakness of the others etc. All the religions teach the people to speak the truth, to be good to others and to do such things, by doing which he and all others will be benefited. Such being the case, there is no scope for specifying this religion or that religion and to differentiate the values in the religion. If any sect or organisation teaches otherwise than that what is stated above, that organisation or sect cannot be called a religion.

Mahatma Gandhi talked many times about Trusteeship. When he said Trusteeship, he kept in view that all properties belong to all and everybody has got a right to enjoy them, according to his need. In other words later on Vinobha Bave has termed it as "work according to capacity and take according to need". What does it mean? It means one should work putting all his abilities and energies for the benefit of the society without any reservation without aspiring for any personal benefits. Because his capacities and energies are nothing but properties of the society and hence his intelligence and physical capacities should be utilised for the benefit of the society. Everybody has got a right to take for his maintenance the things necessary for such a maintenance but not more. Work according to capacity and take according to need. If this small principal is rightly understood and followed by at least 50 per cent of the human beings on earth, the earth will not remain as earth and it will be more than heaven. In such a case nobody would like to aspire to go to heaven after death. They would all pray for being born again on the earth as human beings. Such is the power of this principle of identifying oneself with the society, working for the society without any selfish motive.

Religion awakens consciousness in the Man. When it happens consciousness alone will become a guiding factor for the Man. He cannot commit sin because he cannot find time and place where he will be away from his consciousness. Thus, he cannot do any bad things at any time. No police is required to stop him from doing anti-social work. No punishment is required to stop him from doing bad. His state of mind will be such that the moment any bad thoughts enter into his mind his consciousness revolts. His condition will be like the state of SATAN described by Milton in his book Paradise Lost:

> "Me Miserable
> Which way shall I fly
> Infinite wrath and Infinite despair
> Which way I fly is hell
> Myself am Hell".

When such will be the development of the minds of the people when they are enthused with religious values what can be said of the work that they undertake. All the great works in the world have been accomplished by persons of high state of consciousness. But for them, the world would have been poor without knowledge and benefits of science.

When the persons of such high conscious work the following things can be seen in their area of operation.

1. Corruption vanishes completely.
2. There will be more energetic work with perfection.
3. None of the workers expect any rewards for performing his duties because work itself gives inner satisfaction and happiness which is more valuable than mere physical results or awards for the work done.
4. All hoardings will stop.
5. There will be no partiality in the dealings.
6. Even the last man in the society will be respected by giving equal importance to him just like any other person in the higher occupations.

Gandhiji imagined such a society and he termed it as '*Rama Rajya*' and his constructive work was aimed at that. But unfortunately the country could not visualise his dream of *Rama Rajya* even after 50 years of freedom, because we have lost all the moral values preached by him and we have all become selfish and narrow minded. Hence consequently we are all fighting with each other neglecting the development of the nation and we have become a laughing stock before the other nations in the world.

4

Rural Industries Galvanising Services (RIGS)

Introduction

Rural Industries will be the thrust area for employment generation, sustainable development and a package of activities will be generated.

There are various organisations/departments and systems which have to be involved in making rural industries programme a success. This is where galvanising concept fits in.

Some of the activities/institutions which have to be involved are:

(1) Project makers
(2) Equipment suppliers
(3) Low Cost Practical Consultants
(4) Heritage, visit, groups
(5) Training
(6) Privatising change

Types of Activities

From Agriculture to Rural Development to Rural Industry to Holistic sustainable development becomes the main theme.

Some of the prominent institutions and people who can be involved are following:

This is a viable and transparency effort which generate jobs through various activities like plantation, cultivation, value addition, package, marketing, servicing, tourism, education, transport and various other themes.

RIGS India Ltd. can be the focussed viable programme of tomorrow.

Sensitising Professionals

Who are Professionals?
Definition
Doctors, Lawyers, Administrators, Writers
Conscious Keepers
all those who are in profession
all those who profess
Wider meaning - those who draw state benefits somehow or other — I I M — I I F.
Inservice - outside service students also.

Role of Professionals

Since they at some stage or other derive state benefits
they must become doubly accountable -
Accountability for what?
Accountability to whom?
Accountability how long?
Role of AG in case of Bureaucracies -

Can today only established Supervisors be questioned?

Policing Role of RBI — AG and other Inspecting authorities -

Everybody wanting to become Inspector — Why so?

How does Inspector function?
Inspector *Vs.* Constable -
Policing Role -

Sensitising - Meaning -
Sense -
Sensitivity
Sensitifying -

Spiritual Sensitivity -
Professionalism and sensitivity -
Importance in Third World countries -
Grant Rebate Subsidies Distribution Perks -
Vacancies Quotas - Distribution Arbitrariness -
Political Social Conditions -
Characteristics of Backward/3rd World Nations -
Unorganised
Remote from Decision makers
Language Barrier
Corruption all-round
arbitrary -
Who matters — Law breakers, powerful exploited and
Accepted - conformist -
No Hope situation.
Methods for Sensitising Professionals.

(1) Need conviction -
(2) Organising Professionals
(3) Revisiting Professionalism from Socio-Eco-Cost effectiveness - sustainability concepts -
(4) Key Parameters for judging performance of Professionals - Changing values -
(5) Input *Vs* Output consideration -
(6) Permanency *Vs* Job assignments -
(7) Role Demarcation -
(8) Making System Performing - (MSP)
(9) Existentialism *Vs* and Moving forward.
(10) Drivers - Conductors - Passengers similar.
(11) TV Radio Electronics
(12) Spiritualism - Vision broadening -
Recycling of Soul

Looking inwards
Time tested Values

(13) Identifying location specific problems and Professionalising Roles —

(14) Team work concept developments -

(15) Role of Materialism, Mussleness, Manpower implication of National Problems like population - corruption, inefficiency - lethargy - SWOT analysis - National regionwise
How do we look around us — Castewise Areawise Groupwise

(16) Politics for Mass awakening

(17) Concepts for Materialistic Development Making Nation proud.

(18) Problems of urbanisation — Root of all evils
City culture — alien to our third World -
Serious Deliberation -
Centralisation *Vs* Decentralisation
Need for computerised monitoring.

(19) Identifying difficult and critical input outputs.

(20) Holidays — need to relook -

(21) Organised *Vs* unorganised — groupism to censure to exploitative capacity.

(22) MPT concepts — as opposed to TP or RT concepts (Research Training)

(23) Holistic concept Developments.

(24) Economics of sensitisation — It involves costs — both recurring and non-recurring — Let us say how we will proceed.

1. Discussions and Seminars
   100 people — Plane expenses Time expenses
2. Report writing.
3. Processing in Secretariat.
4. Starting a National Institute as sensitising Training -

5. State level Institutions — Concept
   Formation
   Budget
   Posts
   Advertisements
   Post filling
   Uniform and Confirmation
   More posts
   More promotions
   Higher scales
6. Need for District level Institutions.
7. Autonomy and N.G.O. Induction -

Implications of Time -
Costs -

Death of Professionalism "In sum amounting to
Creation of JOBS. Rape of sensitisation".

(25) How to kill good concepts.
Guarding against Rape -
Hence self supporting system Development
Creating conditions within existing systems for
Replicable models development.

(26) Have faith in people and ourselves -
We are capable of doing it.

(27) Vivekananda said
"Lion Body
Sheep feeling"

(28) Need for sustained National debate on:-
Appropriate Technologies
Low Cost Extension systems
Human behaviour.
Essential Unity of Religions and spirituality
SWOT of society
Glaring problems like population
Cruelty to animals
Work culture
Punctuality

Discipline
Cost effectiveness and corruption
Economics and openness
Sustainability
Success stories
Hope generating models
Holistic programmes
Foreign Departments
Individuality of Regions
History and Lessons
Attitudes formation
Communication
Women Power Pressure groups.

5

Rural Industrialisation : Organisational Structure

For provision of adequate guidance and support and exercise of effective supervision and control by the government in connection with rural industrialization, it becomes necessary to create an organizational structure. Organization means the "planned coordination of the activities of two or more people in order to achieve some common and explicit goal through division of labour and a hierarchy of authority" (Robbine, 1983:6). It is the living structure which furnishes the necessary tool by which the management achieves the ends (Singh, 1977:128). The term structure is generally used to refer to "a set of relatively stable patterned relationship of social units" (Coser and Rosenberg, 1982:463). It is being used here to denote "the differentiated interrelated parts in a collectivity" (Blau, 1982:480) Organizational structure, thus, means the planned coordination of the activities of the differentiated interrelated parts having well defined statuses and roles in a collectivity.

Here it means the differentiated, interrelated and stable parts of the existing machinery of the government autonomous institutions, cooperative organisations and voluntary agencies concerned with promoting the growth and development, exercising necessary supervision and control and bringing about necessary coordination and integration in the field of rural industrialisation.

According to the provisions of Constitution of India development of village and small scale industries sector is the responsibility of state governments. Except for the industries declared by Parliament by law to be necessary for the purpose of defence or the prosecution of war and industries the control of which by the Union is declared by Parliament by law to be expedient in the public interest and specified in List I-Union List of Seventh Schedule of the Constitution of India, all other industries are within the jurisdiction of the State Governments as per List II-State List of the Seventh Schedule of the Indian Constitution. However, over the years, particularly after Independence, Government of India has shown keen interest in the area of preservation of traditional industries and development of cottage and village industries, and has come forward to set up a number of national level agencies which provide inputs in the form of finance, organizational support technical guidance and training technological upgradation and marketing assistance.

According to the present set-up, Government of India provides funds to the Khadi and Village Industries Commission for promotion of Khadi and Village Industries. The Commission in trun allocates money to various State Boards and simultaneously provides financial assistance to voluntary organisations directly so that they may themselves be able to establish and run Khadi and village industries without facing any financial hardship.

Government of India has also set up various financial institutions as discussed supra to provide liberal financial support to entrepreneurs, particularly those who are poor and belong to Scheduled Castes and Scheduled Tribes in rural areas, coming forward to establish cottage and village industries. Moreover, it has been issuing guidelines, instructions and even directives to banks, particularly to those Banks which have been nationalised from time to time ever since nationalisation of banks, to liberally provide financial support for the cause of rural industrialization even at the cost of risk of non-realisation of funds distributed by them.

At the level of Central Government, Small Industries Development Organisation with Development Commissioner Small Scale Industries as its head functioning under the Minister of Industries is looking after small scale industries. Khadi and Village Industries Commission having Chief Executive Officer as the executive head under the Ministry of Industries; Chairman, Central Coir Board working under the Ministry of Industries is dealing with Coir Industry; handloom is being looked after by the Handloom Board with Development Commissioner, Handloom as its Chief Executive Working under the Ministry of Textiles. All India Handicrafts Board with Development Commissioner, Handicrafts as its Chief Executive working under the Ministry of Commerce has the responsibility of matters relating to handicrafts; and sericulture is being dealt with by the Central Silk Board with its Chairman as the head functioning under the Ministry of Textile. This makes it amply clear that different authorities functioning under different Ministries of Government of India are looking after the matters connected with rural industrialization.

At the State level with particular reference to State of U.P. and other States in general Director of Industries functioning under the Department of Industries is looking after small scale and village Industries, Chairman, KVIC as Chairman and Executive head.

Working under the Ministry of Industries

Department of Small Scale, Agro and Rural Industry, Government of India is taking care of Khadi and Village Industries; Coir Industry is also generally being looked after by Department of Industries. However, the organisation and the department under which this organisation functions, vary from one State to another, Director, Handloom Development Commissioner, Handloom working under the Department of Industries is dealing with handloom industry; Handicrafts are being looked after by Director of Industries working under the Department of Small Scale Industries; and Director, Sericulture operating under the Department of Small Scale Industries is taking care of Sericulture. This abundantly unravels that different authorities working under the aegis of different departments of the State Governments are looking after the affairs of various types of industries which exist in rural areas in our country. There are certain industries in case of which the administrative organisation at the State level varies from State to State.

The district level administrative organisation created for manning rural industrialisation varies from one State to another. In the State of Uttar Pradesh, General Manager, District Industries Centre is entrusted with the responsibility of matters relating to small scale industries; District Village Industries Officer looks after the matters relating to Khadi and Village Industries; handloom industry is taken care of by General Manager, District Industries Centre Officers of the State Handloom Boards; General Manager, District Industries Centre is looking after the affairs of handicrafts; and sericulture is being regulated and promoted by Project Officers (Sericulture) District Sericulture Officer. This clearly indicates that like the Central and State levels, at the district level also, there is a multiplicity of industries;

and in some cases more than one organisation/officers has the responsibility due to which a lot of wastage of resources takes place and integrated approach to development of village industries gets thwarted.

The entire organisational set-up at different levels of public administration — Centre, State and District is being depicted at Annexure-A.

Various organisations/agencies have been associated with the work of promotion and development of village industries after Independence. All India Handicrafts Board, Handloom Boards and the Central Silk Board were set up way back in 1952. After a period of two years the Small Scale Industries Board and the Coir Board were established in 1954. In 1957, Khadi and Village Industries Commission was established by an Act of Parliament covering production of Khadi and a set of 25 other village industries whose number has since gone up to 97. These and various other central development agencies engaged in the field of rural industrialisation are being described here in a classified manner under the categories of (1) multi-purpose institutions; (2) training institutions, (3) marketing institutions, and (4) financial institutions.

Multipurpose Institutions

Among the institutions falling within this category, the Small Industries Development Organisation is the most important institution which practically works as a nodal agency for formulating and coordinating policies and programmes for promotion of small scale industries in the country. Besides maintaining close liaison with the Central ministries, Planning Commission, State Governments, financial institutions, etc., the Small Industries Development Corporation makes arrangements for comprehensive consultancy services covering technical, financial managerial aspects, for establishment of small scale industrial units. It also provides for common processing and testing, marketing and training to workers and entrepreneurs. The services are provided to Small Industries Services Institutes, Extension Centres, Regional Testing Centres, Products-cum-Process Development Centres besides some important specialised institutions. The Development Commissioner, Small Scale Industries Working as the Chief Executive of the Small Industries Development Organisation is also the national coordinator of the District Industries Centres which are expected to work as a 'single window' in assisting entrepreneurs for providing varied kinds of promotional assistance. The General Manager, District Industries Centre assisted by functional managers is expected to reader all possible help to the present and prospective entrepreneurs from single window covering small scale industries, Khadi and Village Industries, Handloom, Handicrafts, Sericulture etc. These district industries centres are also looking after the scheme of 'Self-Employment of Educated Unemployed Youth' covering young persons who are aged between 18 and 35 years and who have passed High School. With the multiplicity of agencies set up by Central and State Governments, the role of Small Industries Development Organisation as also of the District Industries centres in discharging the duties and responsibilities entrusted to them requires thorough scientific evaluation.

The Khadi and Village Industries Commission which came into being in April 1957, enjoys a unique position. It is a statutory organisation envisaged with a view to providing package of services in an integrated manner on the doorsteps of artisans in the shape of finance, raw materials, tools and equipments besides training, marketing facilities, etc. The KVIC has been able to build up a solid organisational network which is evident from the fact that in the year 1990-91, there have been 28 State Khadi and Village Industries Boards, 1172 Registered Institutions and 23,581 Industrial Cooperatives. Besides 13,000 sales outlets have been functioning throughout the country. There is, however, bad experience of functioning of the Khadi and Village Industries Commission as it has been functioning in isolation without forming an integral part of the national mainstream; and so have been its various allied agencies.

The Khadi and Village Industries Boards functioning in States are also statutory bodies; and in a sense, they are also autonomous with the result that there is not only lack of coordination between the Khadi and Village Industries Commission and the State Boards but also on occasions a clear conflict between them has been distinctly visible on matters of policy and methods and techniques of implementation. Undoubtedly, the Khadi and Village Industries Commission has done excellent and commendable job in various fields and has a team of dedicated workers as employees of various Gandhi Ashrams who follow the Gandhian philosophy and work on the principle of service to the nation. However, it is really sad that despite such a dedicated band of workers, efforts made in the direction of promotion of Khadi have not been self-supporting and sustaining.

Sometimes an impression does develop that there is undue emphasis on Khadi and a lot of financial support has to be made available by the Government to make various Khadi products marketable. It also seems to be relevant to point out here that inspite of rebate and subsidy, cotton and silk Khadi is beyond the reach of a common man due to its higher prices compared to non-Khadi cotton and silk products in the market. The main reasons for these high prices seem to be non-availability of appropriate technology with the help of which production of cotton and silk khadi products may be made cheaper and inability of the producers of Khadi products to produce according to requirements and particular taste of comsumers. What therefore is urgently required is that upgradation of technology used for producing Khadi products which have great potential of being more competitive in the market, should be continuously pursued; and after conducting marketing and consumer interest surveys, Khadi products should be manufactured according to the taste and needs of consumers. The entire organisational structure of Khadi and Village Industries viz. Khadi and Village Industries Commission at the Central level, Khadi and Village Industries Board at the State level and district village industries officers at the district level, its *modus operandi*, its suitability to the present conditions, its adaptability to changing times, expertise of the personnel, its ability to promote and develop appropriate technology, its willingness to sponsor and conduct surveys of the tastes and requirements of people in different parts of the country, Conditions and mode of delivery of credit, raw material, training consultancy etc. to entrepreneurs, requires thorough examination; and if need be, drastic changes in its purposes, plans, policies, procedures and programmes be introduced at the earliest to overhaul it.

Coir Board is again a statutory body established under the Coir Industry Act, 1953. Coir and its products have great potential for exports. The Board has its Research Institutes, Training and Design Centres, etc. Despite the fact that Coir Industry is well developed in some southern States like Kerala and a lot of co-operativisation has also taken place, the industry still has not been in a position to make use of the best possible appropriate technology. India, even today, is the only country still continuing to employ ratling process of extraction of Coir Fibres. Although it is said that the coir produced by making use of ratling process is superior, it involves pollution, health hazards and ecological damage. Mechanisation in Coir Industry has not been brought in mainly because of fear of unemployment. Therefore there is an urgent need for conducting scientific studies to explore the possibility of rationalisation without tears as also of product diversification and alternative uses of coir.

The All India Handloom Board is engaged in promoting handloom industry which is the largest cottage industry in the country as nearly one-third of the total requirements of cloth in the country is provided by this sector, and in terms of providing employment also it is next to agriculture only. It is estimated that there are about 4 million handlooms in the country with concentration in the north-east region. According to the textile policy of the Government, it has been envisaged that clothing needs of the masses should be met from this sector itself as far as possible because of its vast employment potential in urban and semi-urban areas of the country. The main objective of the handloom development programme of the All India Handloom Board is to provide uninterrupted employment to weavers, increase their productivity and promote marketing of handloom products. Government has taken a number of steps to promote the handloom sector such as help in formation of cooperatives, managerial expertise, subsidy, modernisation, renovation and purchase of looms, etc. The industry, despite of these efforts, has not been able to function effectively mainly because of these two major problems; (1) high cost of production, and (2) low productivity. Technology-wise, powerlooms are naturally more efficient, yielding higher productivity and providing cheaper cloths. Handlooms, therefore, need be given supported market, and some of the handloom products which cannot be manufactured by power looms will have to be paid more attention.

The All India Handicrafts Board and Development Commissioner, handicrafts, working under the Ministry of Commerce, Government of India are concerned with the Development of handicrafts. This sector consists of quite a wide range of products like dolls and toys, carpets, art metal wares, wood wares, printed textiles, cane and bamboo articles, ivory products etc. The craftsmen generally belong to weaker sections of society particularly to Scheduled Castes. It is estimated that about 25 million workers are engaged in this sector. There is an urgent need for creation of additional employment avenues, preservation of skills, extension of market and improvement in quality.

Central Silk Board is engaged in various types of activities required for pormotion of silk industry in the country. India is fortunately the only country in the world which produces all varieties of natural silk. In terms of employment potential, sericulture is providing employment to about 4 million persons. Central Silk Board shoulders the responsibility for providing training to entrepreneurs going for sericulture, takes up researches in various connected areas, fulfils the basic needs of this industry, promotes price stabilisation and undertakes a host of other activities instrument in the development of silk. Despite various promotional measures, per hectare output of mulberry silk in India is quite low as compared to that in Japan and the cost of production too is very high with the result that silk is a luxury item beyond the reach of a common man. Measures, therefore, will have to be undertaken to adopt appropriate technology to improve production and launch a movement for getting sericulture accepted by the people in this country.

Training Institutions

The multi-purpose institutions discussed above have also been imparting training in their respective fields and operating technical schemes. However, there have been some institutions, in addition to these, which have been concerned with providing training required for effective functioning of rural industries. Some of such institutions having separate identity include the National Industries Corporation, New Delhi, the National Institute of Design, Ahemedabad; Small Industry Extension Training Institute, Hyderabad; Council for People's Action and Advancement of Rural Technology, New Delhi; National Handloom Development Corporation, Lucknow; Indian Institute of Handloom Technology, Varanasi, Salem and Gauhati; International Centre for Training and Research in Tropical Sericulture, Mysore; Cane and Bamboo Development Institute, Agartala, etc. In addition to these independent and specialised training institutions,various major public undertakings such as Bharat Leather Corporation, Agra and National Laboratories like the Central Leather Institute, Madras organise various types of R and D schemes and training programmes and provide a wide variety of benefits to small scale and village industries. The National Research Development Corporation of India is also there to promote and exploit indigenous inventions. The technologies developed by all India research organisations like Council of Scientific and Industrial Research, Indian Council of Medical

Research, Indian Institute of Technology, etc. have also been given licence by the National Research Development Corporation of India to impart training to entrepreneurs in private and public industries. KVI Sector consisting of Khadi and Village Industries Commission various Khadi and V.I. Boards and number of Institutions have also old and new infrastructure for training facility with inadequate infrastructure. Greatest problem has been its inadequacy to meet the challenges of internal resource generating marketing developing confidence for self employment.

Marketing Institutions

The National Small Industries Corporation has formulated a comprehensive scheme for internal marketing of various products of small scale industries. In this connection, it has been undertaking a wide variety of programmes such as quality control, common brand name, upgradation of technology, publicity of various goods produced etc. It also provides facilities for hire-purchase of machinery, tools and equipments, training and orientation, etc. through a network of its branches. The State emporia and the Central Cottage Industries Emporium also act as sales outlets. The Khadi and Village Industries Commission and various Khadi and Village Industries Boards functioning in different States have their own emporia; and many other institutions/organisations have also set up their Bhandars/Bhavans at various points in different parts of the country exclusively for the sale of Khadi and Village Industries products. The Coir Board has also opened showrooms and sales depots in important towns. The Indian Silk Export Promotion Council established at Bombay is engaged in the work of encouraging sale of natural silk outside the country.

Besides these various organisations mentioned here, there are a number of cooperative societies and federations and many other agencies which have been concerned with promotion of marketing of rural industries products. Recently, a new experiment of establishing District Society for Marketing Support is being undertaken in the State of Uttar Pradesh. The objective of these societies is package delivery of various types of required help. These societies are performing the functions of making arrangement for needed raw-materials, training and quality control, supplying tools and equipments, and purchase and sale of finished goods. A perusal of these functions performed by these district societies of Marketing Support clearly reveals that one of the essential constituents of their effective functioning from the standpoint of providing help to village industries in an integrated manner viz., financial support has been missing with the result that this experiment is also getting a big jolt and is at the brink of meeting failure. Assistance from various voluntary organizations is also being sought for; and in some States like Uttar Pradesh, voluntary agencies and agents have been entrusted with the responsibility of selling the products of village industries on commission basis; and this experiment has proved to be quite successful. Despite all these efforts, there is hardly any arrangement for the sale of products of rural industries at the village level, especially in remote rural areas; and Districts Village Industries Officers can play an important role in this regard by identifying the entrepreneurs, especially those who are unemployed, and belong to weaker sections, and motivate them to take up the work of sale of village industries products on commission basis as also by organising cooperative marketing societies at the village level.

Financial Institutions

The Industrial Development Bank of India provides funds to commercial banks and State Finance Corporations through the scheme of refinance of industrial loans. The Commercial Banks, Cooperative Banks, Regional Rural Banks, State Finance Corporations, etc. constitute the organisational structure existing at present with a view to providing financial support for rural industrialisation. The Khadi and Village Industries sector is mostly being financed by the Khadi and Village Industries Commission from the funds made available by Government of India. The Commission provides funds to the Khadi and Village Industries Boards functioning at the State level which, in turn, allot them to various districts keeping in view their potentials in the field of Khadi and Village Industries. National Bank of Agriculture and Rural Development has come in a big way to refinance almost all the village and cottage industries including handloom, sericulture, coir, etc. It has also been providing refinance facilities for loans given for industry Service Business (ISB) component under the Integrated Rural Development Programme. The National Small Industries Corporation has also been providing loans to small scale industries in the country. The Small Industries Development Bank of India as a subsidiary of the Industrial Development Bank of India has been providing financial assistance to small industries including cottage and village industries in India since 1989. However, despite all these multiple institutions created for providing financial assistance for rural industrialisation, flow of finance to this sector has not been smooth and satisfactory due to a multiplicity of constraints such as cumbersome and complicated procedure of loaning, widely rampant corruption in the administrative machinery, lack of awareness among the organisation of entrepreneurs, weak cooperative movement, non-availability of expert advice required for preparation of economically viable projects, poor arrangement for marketing, shortage of raw materials, lack of coordination etc. In order to ensure adequate and timely financial support for rural industrialisation what is immediately required is the creation of separate apex financial institution for traditional and modern rural industries after separating the rural industries from the presently clubbed Village and Small Industries sector, establishment of their branches at the district level and timely provision of full loans to the prospective entrepreneurs, generally without any subsidy, in a simplified manner without unnecessary procedural delays and corrupt practices.

Gaps in the Existing Organisational Structure

A perusal of the existing organisational structure reveals the following gaps:

1. Different types of village industries have different types of organisational structure.
2. Different organisational set-ups are operating in isolation.
3. There is a dire lack of coordination not only among different types of organisational set-ups dealing with different types of industries by operating at one particular level of government but also among different levels of government in respect of organisational structure evolved for catering to the needs and promoting the interest of same village industry.
4. There is duplication in coverage of rural target population as also in information which is supplied by different organizational set-ups

leading to wastes of funds earmarked for rural industrialisation by different Ministries/ Departments of the Government.

5. There is no linkage anywhere.

Measures Required to be Undertaken

In order to develop an effective organisational structure that may be able to promote rural industrialisation by properly taking care of various aspects of different types of village industries, the following measures are required to be undertaken:

(1) A unified but decentralised organisational structure will have to be evolved for all the different types of village industries. A separate department of village industries should be created within the Ministry of Industries which should be given authority to function as a nodal government department dealing with the entire gamut of rural industrialisation. Khadi and Village Industries Commission functioning under the proposed department of Village Industries of Ministry of Industries, Government of India should be entrusted with the responsibility of developing all kinds of village industries. Various divisions should be created within the Khadi and Village Industries Commission itself to cater to specific needs of different types of village industries. All the policies relating to rural industrialisation in general and different types of village industries in particular should be decided by the commission. At the State level, Khadi and Village Industries Boards should be accepted as the nodal agency. Likewise, Khadi and Village Industries

Centres should be established at the district level with District Village Industries Officers as their head having Khadi and Village Industries Officers functioning under the Block Development Officers at the block level.

(2) Plans for development of village industries should be prepared industry and village-wise at the block level so that they may become realistic, and financial allocations may be made accordingly.

(3) Present culture of subsidies and rebates should be kept confined only up to weaker sections of society so that its present abuse may be minimised. Cheaper term loans repayable in easy instalments should be made available to those going for setting up industries in rural areas. Preference in allotment of land and concessions in power supply should also be made available to rural entrepreneurs. Zero-base budgeting involving *de novo* financial allocations every time may be followed to run the small scale industrial organisations existing in rural areas.

(4) A built-in system of adequate monitoring with multiple points to check irregularities and ascertain progress should be developed right from the block-level in order to ensure proper utilisation of loans given for rural industrialisation and to provide timely necessary guidance to the entrepreneurs to remove varied kinds of obstructions in the way of effective functioning of industrial units.

(5) Proper training institutions already functioning in society should be identified and optimally utilised. Self-supporting training institutions should be developed, preferably at the district level, to cater to the

training needs of rural entrepreneurs at nearest point.

(6) Organisational procedures should be simplified in the interest of rural entrepreneurs, paper work should be reduced to minimum and organisational climate should be made conducive on the following lines suggested by S.K. Bhatia (*The Hindu*, 1988).

"From internal focus to focus on environment.

From focus on process to focus on structure and process.

From focus on management to focus on all levels.

Shift from narrow to broader knowledge base.

Shift from specialist to generalist or team approach.

From consultant to line manager as change agent.

From single intervention to multiple interventions.

From truth and love to power and politics.

From participation to contingency approach.

From singly country to multi-national."

(7) Effective control mechanism should be evolved. Inspection registers should be maintained right from the level of industrial unit itself at different levels in different types of organizations and inspection notes highlighting irregularities and necessary directions, instructions and suggestions should be recorded in the register at the time of on the spot visit, instead of reporting at the headquarters and therefrom to the concerned organizational unit. Adequate system of establishing accountability should be evolved and those found guilty of non-

feasance or mal-feasance should be identified and punished.

(8) Suitable marketing network should be evolved on the lines of District Society for Marketing Support initiated by the Khadi and Village Industries Board, U.P. Technical expertise and guidance should be taken from the specialised institutions working in this field. Voluntary organisations and enterprising individuals should be involved in the work of promoting marketing of rural industries products on commission basis. Efforts should particularly be made in the direction of exporting village industries products by exploring foreign markets and establishing credit in them.

(9) Organizations of rural entrepreneurs should be created at different levels with a federation at central level in order to exert pressure on the Government to chalk out and pursue policies conducive to the promotion of village industries as also to counteract the pressure of big industrialists lobby on the Government which usually manipulates the policies of Government successfully in favour of urban and semi-urban based industrial organisations, obviously at the cost of small and tiny village industries.

(10) Open door communication policy should be followed within the organisational set-up under which free and frank expression of ideas should be encouraged, suggestions from all categories of employees should be invited and timely scrutinised and those found worthwhile should be implemented; and genuine grievances and complaints of employees should be redressed.

(11) A suitable management information system should be developed in order that information required for decision making may become readily available and lessons may be learnt from past experiences. Suitable use of computers and mass communications strategies may also be made according to the need.

(12) The real future of rural industrialisation will come through identification of proper SWOT, hence traditional and non-traditional industries will have to be suitably braketed, linked up and market oriented approach will have to be developed. This also means basic changes in the attitude of various goods.

(13) Organisations are not an end in themselves or they are not meant for people getting salaries or facilities from them. There was a suggestion to hand over D.I.Cs. to institutions of industrialists in each district. How that will be ever possible. Why conflicting groups. Can some D.I.Cs. be earmarked to look after rural industries only.

(14) Organisations have to develop capacity for sustaining and generating resource internally. How can they do it. Does marketing concept needs to imbibe in a big way.

(15) Planning, Action, Research, Codification, Extension (PARCE) will have to be the basis of organisational development. This means accept the differences of region, target group, extension machinery and time factor.

(16) Planning Commission, Department of Economic Affairs, Plan implementation have to play a very active role in coordinating monitoring and guidance as the scarce resource allocator distributor, monitor and

as apex bodies their coordinating role will go a long way in quality implementation of Rural Industrialisation programme. Since linkages between rural industries sector and Rural Development Department would be the prime need of the day for sustainable rural employment oriented industrialisation. There is no option.

(17) Some of the tactful issues brought out by KVIC in its approach for Eighth Five Year Plan also need to be attended.

Time has come to open up organisation for competition, hence the bankers, the publicisers, trainers, the organisation developers, evaluators all will have to pool their collective strength.

Annexure A

Existing Organizational Structure of the Government for Rural Industrialisation in India

Sr. No.	Name of the Industry	Central Structure Organisation	Ministry	Organisation	State Structure Ministry	District Structure
1	2	3	4	5	6	7
1.	Small Scale Industries	Small Industries Development Organisation with Development Commissioner, Small Scale Industries as its Chief Executive.	Ministry of S.S. Agro & Rural Ind.	Directorate of Industries with Director, Industries as its Chief Executive.	Department of Small Scale and Village Industries.	General Manager, District Industries Centre-SSSI, Etc.
2.	Khadi and Village Industries.	Khadi and Village Industries Commission with Chairman as its Head and Chief Executive Officer as its Chief Executive.	Ministry of S.S., Agro & Rural Ind.	Khadi and Village Industries Board with Chairman as its Head and Chief Executive Officers as its Chief Executive.	Department of Small Scale and Village Industries.	District Village Industries Offices/Manager, Khadi and Village Industries Board.

1	2	3	4	5	6	7
3.	Coir	Central Coir Board with Chairman as its Head.	Ministry of S.S., Agro & Rural Ind.	Varies from State to State.	Varies from State to State.	Varies from District to District.
4.	Handloom	Handloom Board with Development Commissioner as its Chief Executive	Ministry of Textile.	Director, Handloom/ Development Commissioner, Handloom.	Department of Industries.	General Manager, District Industries Centre/Officers of the State Handloom Board.
5.	Handicrafts	All India Handicraft Board with Development Commissioner, Handicrafts as its Chief Executive.	Ministry of Commerce.	Directorate of Industries with Director, Industries as its Chief Executive.	Department of Small Scale Industries.	General Manager District Industries Centre.
6.	Sericulture	Central Silk Board with Chairman as its Head.	Ministry of Textile.	Director, Sericulture.	Department of Small Scale Industries varies from State to State.	Project Officer/ District Sericulture Officer.

6

Self Supporting Integrated Rural Development through Rural Industrialisation

Introduction

Our experience in rural development/rural industrialisation has been that, despite massive input of money and other resources, including manpower and infrastructure due to lack of proper linkages, the programmes have not succeeded to the desired extent. The other reasons for low success has been unawareness of the requirement of self-supporting models. This is primarily due to the fact that the organisations work in isolation and they have hardly any regular forum for interaction with beneficiaries.

There are also some important on-going programmes in rural areas. Without duplicating the efforts if they could be pulled better results would definitely accrue in a short duration.

1. What is the scheme?

It is the cluster approach for development based on pulling resources of various on-going programmes for the overall development of rural areas as will be seen from the following. The scheme is to involve various on-going programmes for linked up activities.

2. Granting that Dairy and Dairy products can have the following advantages

The Dairy Industry after operation flood has become a very viable industry and all State Governments/ National Governments are encouraging establishment of such Dairy all over the country. In fact, NDBD as an apex body have been doing significant work in this direction.

Relevant to this dairy activities, it has many added advantages as enumerated below:

(i) Milk is one of the most nutritious food and thus supplements eradicating of malnutrition;

(ii) Dairy activity leads to promotion of its many value added products such as curd, srikhand, yoghurt and allied confectionery farm items of milk which is an income generation activity in the rural areas;

(iii) Establishment of Dairy makes the location a viable place for establishment of Biogas Plant of equivalent capacity and size. Establishment of Biogas Plant has its application in the following target benefits;

   (a) can be used as a fuel for cooking purposes;

   (b) can be used for lighting purpose;

   (c) can be used as an energy input to generate site for production of electricity when its requirement in the ratio of 8 : 2 with diesel can generate foolproof electricity depending upon the capacity of the plant and thus motivate power in the form of high power motive power could be obtained. Related to generation of such motive power, this could be utilised for the purpose of running water pumps, portable concentrate distribution on the one hand and scientific handling of cattle dung will lead in other benefits in the form of arresting affluent disposal, clean cooking conditions, free environment etc.

(d) The motive power could also be utilised for running appropriate technology activities at a conceivable low level of unit production which is promoted by KVIC such as Shaila Wheel in Pottery Industry, Paddy Processing in PCPI, Masala, Atta grinding, bakery, oil extraction etc.

(e) The output of slurry of such a biogas plant is a very good enriched manure which could be utilised for cultivation of various types of agricultural produces, vegetables etc. Such bio-manure application for cultivation of crops yields high level food without danger of chemical fertilizer residual changes and is not only tasty but also nutritious.

(f) Related to above benefit is another aspect of the preservation of soil for a considerable longer period to time when application of bio-manure makes the soil more humus, porous and arrests its deterioration which otherwise rich soil is subjected to put for use of synthetic manure.

(iv) Thus the promotion of Dairy activity along with biogas integrated benefits by rural employment generation, healthy surrounding, fuel saving, healthy food, environment protection.

(v) The integrated product envisaged aims at creating such cluster of activities when these centres become a model of demonstration and can be a viable rural resort for urban dwellers.

3. Other on-going programmes will be based on biogas as the centre point for power in rural area. Biogas, solar energy improved chulah, pressure cooker, wind mill when applied in integrated manner will have the following advantages.

The Centre will be a nodal agency in implementation of various non-conventional energy programmes such as installation of biogas plant, solar devices, improved chulhas, wind mill for lifting product, use of pressure cooker etc. which will ultimately be a cause for creation of alternative renewable energy resources on the one hand and on the other make the rural people adopt to use of this natural resources for a better purpose. These activities will be promoted by the centre for its extension programme so that not only in the village of location of the project but also in and around the village these non-conventional energy programmes could be promoted in a big way. The Centre by itself while owning a Dairy plant will establish an institutional biogas plant on adequate capacity to ensure that atleast 50 per cent of its energy needs which are required for commencement of various village industries activities are met from the biogas input through establishment of generator set of its own. Community solar cooker would be used for cooking foods of centres inhabitants who would be associated in running the activities of the project at the site of location. Water solar heater would be utilised for not only use of domestic purposes but also in such industrial application which may be needed for the activities proposed to be run under the project.

Use of improved chulha in its modified form for running a Bakery, Murmura making, Poha making, parboil rice cooking will conserve substantial quantity of fire wood and this will be directly saving wood of forest. In the same manner wind mill will be used for low height high discharge lift irrigation purposes for on-going programmes in campus but within the location where whole food made out of Bio-manure will be produced. Similarly potential skill will be used for running such electronics/electrical appliances like T.V., street light, solar lamp etc., etc.

On an average once such a project with atleast 3 village industry, 25 cow dairy is established providing employment to about 100 people out of the total energy requirement of the project atleast 50% thereof can be met from use of Non-Conventional Energy input.

4.1 Optimising input for Biogas—Human excreta at Railway Stations, in railways can be collected and suitably mixed with cattle dung, agricultural waste etc.

The concept for establishment of community toilet has already come into existence when the target group has been identified as slum dwellers. Many potential areas have establishment of such community toilet remains to be explored such as railway station, city bus stops, picnic gardens, place of cinema theatres, entertainment parks etc. where such community toilet if not in fixed manner it could be established as a mobile toilet. The resources so collected of nightsoil could be proportionately mixed to cattle dung and they could be centrally used for running big capacity institutional biogas plant and thus these biogas resources can be converted into electric power or mechanical motive power for various application and uses.

4.2 Slum areas — and Sulabh Souchalayas.

The benefits of Non-Conventional Energy Resources can as well be made by the apex agency by adopting some slum areas in its adjacent urban location whereby could establish mobile toilet for use of slum dwellers or a community toilet in line with Sulabh Souchalaya scheme. Establishment of such community toilet on one hand will provide employment to scavengers who are till today in many areas cursed with activities of carrying nightsoil and on the other hand may keep a clean environment in their locality while making use of nightsoil as raw material for production of biogas. Benefit of use of Biogas could be extended to the slum dwellers themselves in the form of cooking gas or lighting facility.

4.3 On roads of highways near Dhaba/Tabela entire integrated models can be installed and linked with hostel, picnic spots to utilise human excreta and human urine.

Dhaba/Tabela in our country has become a best model of roadside hotel for common people who are travelling on the road. These roadside hotels are also targetted as an area for promotion of the integrated proposed scheme. Such Dhaba/Tabela scheme has already been approved by commission for its implementation in the country and the response from the field is not discouraging. These Dhabas can be very well integrated in the proposed project and as an additional input to the scheme the community toilet on road side location can be promoted under the project.

7

Integrated Rural Industrialisation through Biogas

Energy — the Basic Need for Development

Conventional Energy	:	Oil, Coal etc.— limited resources. Normally environmentally pollutant.
Non-Conventional Energy	:	Biogas, Solar, Windmill, Improved Chulha, Briquette etc. — unlimited potential. Environmentally clean fuel.

Meaning of Rural Industrialisation

Rural Industrialisation means—

Value addition on local raw material like

Agriculture

Forest

Horticulture

Chemical etc. Or demand based Industries thus making marketable products and marketing either in villages and/or cities or export etc.

Importance and Linkage of Agricultural, Rural Development and Rural Industrialisation Development Models

Agriculture	Rural Development	Rural Industries
1	2	3
Agriculture, Horticulture, Forestry, Sericulture etc. Animal husbandry, Fisheries etc.	Health, Small Saving, Pollution, Environment, Ecology, Drinking water, education, IRDP, Roads Housing, Tourism, S & T etc.	Rural Industries means activities which enable Value addition on local raw materials like agriculture, forest, horticulture, chemical etc. or demand based industries such as KVI, Handloom Coir, Handicrafts etc. with the following benefits: 1. Low cost employment in rural areas, 2. Simple technology 3. Self employment 4. Employment at doorstep etc.

Integrated Rural Industrialisation through Biogas

Non-Conventional Energy Sources	- Biogas - Solar - Wind - Improved Chulha - Afforestation - Recycling of wastes

Biogas - KVIC is the 'PIONEER' started in 1961-62
- Installed over 2 lakhs biogas plants.

Integrated Rural Industrialisation through Biogas

KVIC model plant most technically sound model.

Highly skilled workmanship for civil construction not necessary

Provides gas at constant pressure

Provides long trouble free service

Importance of Science & Technology

For improving quality

Minimising cost of production

Reducing drudgery

Sustained development of rural economy

Components of Science and Technology

1. Technology generation (R&D)
2. Technology transfer (Lab. to Land)
3. Technology Demonstration (Exhibitions)
4. Adoption Research (Adoption of new areas)
5. Training in improved technology
6. Analysis/Testing of productivity
7. Quality control/standardisation
8. Supply of improved tools and equipments.

Integrated Rural Industrialisation through Biogas

Benefits of Biogas plant :

Provides neat, clean, instantly lit efficient fuel

Provides enriched manure rich in nitrogen and humus

Useful to run engines, pumpsets

Electricity generation possible

Cluster Approach for Development

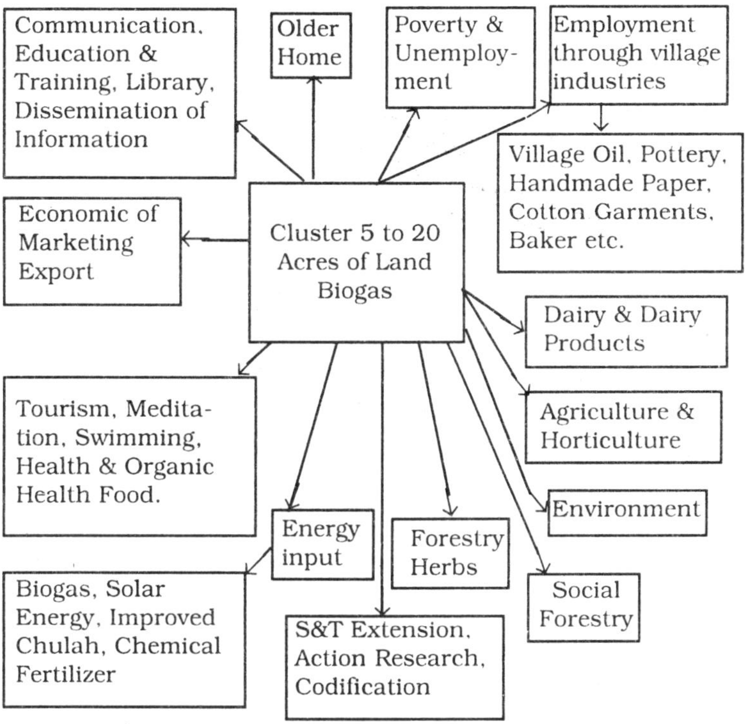

Helps in rural sanitation
Helps in reducing deforestation
Reduces smoke, relief to housewife.

Costs Planning

Self Supporting Integrated Rural Development
"Have Fruits - Not Roots".

Some of the Sectors where Biogas could be used are:

Fuel for Bakery, Laundry, Soap making units etc.
To energise pumps for irrigation
Provides heat required for rearing of chicks in poultry farms

Diagrammatic Dhaba/Tabela scheme of KVIC

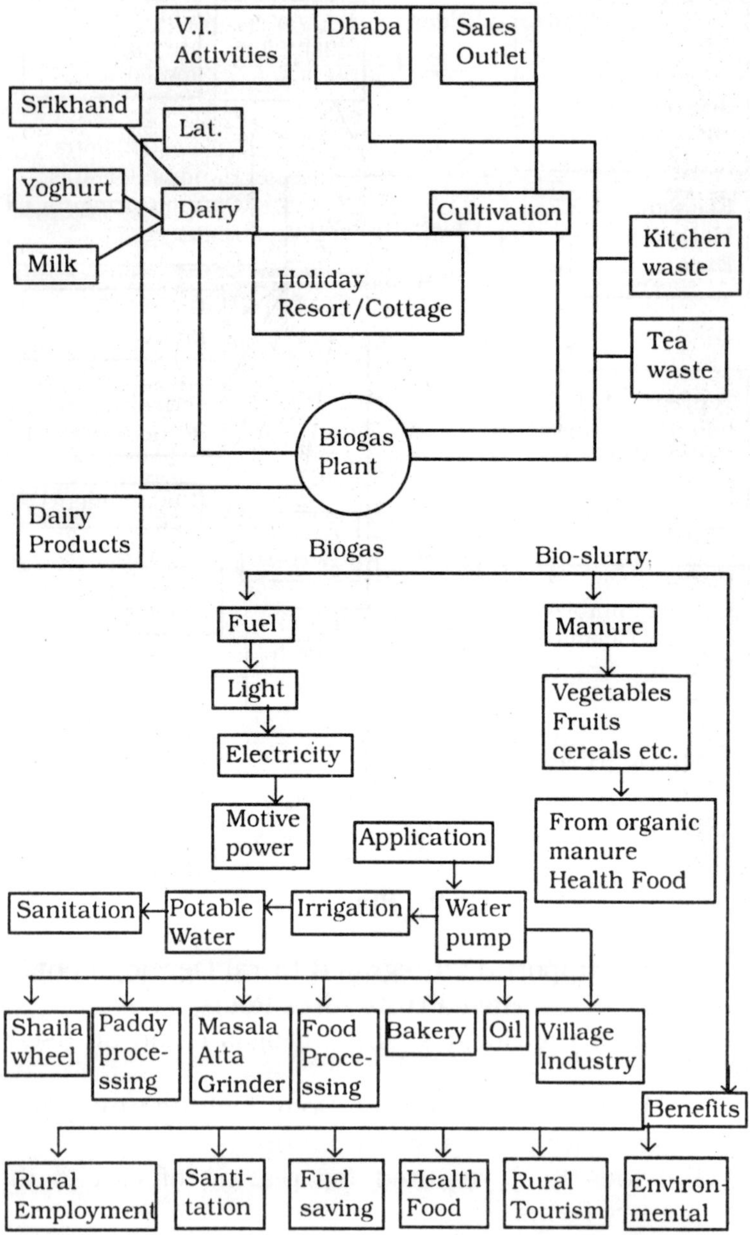

For running flour mills
For running chaff cutter
Conversion of milk products for Paneer, Butter etc.

An integrated approach for Rural Industrialisation through Dhaba/Tabela Scheme of KVIC is pictorially demonstrated separately.

Perception of S&T Gap Area for Rural Industrialisation

1. Codification of existing improvements
2. Role of training centre
3. Role of funding
4. Cost effectiveness
5. Productivity
6. Role of Beneficiaries
7. Problems of coordination
8. Monitoring systems and role of computer
9. Import of technology for Rural Industrialisation
10. Export of equipments to third world countries for rural industries.

Assistance from KVIC

(A) Free Technical Guidance through trained worker
(B) Financial Assistance in the form of Bank Finance.
(C) Backward forward linkages for total rural development
(D) Sustainability

Five Powers

Policy power
Women power
Technological power as Economic power

Power of Spirituality
Power of Faith.

Calculations

Biogas plant based on cows	*Cost*	*Employment*
Capacity of plant - 15 cum	Rs. 35,000/-	300 man days
Bio-manure - 65 tons	Rs. 13,000/-	365 man days

Biogas equivalent to Kerosene - 3285 Lit. Rs. 9,855/-

Essentials for Replication

Sensitivity
Extendability
Holistic
Roots probing
Meditative
Local Linkages with colleges and other Institutions
ACR — Action, Research, Codification
Pooling up of resources — expertise
Killing of Ego
Performance related remuneration/incentives
Cost effectiveness
Basics of training
Training for wage employment/self employment/ competitive work
Marketing of production and training
Internal Resource Generation.

Calculation

Rural Industries

Industry	*Production*	*Employment*
1. Village Oil Industry	400 Qtls	50 nos
2. Processing of Cereals & Pulses		
a. Paddy Processing	Rs. 10.30 lakhs	12 nos.
b. Masala & Atta Chakki	Rs. 1.62 lakh	7 nos.
c. Bakery — A Type	Rs. 2.06 lakhs	6 nos.
3. Fruit & Vegetable processing	Rs. 9.51 lakhs	57 nos.
4. Village Pottery (Shaila wheel)	Rs. 0.08 lakh	3 nos.

Calculation

Essential Linkages for Successful Implementation

1. Co-ordination
2. Cost effectiveness
3. Replicable
4. Bankable
5. Integrated approach
6. Protection Ecology
    1. Pollution free production process
    2. No adverse impact on water resources, forest etc.
    3. Conversion of waste into wealth
7. Gandhian Thought - 1. Co-existence
    2. Dignity of labour
    3. Social harmony
    4. Hope for future.

Synopsis — Need for Revisiting Success

1. To carry out review/evaluation/introspection/ chalking of the schemes, programmes, items etc. which were acclaimed in the past as a very successful model.
2. Examine cost effectiveness, replicability, sustainability of that activity.

Financial Linkages

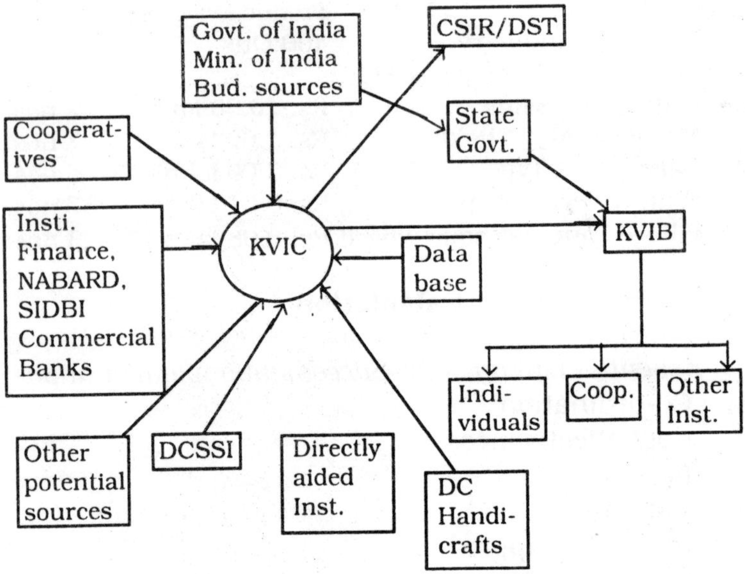

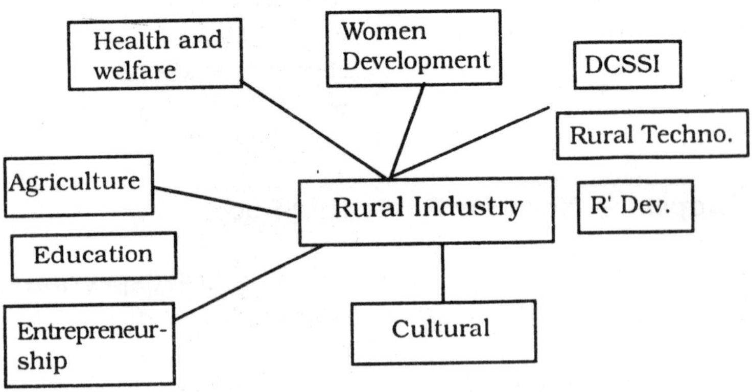

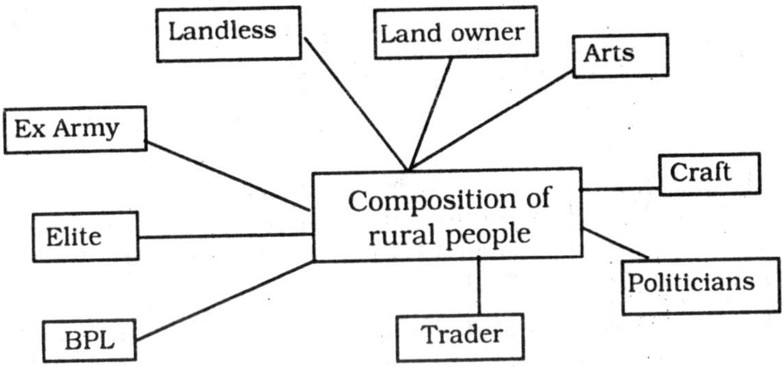

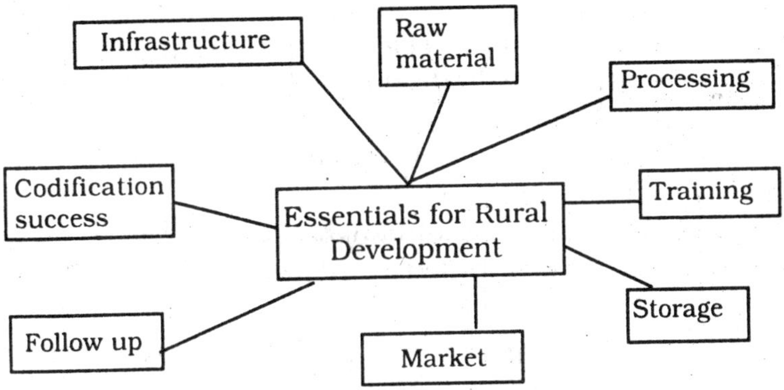

3. Examine how social, economic, environmental, political, factors have affected that scheme.
4. What precautions could have been taken by the formulator, originator, implementor or monitor of that programme before hand to ensure the success of that programme over a period of time.
5. To see the implications of easy availability of funds, indifference to environmental and ecological consideration in the field and to make the programme a success what mistakes were committed?
6. Scheme, re-visiting successes:

(i) Preferably who claim success for that programme should be invited to present a programme on the past, present and future of the scheme.

(ii) What cost was incurred and how the programmes were successful or unsuccessful.

(iii) Proposal is that they should on a voluntary basis, present their experiments of the successes and its revisit and be prepared for criticism from the audience. The idea is to ensure that one who was involved in the project should be able to present its various angles and linkages. Disadvantages of any professor or successor or other independent going to evaluate the programme at this stage that he will have no appreciation and secondly he may not be able to study all the linkages.

(iv) We must accept many people have done many good work; but the greatest step for success is that of 'time'. Only those programmes can be successful which prove their worth over a period of time and we should have no fear to say that in the last few decades various programmes were taken up and they have really become successful as we understand success today.

(v) This exercise should not cost much because the presentor will be expected to bear their own expenses. Some expenses will be required for writing letters inviting of those foreigners who would like to revisit their successes in the open forum. Mostly they will be NGOs, Govt. servants or few individuals. If need be their T.A., D.A. can be arranged but mostly there should be no need of any T.A., D.A. except some literature etc.

There is also need for this sort of exercise to get away examination of routine nature of most of our programmes. As is well known the HRD, Training Motivation is mostly failing in Government or semi-government sector despite good intention of every one. One reason is that we are not prepared to examine our avowed conviction in the light of other's views and there is often lack of linkages in this examination.

For the success of any programme apart from replicability, sustainability, extendability, involvement of below proverty line group, or unemployed, women power, rural development and holistic developmental approach will be must. How many of our programme can meet this state with the scarcity of resources, the time has come to reexamine and revisit various programmes, which were basically well intentioned but also well spent. Now with the scarcity of resources all round and apathy to work and all pervading indiscipline, the time has come to take this programme with new vision and based on our experience, we should revisit successes.

As the premier institution at national, international level I.I.P.A. should come forward to take lead in this innovative, bold, difficult experiment. Money should genuinely be not a problem because exercise itself will be very low cost. But if need be other departments must be involved to make the fruits of this experiment, experience available to others at a very very low cost.

The following will be the time frame for re-visiting successes:

1. General appeal to be publicised widely inviting volunteers to present their successes which were acclaimed in the last 40 years or so. This can be from any field. But the presentation should be maximum in one hour giving, origin, historical

development, linkages, money spent, objectives, successes claimed and replicability, extendability, economics etc. of the programme and how it stood after the experimentor left the scheme and the latest position with reference to the objective.

2. Invite synopsis and circulate it widely to all those who would like to participate in this exercise preferably at I.I.P.A. Delhi and regional branches.
3. Actual presentation of the successes and the question-answer session along with codification thereof.
4. Circulation of the gist to the present officialdom of the scene of success and inviting their views on the feeling of the experimentor.
5. Identify certain common lacuna which does not allow the experiment to succeed *in toto* over a period of time.
6. Codification of those points and ensuring their induction and infusion in the programme being formulated and implemented today.
7. Identifying certain common linkages which are difficult, normally mixed and vital for the success of the programme.

8

Professionalism and Civil Servants

The scope of Government activities has expanded manifold due to the acceptance of the concept of welfare state in our Constitution. The wide diversity of the activities of a welfare state has, however, made the entire administration a complex one. Dependence of public on Government, on one hand, has increased enormously but the administration has not come up to the expectations of the vast majority of the populace. The rise in people's aspirations and expectations, spurred on by prodigal promises by political leaders without any regard to the limitations of resources and procedural difficulties, make the people dejected and disappointed when they go to the government departments for the reparation of their grievances. The people do not depend on the government to conduct civil service examinations, carry on budgets and other such things. These are incidental. People expect the government to carry on programmes of general benefit and it is the execution of these programmes that is the proper focus of administration. In short, political awakening and consciousness of rising expectations had offered a new challenge to the administration.

The governance of man is the grandest of all professions. It is easier to seize power than to exercise it. Many, indeed, are the duties of the man who has chosen the work of rendering service to another. Even

'Yogis' do not find it easy. There are many opportunities in the service to do jobs that give one the satisfaction of having created something. The supply of service by the state is not governed by market price. For the most part, the aim of the democratic state is to supply its services to all who need them and to treat all consumers equally. The services performed by the state are more urgent than those performed by private institutions. It is also a general belief that the ethical standards of public officials are probably higher than those prevailing in business and other walks of life. The profound and special obligations which rest upon public servants as the instruments of government of the people and for the people, have long been close to the heart of the political and administrative development in every democracy. The significance of the outlook and behaviour of the government servants, both on duty and off, is substantial because of their pre-eminent position and because of the extent to which they represent the government in the everyday life of their fellow countrymen. Officers and employees of the government are servants of the people. Those holding public office, as servants of the public, are not owners of authority but agents of public purpose. Contentment of the people is the desired goal of administration. To quote the words of eminent person Wudrow Wilson:

> "Public administration should crown its duties with dutifulness. It should be responsive and responsible."

A time has come to more towards greater administrative efficiency and re-awaken a sense of response to the needs of the people. When the administrator closes his ears, the public opens its mouth. The rapport between the public and the administration must be direct. The latter must be in a position to sense the mood of the people and work towards goals meant for the benefit of the public at large. An administrator must have a first hand knowledge of what the common men say and do. The fate of the rural masses should not be left entirely at the mercy of the village level workers who not only show general apathy towards the development of villages but sometimes create obstacles in the smooth functioning of various schemes launched for the betterment of the villages. The implementation of important government schemes remain incomplete because of this half hearted and incomprehensive approach. Taking of government schemes to the doorsteps of the rural masses and to bring administration closer to people is the greatest need of the hour. Grudging acceptance by an individual of his responsibility and duties in a democratic, socialistic and welfare state, the desire to achieve successful results without hard work, lack of public interest, co-operation, non-adherence to truth and integrity as social norms, require extensive investigation and drastic change. As Edmund Burke has mentioned:

> "Those who are connected in the social work of real worth should be proof against fatiguing delays, mortifying disappointment, shocking insult and what is worst of all the presumptuous judgement of the ignorant."

Less and less people wanted to work in the sectors connected with poverty eradication and social upliftment. In a New Year Greetings (1987) sent by Sri D. Bandyopadhyay, Secretary, Rural Development,

Government of India, the following sentence seems to speak everything:

> 'Can we in the Rural Development by our empathy, dedication and diligence lessen the apprehension, the uncertainty, the drudgery of those who are looking towards the new year as awesome repetition of the old? May we resolve to wipe the tear from every eye.'

No amount of mechanical engineering can improve the edifice till social and ethical values continue to remain at their lowest ebb. Although the Government is not particularly interested in the private lives of its employees, it does expect them to be honest, reliable, trustworthy and of good character and reputation. They are expected to be loyal to the government and to the department or agency in which they are employed. A government servant should not subordinate his duty to his private interests, but neither is he to put himself in a position where his duty conflicts with his interests. Even senior government officers want to be in the corporate sector where facilities are in abundance and comparatively accountability less. No wonder those at the top of the hierarchy of public services prefer soft options. Allowed slowly but surely '*Bhrashtachar*' becoming '*Shishtachar*' as Vinobaji has said. The entire machinery can work honestly only if integrity and sincerity exist at the top of the organisation and the top has not merely got to be honest but has got to appear to be honest.

With the rising expectations from Government, the role of Government servant has definitely undergone a vast change. Along with the changes in the system, the professionalism of the Government servant also underwent drastic changes. When we talk of professionalism, we must be clear about the concept itself. According to Roscoe Pound, "There is much more in a profession than a traditional trade dignified calling. The terms refer to a group of men pursuing art as common calling in the spirit of public service, no less the public service because it may be incidentally a means of livelihood. Pursuit of the learned art in the spirit of public service is primary purpose." Webster has a different connotation. According to him, it is "a calling requiring specialised knowledge and often long and intensive preparation including instruction in skills and methods and committing its member to continued study and to a kind of work which has for its primary purpose the rendering of a public service."

When we look at our public services with important characteristic of professionalism, we obviously find something missing. The development of skills and methods may have been partly corrected but "the aspect of spirit" seems to be missing. When a person joins defence services, he has also in mind the concept of adventure, challenges, rewarding carrier. The war and other hazard like separation etc. are professional inconveniences. It would be pertinent to mention something about politics because no study of civil servant can be done in isolation. The politicians have their own professional hazards. The permanent administrators have to possess great amount of sagacity and tolerance. An administrator under obligation is weak and cannot function on his own. Even in the altered circumstances of today when administrators are subjected to pressure from various quarters, they must stand firm and refuse to give up the fundamental values of integrity, courage and objectivity. As somebody has said, "Managers of the future will need intellectual breadth, strategic capability, social sensibility, political sophistication, cool-mindedness and, above all, the capacity to keep their poise amid bewildering changes." No wonder in the fast changing situation, senior government servants and specially at senior level would have to have the capacity to play conflicting roles. They have to combine at times even mutually conflicting job. The integrating role they will have to play in promoting the neglected sector would be much more challenging. In a lecture delivered by Prof. R.C. Bhandarkar of the Deccan College of Poona and quoted in a short history of Indian Politics by Sir Vermy Lovett of Indian Civil Service (1919) reads:

> "We have been subjected to three fold political tyranny, priestly tyranny and social tyranny or the tyranny of castes. Crushed down by these, no man has dared to stand and assert himself. Even religious refuse have shunned the legitimate consequences of their doctrines to avoid coming into conflict with the established order of influence. At the present though we live in a foreign domination we enjoy freedom of thought and action as much as we never enjoyed before under our Hindu princes. But have we shown a capacity to shake ourselves free from priestly and social tyranny? I am afraid, not much."

Things are seldom very good or very bad. The system is as good or bad as people make it. What is right and wrong in administration is difficult to answer. Everything is right and wrong in its place. The secret of success in the service lies not in just being superficially smart but in hard work, in close study of the problems that come up and in their analysis, in observation of economic and social conditions, in appreciating the needs of the people and finding speedy and, if possible, simple means of satisfying them. The goal of our work, therefore, is not merely the disposal of files or papers or passing them around but satisfying human needs and human requirements. Behind every letter, application or file stands one or more human beings with their needs and requirements legitimate or otherwise.

One often hears the routine bound administrator bemoaning his lack of time to do anything constructive. He is probably working himself to death, penning over reams of paper, signing hundreds of letters and forms and sorting out little problems which should never have been brought to him. An untraced appraisal of his routine will reveal that he is probably spending half of his time on matters which could and should have been handled by his subordinates. Surely, an organisation does not hire a highly paid officer to deputise for a senior clerk. Making the best use of the best people, insisting on the highest standard of integrity and promoting mutual understanding and proper adjustment of human relations and reorganization will definitely ensure greater speed, effectiveness, responsiveness and efficiency.

Administrative talent means the capacity to understand and direct the work of others, to accept responsibility, to exercise good judgements in making difficult decisions and to infuse confidence in others in trying situations. Efficiency in action is Yoga. The best professional is one who has enough sense to pick up the right man for the right job, basing his selection on a correct judgement and assessment of the abilities of his officers and men. A professional should be aware of what is expected of him and what end he is working for. It is only when the field of responsibility is clear that one can find out ways and means to achieve an objective. An executive is like a carpenter and manpower are his tools. By skilful and methodical use of his tools, a carpenter, can shape the wood to a required design and pattern. With the same set of tools, one carpenter is able to make a crude bench, another a good chair and yet a third one, a shining almirah. What does this mean? It simply means that it is not so much in the tools but in the person using them that the key to good workmanship lies. Lot depends upon the persons who are manning the organization. Officers at the helm of affairs cannot be absolved of the responsibilities if the system is not functioning properly.

In a State like Uttar Pradesh and Bihar the former Cabinet Secretary to the Government of India have criticised both politicians and bureaucrats. Many experienced people have opined that if between IAS and politicians blame has to be contributed, then more will go in favour of IAS. This is the area for professionals as it concern the top service. The challenging time like ours require that we take up professionalism as very important aspect and develop suitable plan of action.

9

Scope for Improvement

The transport organisation is very old and it also mainly a Non-Plan Department. The office buildings are very old and working conditions are not public service oriented. Since new procedures have not been evolved, the speed of disposal of the work is slow and movement of papers involves handling by a number of functionaries. It is, therefore, impossible for the public to get the job done directly. A number of touts and Dalals have mushroomed and even if somebody dares to introduce change in the working culture, it is not allowed by the vested interests. To add, forms, information system, file covers and adequate stationery are not available and rates of taxes are not widely publicised. The frequency of visits of customers to get the job done has also not been reduced. The dirt, filth, unhygienic conditions and primitive filing system make things really unbearably frustrating.

Whenever any increase in staff or building space has been done, it has not kept pace with the increased work-load. Though the potential of the Department to augment revenue for the Government and to give better working facilities to public is stupendous, no systematic effort has ever been made to improve upon the situation.

Nature of the Problem

To make any improvements fruitful and lasting, it is essential that the problems are identified. The following were observed to be the major problems:

(a) No clarity as to what are the major works being performed?
(b) What was the frequency of visit of people, for what job, total financial implication of person who came to the office.
(c) No consideration of efforts of the past to improve the situation and with very little or no impact.

Observations: Once the nature of the problem was identified, the following observations were recorded by an inspecting officer after sitting with all officers of the Department in the place of working for 5 days:

Nature of Work Performed

		Broadly in two categories	
		of heavy vehicles	of light vehicles
		1	2
(i)	Type of vehicle	Truck /Bus/ Matador/Taxis, i.e. heavy vehicles.	Private Scooter, Cars, Mopeds/ Govt. Cars, i.e. light vehicles.
(ii)	Type of client	Professional Transport Coys., Govt. Heavy vehicles; individual heavy vehicles etc.	Doctors/ Advocates, Lower, Middle Class for Car etc. & Light vehicle owners. Farmers for tractors etc.
(iii)	Nature of work frequency & fees to be paid.	Registration of vehicles, obtain fitness certificates, collect permits for three years or 4 months temporary; or 28 days outside the State, pay taxes.	To get registration of vehicles (only one in lifetime of the vehicles).

		1	2
(iv)	Pay taxes of vehicles and permits.	Every 3 months. Road Tax for 3 months Rs. 1800; Goods tax 3 months Rs. 1350; Passenger tax - different amounts, different routes.	Pay taxes (annually) - Moped Rs. 35; Schooter Rs. 55; Car Rs. 150.
(v)	Permit fees	Varying from Rs. 50 to Rs. 160 for 4 months to 3 years. For National Permits an extra fee of Rs. 500 per annum.	
(vi)	Driving Licence Fees	Rs. 15/- for 3 years	Rs. 15/- for 5 years.
	Quantum of work load	10%	90%
	Percentage of revenue collected.	90%	10%
	Distribution of staff (clerical level)	30%	70%
	Supervisory level	80%	20%
	Rules and procedures for jobs to be done.	Same for both types of clients.	
	Number of new vehicles added annually (approx)	700	30,000
	Issue of new driving licences etc.	1,000	10,000
	Procedure of accounting and receipt of taxes; granting of registration numbers etc.	Same registers and Same procedures.	
	Total number of forms etc. required for completing various formalities.	100	20

Conclusions

From the above observations, the following conclusions were drawn:

(1) Work load was heavy on light vehicles but revenues were from heavy vehicles;

(2) Clientele of light vehicles owners consists of educated middle and higher class. They normally prefer to get their jobs done directly, without involving Dalals if working conditions are conducive to direct work.

(3) Frequency of coming to office is annual in case of light vehicle owners. The aspects of time, behaviour, courtesy, promptness etc. were more important for them. To reduce their coming more often, taxes of more than one year could be accepted and better facilities could be provided.

(4) Owners of heavy vehicles have to come more frequently (at times even weekly) to get various jobs done. They tend to develop contacts with staff of office and mostly prefer to get their jobs done through Dalals since it also helps them in saving time and energy.

(5) Chances and temptation to avoid taxes were more with heavy vehicles owners since rates of taxes are much higher and chances of detection were less.

(6) It also means if more attention could be paid to monitoring of taxes, checking, etc. of heavy vehicles, more revenue would accrue to Government with minimum of effort.

(7) Urgent need to bifurcate accounting, collection and registration number granting process for both types of vehicles.

(8) Since two different types of clientele are

involved, it is imperative that they need two different types of behaviour from the same office. It is a very difficult requirement.

(9) Rules and procedures have to be suitably modified to give them differential treatment. This may, at times, need Government sanction.

Constraints to Action Plan (On Observations and Conclusions)

1. Government will not easily sanction new posts of clerks etc. and funds for construction of own buildings according to actual requirements.
2. For separating workload of the two types of vehicles, registers, account books, etc. will be needed. How to print them? This would involve extra expenditure.
3. How to change established working norms, patterns, system of movement of paper and set working culture, working since decades?
4. How to make extra working space available? If separation of heavy and light vehicles workload has to be done, Finance Department would not accept heavy rental burden so easily?
5. Departmental senior officers, clerks of the office and on top of them touts or Dalals who have been working since many years would not allow this rational change to take place without lot of resistance. So to make it a success, this change has to be gradual, concerted and staff has to be motivated and convinced.

What was Done?

(1) Separation of allotments of numbers relating to light vehicles and shifting this work to Headquarters

Office. This necessitated vacation of three ground floor rooms in Head Office and construction of a shed in front for people to stand. The rooms were already available at no extra cost as Government had recently spent about Rs. 20 lakhs on building-expansion for the Head Office. Now it cost only Rs. 9,000 for shed which was within the powers of the Head of Department. The windows towards shed were adjusted to work as counters.

(2) Comparatively younger clerks already working in office were selected, trained and motivated to work in new counters. (It was made very clear that otherwise their services were at stake).

(3) Some exercise was conducted and specific steps were taken to :

(a) reduce movement of paper;
(b) reduce number of forms;
(c) print forms on both sides of paper;
(d) reduce size of forms to be used;
(e) motivate people to deposit taxes for more than one year;
(f) accept taxes all the year-round instead of only in the month of December; and
(g) involve dealers of light vehicles in filling up of forms, guidance to public about rates of taxes, procedure of registration etc.

(4) Required forms, registers, etc. were printed in sufficient number at Government Press. For this, personal liaison was established with the Superintendent, Printing and Stationery, U.P., Headquarters Office had to centralise printing work instead of 25 different offices doing it earlier.

(5) Supervisory staff was motivated to sit in the shed and were exposed to public.

(6) Communication with public was better achieved

through loud-speaker announcement and by making forms, table, bench, etc. available in the shed. 'At your service' boards were displayed prominently where 'helpers' were sitting in the shed. People were requested to 'co-operate and help' in the beginning.

(7) Rates of taxes, procedure, facilities, etc. were all prominently written on a big board. This was by courtesy of a reputed dealer of light vehicles.

(8) Names of clerks who were collecting taxes, issuing receipts, giving licences, taking tests, etc. were displayed boldly and prominently. These were announced through loud-speaker also.

(9) An enquiry counter was established which also supplied forms and which was manned by a trained 'blind' girl. Enough space was made available for people to move about and park their light vehicles.

(9A) The lay-out of the office complex was designed to suit the total need of the user. The following chart would explain:

Corridor		Portico	
6	6	6	6
1	1	1	1
2	2	3	3
5	5	5	
Vacant		space	
4		4	
Main Road			

1. Clerks sitting behind window.
2. Technical Inspector and Clerk and spare table in the shed.
3. Inquiry and Notice boards.
4. Vacant space.
5. Place for public to sit.
6. Clerks & Head Clerk.

(10) Work of VIPs or of people who brought bulk

work of big departments etc. was done after 2 O'clock. This was to attend to 'direct comers' first.

(11) Effort was made to send teams to major offices where all work would be done there only. This was to offer home facilities to 'honoured customers'. Days were fixed at the request of these major offices.

(12) More and more emphasis was placed on efficiency, quickness and concurrent monitoring and evaluation of workload. Quick follow-up action was taken wherever necessary. Internal Audit Party was deputed to carry out timely audit. Earlier, vested interests were fought with public confidence and by creating conditions for direct work in minimum time.

(13) Wide publicity was given to cases to forgery, false licences, etc. which were caught by the Department, through papers and loud-speaker. The hand of touts was exposed and surprise raids were conducted to get rid of touts from new premises of office.

(14) Officials/clerks reporting forgeries were given special entries and their achievements were circulated to all other officers for encouraging them to perform better.

(15) Since work was being done smoothly, people did not go to touts. Lesson learnt, "to get rid of touts, your efficiency is the best remedy."

(16) No money was spent on purchasing of loud-speaker. They were already available in the Department lying dead and silent. They were only made to use. Office furniture, almirah, etc. were all brought from old office only. They were only made to look new and life was put into them.

(17) Work at old R.T.O. office was systematised due to increased availability of space. Cleanliness and orderliness ushered in. More attention was paid to monitoring of taxes, evasion, forgery and many other steps which were not taken since years together.

Responsibility could now be fixed. Permits, routes upgradation, transfers, seizure about heavy vehicles could now be looked into because 90% of total workload had been shifted somewhere else and senior officers of the office could get sufficient time to look into cases of heavy vehicle owners.

(18) Continuous effort was made to involve users into the whole operation. For a few months, office was opened even on Sundays to offer better services to light vehicle owners. It was a happy sight to see people coming with their families and after getting their jobs done, going to buy vegetables on Sunday morning.

(19) The total effect of this was increase in revenue from light vehicles, better services to users, recovery of very heavy old dues and detection of innumerable cases of forgery and cheating to Government. The office was geared to its maximum efficiency. The availability of better working conditions, forms, registers, file covers, information and on top recognition of good work and quick admonition to bad workers brought good results.

(20) Incentive scheme for catching major tax evasion was sent to Government, but it could not see the light of the day.

(21) Monthly systematic monitoring was started direct by Headquarters to reduce time factor and to relieve all supervisory, field officers for field work.

Conclusions

Longfellow says:

> "Each morning, sees some task begun,
> Each evening, sees it close;
> Something attempted something done,
> Has earned a night's repose."

He has also at other place mentioned:

> "Trust no future, however pleasant,
> Let the dead past bury its dead;
> Act, act in the living present,
> Heart within and God o'er head.

Off and on changes are introduced in our system. Some changes stand the test of time. The change agent plays his role according to his perception, training, motivation and orders. Granting that change agent tries to put his best in a given situation, he has to be aware of his limitations and also the characteristics and peculiarities of the system in which he is operating. The constraints of continuity also plays a very important role. Many times, changes introduced may not stand the test of time. It would not be very proper to highlight again the points which have already been highlighted somewhere. Here we have a report by Mr. Anil Kumar Lakhina, published in the Indian Institute of Public Administration Journal. The study was about the reforms in the Collectorate of Ahmednagar and in the concluding portions, Mr. Lakhina, the author, who was instrumental in conceiving and implementing reforms has brought out very succinctly the problems of the change agent. He mentions, "One of the weaknesses in the reforms introduced in the Collectorate is its local approach. A bureaucratic machinery is notorious for the preference to *status quo*. It has `extraordinary resilience to come back to its original form no matter what interventions were made at any time, unless these interventions also brought simultaneous changes at Central or State level' (Anil K. Gupta of IIM Ahmedabad). Though it is heartening to note that senior officials and non-officials have appreciated this effort yet the will to carry them elsewhere has to crystallise itself."

"The element of giving importance to clerical staff, it appears, has been given a concession. The office has Class I officers (30), Class II officers (34) and Class III staff (1171). It is the last category which determines the personality of the administrative apparatus by its sheer number. Addressed in other way, the ego aspect remains important. Reforms introduced have to provide for the filler which promote self-esteem. It is all right to have pride in changes introduced and for being instrumental in doing so. But the euphoria may not last long. Then what?"

"The aspect of inspiration is also critical. It is beyond doubt that the present Collector could inspire and motivate his team and staff to stir change. Before taking this leap, the self of the inspirer has to wield an iron will. So long the will pervades, the system obeys. The moment the will fades, the system recoils. A strong fear lurks that these reforms may not be long standing."

"Complete severance of clerk-public contact may never succeed nor is it necessary. Certain levels of public will not get convinced unless the windows open up in clerical ranks. However, it would be an interesting exercise to regulate this contact. The effort is to make the system more public oriented. The idea to limit the clerk-public contact is intended to minimise the favours that creep in and not because there is less confidence in clerical ranks. It can also be hypothesized that if the perceptions are enlarged at the lowest levels, better changes may surface."

Having mentioned what Mr. Lakhina has written about his experience in the field of reforms in the Collectorate, one may venture to look back and think over the failure of the reform conceived and implemented systematically. We will have to go in for introduction of gradual mechanization of our activities.

A machine costing about ten thousand rupees was purchased but subsequently, it was found that it was of no use. These experiments could have been successful provided initial thinking was proper.

With best of efforts, the will and skill of the people who work has to be properly developed and maintained. In recent years, emphasis on training of the highest level is a welcome step. What is needed is the development of right type of attitude towards training content. This can be done only by committed, suitably trained and practical trainer.

Need to highlight good work done and to sustain it over a period of time is another single, important work which needs attention. The publicity of success stories and good work done anywhere needs proper exposer. After all in a society where ordinary work hardly matters, at every level it is important to highlight good work done.

Need to integrate the activities of training centres and practical administrators must be emphasised. At the moment, training institutions and men in the field operate at cross purposes. At times, they even criticise the ignorance and indifference of each other. Policy making level would have to co-ordinate and suitably demarcate the role of each other.

This case study was written sometime in 1991-92. Since then many changes have taken place around transport sector. Many vehicles have been exempted while other taxes have been made simpler.

The idea is to explore the potential of long term mind-setting in continuously searching for improvement.

10

This is just to Thank You — God

Somebody has said, "For every ailment under the sun; there is a remedy or there is none. If there is one, try to find it; if there is none, never mind it."

We are all daily confronted with problems. We have social problems, family problems, settlement problems and plethora of other problems. According to our background, training, will and perception, we try to solve them. Problems are the part of life. We cannot have any person engaged in any occupation without problem. Then there are national and international problems. They are the problems of very high magnitude and require cohesive acumen and sagacity to get over those problems.

There are many scientific ways of solving problems, but it all depends on the will and skill of the problem-solver as to how he solves it.

In this connection, I am reminded of a quotation. It reads, "God, give me strength, to change the things I can, to accept the things I cannot change, and the wisdom to know the difference."

The above golden quotation makes us well-equipped to face the problems. The greatest problem of our time is the problem of frustration; with our best of efforts and intentions, how to know our limitations? Initially, we start with idealism. Without going into the practicalities we impose our perceived solutions. Sometimes they work and many times they don't. When they don't work, we find fault — mostly in others. Finding faults is not bad in itself, provided it is with open mind. The real problem starts here. Once the stage of getting over the problem is over, sponsored criticism of the system and machinery begins. This is the stage when one must be very careful lest one may become disgruntled and confirmist. It is here, the quotation enjoins us to accept the things we cannot change. But this acceptance is not total. It has to be qualified by objectivity of the problems. Somebody has also said that if things were that easy, everybody could have done them. Needless to say, explorers of results cannot give up so easily. Desires to keep trying depends again on our confidence. This confidence is to be developed in yourself and also others. After every mishap, one can also say that it could have been even worst. The very fact that things are still not in the category of worst, think, still good things are there. Obviously, change agent or pursuer of objectives has to be self-motivated and man of conviction. He has to experiment. Even the worse of people have some good buttons. It is on the confidence and experience of the button-pusher that the reaction depends.

Having known the limitations of the efforts and the hard work, it is very essential that one knows the meaning of "the wisdom to know the difference". If one cares to decipher the message of failures, as explained above, every person has his perceptions and if every one has to succeed in his pursued aims, things would be in an utter disarray. It is great fun to hear these perceptions. Sometimes one shudders to think as to what would happen if the perceptions of some figures were to materialize! We do not have to go any far off to see people of this type. They are our near and dears. Even the most positive person might create grave complications for the society, if all his self-perceived positive ideas were to materialize! Needless to emphasize that as it is bad for all ideas to fail, same way, all ideas must not succeed. We are human beings. Only machines can bring uniformity. Hence, we must accept that difference in what you are able to achieve and what you are not able to, can be explained very rationally and analytically.

If one can understand the great philosophy behind this type of quotation, life would be much enjoyable. After all, the worst of tragedies also need justification. The best of rational, the worst of irrational—both have justifications. Even the worst squanderer can produce evidence to adduce their cause. In this connection, one must thank God if one gets the wisdom to understand the complexities in which we are not only to live but have to survive and die. Thank you, God, once again.

11

Mahatma Gandhi and Peaceful World Order

In the twentieth century two prominent economic philosophies have changed the world beyond recognition. One is Marxist philosophy and the other is Gandhian philosophy. Emancipation of man from all types of exploitation were the aims of both Karl Marx and Mahatma Gandhi. However, peace is the precondition of Gandhian thought. As violence breeds further violence and for economic prosperity, peace or non-violence is the prime condition, Gandhiji wanted to eschew violence from all institutions of life. It goes without saying that a peaceful world order, can only come by the practice of non-violence by the majority of the nations of the world.

In the decades of forties and fifties, some of the newly freed under-developed countries of the world were attracted towards violent struggle against the colonial powers and wanted to follow the marxian path. However, many of these republics could not remain peaceful after their hard gained independence. As a pioneer of the freedom movement of India, Gandhiji knew, too well that if India earns her freedom by a violent struggle, violence would continue for a long time after freedom. Thus, although quitting of the British from India was the *summum bonum* of his life's mission, Gandhiji never wanted a bloody violent struggle for removing the British, because of its aftermath.

Gandhiji considered the entire world as one unit and all mankind as his brethren. As the colonial powers were not following the principle of equality of man, which Gandhiji considered as the law of God, he had to fight relentlessly against them but he had no personal hatred against any particular nation or race. Gandhiji had fine rapport with the British labourers and intellectuals.

In a discussion with Lord Irwin, he said picking up the "Holy Bible" from the viceroy's table that "all problems of your country and my country can be solved if Jesus Christ's teachings given in the sermon on the Mount can be followed by the people of England and India together". By this, Gandhi meant to say that if the people of the ruling country and the ruled country realise God's wish that no one should exploit another and behave with a brotherly attitude and help each other in a spirit of equality and gain prosperity through hard work, all problems of all countries would be naturally solved.

A peaceful world-order is only possible, if this proposition of Mahatma Gandhi is applied in the International Affairs of today. Actually, it is not invented by Gandhiji but is the oldest principle of peace.

All religious scriptures of the world, say although in different languages that God loves peace. A peaceful man and a peaceful nation is liked by God and get all his grace. Mahatma Gandhi was a deeply religious man, and professed that Truth is God and God is Truth. He was religious, not in a parochial sense but in a very broad sense. It is only a great soul like him can embrace truths from all religions — Hinduism, Islam, Christianity etc. This broad framework of mind elevated him to the greatest statesman and political thinker of all times of the world. It may sound little exaggerated today. But in years to come, in the coming generations, Gandhian views on world Affairs and political thinking would prove correct.

Gandhiji, said that *Satyagraha* is meant for the common people, not merely for saints. It is war without violence. It is based on love, not on hate. It is based on loving one's opponents and suffering to convince them. It differentiates between the sin and the sinner, between the evil and the evil-doer. It is the weapon of the brave, not of the weak. It demands discipline and may entail self-sacrifice, suffering, fasting, imprisonment and death, yet it is the supreme virtue of providing means consonant with the highest ends. (Ref: Homer Jack).

Mahatma Gandhi's political doctrine of peace and Non-Violence was prescribed not only for the Indian sub-continent but for the whole of the world. Gandhiji shared contemporary regard with statesman like Churchill and Roosevelt as well as with creative thinkers like Einstein and Schweitzer. His concern for a peaceful world-order is reflected in his comments and thoughts on the American Negros, persecution of the Jews by the Christians, Jews and Palestine, Zionisim and Anti-semitism, Jewish people's craze for a home land, Socialism and Communism, the Czech problem, combating Hitlerism and even on Atomic warfare. Mahatma Gandhiji's letters to Franklin D. Roosevelt, Chiang-kai-Shek, Lord Linlithgow etc. shows his clear understanding of the world politics and his impressions on it. To the then US President Roosevelt, Gandhiji wrote, "I hate all war" (Ref. July 1, 1942).

Mahatma Gandhi's Views on a Peaceful World-Order

Mahatma Gandhi was not a political theorist but he was a political engineer. He did not like him to be labelled as a saint-turned politician but a politician aspiring to be a saint. His love for Truth and God, instilled in him a burning faith in Non-violent freedom movement. He advised this path not for India alone but for the whole of the world. Regarding persecution or Jewish community in different European countries, he advised them the stick to their century-old home-country and not to crave for a separate home land. He advised all, who are exploited and persecuted to offer passive resistance to the authorities that exploit.

Gandhiji — Lessons for Action

We celebrated his 125th birth anniversary of father of the nation. As the time passes the need to look at Mahatma Gandhi from practical utility with reference to action becomes important. Nations like individuals possess their own responsibility and distinct characteristics based upon the requirement of change, aspiration of the people, changing value system, need to reexamine becomes paramount. The whole gamut of synergisation of truth, non-voilence, simplicity, characteristics, mission and on the whole a personification of action.

This is supposed to be the time of the masses. The day of personalised systems would be turned around by a principled system. There will be need to relook at things from various angles. Professionals are required to be substituted by objectivity. Principle have to have transparency.

The 125th anniversary of Mahatma Gandhi presented a golden opportunity. The strength, weaknesses and opportunity, sustained analysis offers reexamination from holistic angles.

It is interesting to study some aspects of the constructive programmes as how implications could be done based on lessons and action — "L & A".

Action Plan required and relevance of 125th anniversary

(1) Identify models which have been developed on the basis of Gandhi-Vinoba. They may include Relegaon Sidhi, Tamil Nadu, Wardha, Rajasthan.
(2) What are the lessons of prohibition in Gujarat and Wardha? Have they brought bad name?
(3) Re-orientation and re-examination of constructive programmes and lessons to be learnt to remodel them.
(4) Free, frank, fearless attitude for examination.
(5) Analysis of the problems from different angles like those who are politicians, industrialists, social service citizens, bureaucracy including administration, police at lower level.
(6) Role of institutions working for Gandhian studies, research, experiments, technology and their views along with need to follow laboratory approach, in carrying out experiments in field with human behaviour.
(7) Changes which were not thought or perceived during his time like generation and availability of small technologies entrepreneurship concepts, lessons or failure of vocational and basic education, decentralisation of ginning, pressing and development of Biogas technology, availability of scientific knowledge on organic manure, development of rural tourism, views of the critics of his time and how those products have been proved right or wrong. What was the basis of the criticism that time and even today and how elite bureaucrats made mockery of values with special reference to prohibition and other religious behaviour patterns etc.
(8) What all he said about certain principles so close to him and how do we find it today?

(9) How business-like approach to his cherished terms is possible since all personalities are ultimately marketed by their failures either to carry on with the work started or to somehow continue their provision? How does the lobby work? What are the pressure points? How did Vinobaji, Sane Guruji, Kumarappaji and many others were being perceived?

(10) What was the role of various programmes like All India Spinners Association, All India Village Industries Association, prohibition, policies, prayers and how the massive funds ultimately were utilised.

(11) How many institutions fared well which were started by him during various phases whether relating to education, technology, employment, language.

(12) What was the life style, values of subsequent followers as also the hope signals developed?

Communal Unity

This programme is meant for bringing different groups together. There was an element of harmony. Unification based on to meet basic essential behavioural principle. Subsequently, various organisations were grouped to develop community. But as time passes, this becomes a serious problem. It seems that ultimately, economic need to have a communal unity will be the only binding forces.

The lessons of history speak in the current time, invariably draws this conclusion. Hence economic consideration will have to be given supreme importance to usher in communal unity.

Removal of Untouchability

Granting that untouchability has been the biggest

curse of India, various efforts were initiated both legally, administratively. The untouchability has been reduced considerably. But caste structure has become dominating. Today, in many States it is at the top. The political compulsions have made it very dominant force. Hence in the final analysis, the caste structure would be weakened only when economic forces dominate. How this will be done? With opening of principle will be changed to honour merit, irrespective of caste or region. The need to perform would leave no option but to honour merit through economic consideration.

Languages

Again some questions can be asked. Why both in provincial languages and national language we have various problems.

Gandhiji's View on Languages

Mahatma Gandhi wanted that in free undivided India, Hindi and Urdu should be used simultaneously i.e. Hindustani language, both in Devanagari script and Persian script, should be used simultaneously. Had this suggestion of Mahatma was accepted, Muslim brethren, would not felt alienated with Sanskritised Hindi, since Hindustani language was in vogue in India, for a very long span of 4/5 centuries as court language and lingua franca in major part of the Indian sub-continent, Mahatma Gandhi's suggestion was quite appropriate.

Promotion of Economic Quality

Can we draw happy picture? To what extent with harmony decentralised mode of monitoring and upgradation of available local technologies could have helped in better economic quality.

In some way, programmes of Cow protection, Nature cure, Bhoodan, Gramdan and Shanti Sena, labour and student need to be examined. What were the reasons with these programmes. Why did they not aspire hope.

All the above constructive programmes with their strength, weaknesses, opportunities need relook. Panchayati Raj institution became more and more important. Many of these programmes of constructive nature have been given to them by constitutional amendment. There are economic issues and have to be examined in totality.

Analysis

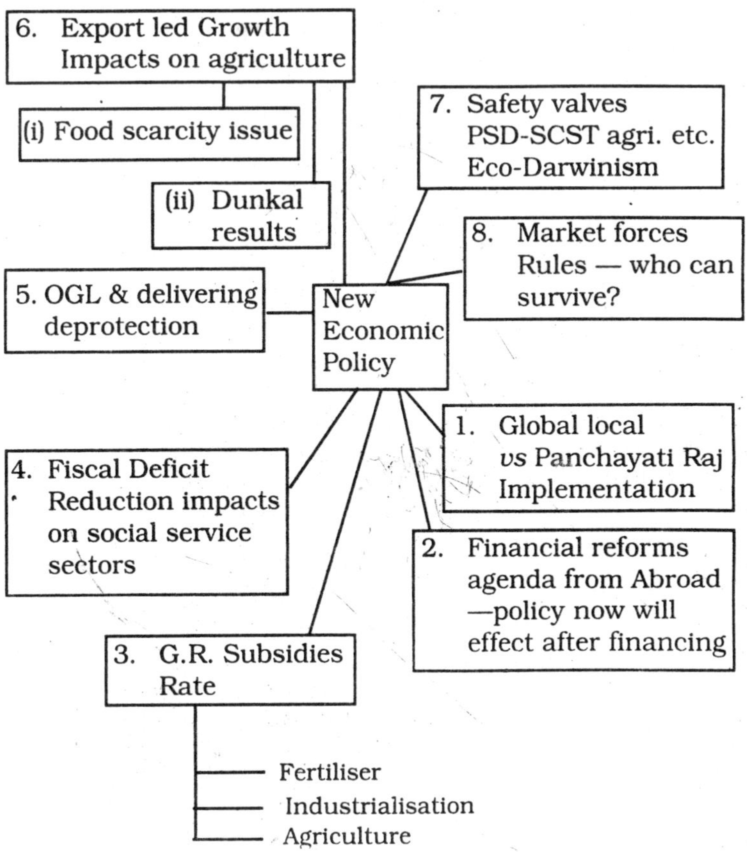

Competitiveness

- Traditional artisan
- Skills - Manpower

Redesigning of Resources - globally
Matching by policies

competitive

- Rate of marketing
- Reframing
- How to do it?
- Priorities
- Better use of Resources

NEP

- Global *vs* local
- Panchayati Raj
- NEP contains

Liberalise - Globalise
Security - Food
High Value Crops
Sustainable agriculture

Balancing Role

— Must have growth
Cravity
Carrying capacities of sources, i.e.
Sustainability Issue in totality.

Major Components:

Agriculture pricing
Linkage in Agriculture & Rural Industrialisation
Rate of Panchayati Raj institutions
Household units— implements
Price ratios—inputs—outputs
Fixed costs etc.

Issues NEP

Promotion — Organisations
Price Policies.

Endless — Beginning to Endlessness — India

1. Habit formation
2. How the habits are formed?
3. How they stay?
4. How the habits are changed?
   (a) With quality, clarity and vocation
   (b) Reasoning
   (c) Scientific analysis
   (d) Role of spiritualism and need to develop spiritual resort — spark into flame — song of heart and prayer as nourishment for happiness.
5. How things appear and disappear — who sees and watches them and role of eye. In this connection of opening and closing.
6. Questions must come automatically. Role of ideas — good and bad ideas — time and need to ponder over goodness or badness with reference to time, people, originator.
7. Light from within Atman, Parikshan — justifying *versus* non-justifying.
8. SWOT of India—
   (i) Spirituality
   (ii) English
   (iii) Ayurvedic
   (iv) Deep understanding, love and family — discarding I — redefining beauty, look, know — luck, now need to act today.
9. Wise from insight. Getting it — Eye, We, They, Us — the importance of the present moment.
10. Experience, importance, vision broadening realising yourself through holistic approach.

12

Economic Issues in Panchayat

With the Constitution Seventy Third Amendment Act 1992, the scope of activities of Panchayati Raj institutions have considerably widened. As a matter of fact, Panchayati Raj system represents people's needs and their aspirations. They can thus give a fillip to all activities operating/operated in rural areas with the sole aim of bringing about rural industrialisation in real sense of the term.

As defined in the Constitution, "Panchayat" means the institution (by whatever name called) of self-government constituted under Article 243B for the rural areas of a Panchayat.

Here, it is pertinent to point out that Panchayati Raj system is not totally new to India. However, with the above amendment the Panchayats have been accorded the recognition as a harbinger of effecting change in rural scene. What is to be noted is that all the 29 items added to Eleventh Schedule of the Constitution were directed towards economic upliftment and with their true implementation, economic status of villagers will be elevated. Following are the 29 items of activities as enunciated in the Constitution:

1. Agriculture, including agricultural extension.
2. Land improvement, implementation of land reforms, land consolidation and soil conservation
3. Minor irrigation, water management and water-

shed development.

4. Animal husbandry, dairying and poultry.
5. Fisheries.
6. Social forestry and farm forestry.
7. Minor forest produce.
8. Small scale industries, including food processing industries.
9. Khadi, village and cottage industries.
10. Rural housing.
11. Drinking water.
12. Fuel and fodder.
13. Roads, culverts, bridges, ferries, waterways and other means of communications.
14. Rural electrification, including distribution of electricity.
15. Non-conventional energy sources.
16. Poverty alleviation programme.
17. Education, including primary and secondary school.
18. Technical training and vocational education.
19. Adult and non-formal education.
20. Libraries.
21. Cultural activities.
22. Markets and fairs.
23. Health and sanitation, including hospitals, primary health centres and dispensaries.
24. Family welfare.
25. Women and child development.
26. Social welfare including welfare of the handicapped and mentally retarded.
27. Welfare of the weaker sections, and in particular of the Sheduled Castes and the Sheduled Tribes.
28. Public distribution system.
29. Maintenance of community assets.

Rural Enterprise development is a must to achieve desired result as expected of Panchayati Raj institutions. Pooling of resources is a *sine qua non* for success of any venture, particularly those related to rural areas. But it has been seen that pooling of existing available resources of both manpower, infrastructure and expertise have been lacking in the past. Hence, it calls for new orientation in the entire gamut of economic activities so that rural sector is endowed with plentiful resources to feed myriads of activities, including 29 aforesaid items.

Panchayati Raj and Action Plan

To concretise rural enterprise development, there is a need for working together for this purpose, we have to give a good bye to callous attitudes now gripping our minds. At the same time, Planning, Action, Research, Codification, Extension and Loaning (PARCEL) concept must be practised. It is so because it pre-supposes policy changes at various levels. This concept also ensures fuller utilisation of investment through organiser entrepreneur with a view to facilitate sustainable self-employment enterprise.

Poverty is directly an offspring of exploitative policy. Hence, it is essential that a participative system is developed. This participative system has to encompass all aspects of life. It has a bearing on various issues influencing the policy planning. The removal of poverty visualise certain amount of co-ordination, linkages, monitoring, funding and internal resource generation through marketing. As far as the monitoring aspect is concerned, it connotes not only social consciousness but also the self-management. This will lead to attitudinal changes in the long run. The diversity of these problems can be understood better with reference to local approach i.e. with active involvement of Panchayati Raj institutions are capable of taking up a holistically designed plan of action for sustainable employment generation. It calls for a well conceived tie up with a programme. In this connection, the case study of Bassi (Rajasthan) would be of great interest. This brings forth the following aspects:

(1) Linkages with Panchayati Raj for income generating programme.
(2) Diversification of income generating activities with greater thrust on women programme.
(3) Long term region-wise plan of action.

It is essential that for evolving co-operative, integrated, well monitored and co-ordinated plan of action, attention ought to be paid on planning, action, research, codification and implementation aspects with Bank Finance. To derive best result, simultaneously there must be a well developed approach.

Panchayati Raj Activities

The Panchayati Raj institutions will have to mobilise resources not only by taxes, fees and licences, but also by borrowing from banks, co-operatives even from private money lenders. Their funds will be required not only by direct activities to be run by the Panchayati Raj institutions themselves but also for the unemployed youths, co-operatives and the institutions wanting to generate the activities in this sphere. It means the question of privatising some of the activities within the villages and it need not be ruled out. Though it may seem a difficult preposition today, but if we look into cost effecting aspect and need to mobilise and galvanise the activities, we will find no other option. Hence, some consideration on proper pricing would be essential if resources have to be mobilised, generated, and properly utilised.

The experience of rural banks or cooperatives has not been very encouraging. Even funding of the Integrated Rural Development Programme by commercial banks has not been satisfactory. In this situation, we have to learn from the past experiences. Why this has failed? Why the tendency has been not to repay the loans? Why social pressure could not be built up? We have to remember that ours had been a starved society. Whether it was consumption, way of life, material resources accumulation, traditionally we have been told to sacrifice and satisfy with the limited resources. Still in the last few decades, there has been clamour for materialisation. Hence, now a situation has developed where the tendency of consuming even the root of programme is discernible. As a result, we find the poor utilisation of resources and investment. Hence, the first lesson to remember is that in a starved society, the human behaviour will need very close, open and interlocked monitoring. This means two things. First, the principles governing bank finance must be so articulated as to provide incentives for outputs. Secondly the strategy and tactical efforts must help the society to develop empathy and broader vision so that the investment, generated surplus and resources itself are not consumed.

Principles to guide mobilisation of resources:

(i) Project must be from small to big.
(ii) Emphasis of social measures for sustaining the project and ensuring recoveries.
(iii) Costing of linkages must be in-built without depending on State interventions
(iv) Activities must be replicable and self-employment oriented.
(v) Emphasis should be on human resources rather than capital resources.

(vi) Existing raw materials must be processed with effective technology and stored to gain maximum economic advantage for the rural areas.

(vii) Transparency and openness should be the hallmark.

Once the principles for formulating the projects, implementing them, monitoring them, as also evolving an integrated and holistically developed model is clear, efforts can be made to mobilise resources with proper strategy and tactics which will include:

(1) Maximum use of existing infrastructure. It may belong to any Banks. The policies must be tailored to the requirements of the Panchayati Raj enterprise.

(2) Regular studies on replicable and failure models should be ensured with the active involvement of schools or academic institutions in that area so that a vocational type of linkages could be built up.

(3) The parameters of judging and grading the good work should be transparently disseminated.

(4) Role of women and weaker sections should always be highlighted.

(5) Self-employment oriented self-supporting model should be developed, training should be linked with it and teachers should be involved in every activities.

(6) All the compatible competitiveness and strengths, weaknesses, opportunities and threats of rural areas are always to be kept in mind.

(7) The social accountability and social pressure should invariably be resorted to.

(8) To achieve this, intermediary interaction with successful Managers as well as unsuccessful Managers should take place.

(9) Emphasis should be laid on self-financing or borrowing from within the village or indirectly minimum dependence on funding agencies. This will indirectly mean building up of self-confidence in enterprise developers who will indirectly call for various policy changes.

Locally Based Economy

In the above perspective, we must view the local economy. Local basically refers to lowest entity, analysis and intervention. Local has to be understood with reference to political, economic and social interest. Overall commonality of interest becomes its inseparable part. It is a qualitative criterion and significant area approach. Panchayats in India have been formed based on population and it has something in common. Hence local enterprise could definitely encompass indigenous commonalities. The enterprise concept with reference to income generating activities in a given area visualises capacity to develop income generating and risk taking entrepreneurial capabilities.

Local approach as opposed to regional or State approach, signifies certain differences. The reason for this emphasis can be explained in Table 12.1

Table 12.1 : Differences in Local and State Approaches

	Point of differences	*Local approach*	*State Approach*
1.	Accountabiliy	Much more	Much less
2.	Distance	Very near	Very far off
3.	Social aspect	Very relevant	Remote
4.	Sensitivity	Much more	Much less
5.	Neatness	Very much	Remote
6.	Trust aspect	Has to be there	Remote
7.	Language	Local language	Different language
8.	Accessibility	Very much	May be

If we understand the point of difference properly, it should not be very difficult to fathom the need to give an economic thrust on Panchayati Raj institutions for developing successful models.

Role of Castes

The castes have played a very important role in sustaining villages both as social and economic homogeneous self-supporting and self-governing institutions. Traditional caste structure, which has undergone a sea change in the last 6-7 decades has to be understood, with reference to latest happenings in some of the backward States. The fact remains that life in India is still governed by caste factors. From birth to death, many activities are governed by this factor. Can it be neglected? The political survival of many parties and personalities solely depends on the way castes can be manipulated. If that is the reality then why not use caste as a source of income generating activities? Various traditional activities are still surviving in villages. Despite efforts to totally do away with them, they are still present. In the stage of liberalisation, they may get impetus because of their competitive capacity and lack of other avenues. With better income generating policy prescription and dignified way of self-employment, it should be possible to give a new thrust on employment generation by properly analysing the Strengths, Weaknesses, Opportunities and Threats (SWOT) of the caste structure. For this purpose, a new vision is essential for sustainable growth with active involvement of Panchayati Raj institutions as detailed below:

When tickets are distributed by political parties, the caste structure is invariably considered. Even Panchayati Raj operates on dominant communities and the caste structure. Can this leadership be motivated to pay attention to dominant industry, service and business activities of the area? Can policy issues with reference to that activity/enterprise be considered like:

(a) Policies with reference to payments;
(b) Policies with reference to thrust on women;
(c) Policies with reference to working hours and local tradition;
(d) Policies with reference to involving local skills and expertise;
(e) Policies with reference to local ownership of resource;
(f) Policies with reference to life style, aspiration and communication possibilities;
(g) Policies with reference to involving traditional structure for offering important facilities; and
(h) Policies with reference to appropriate tools and machinery for reducing drudgery, maximising output without compromising on quality.

The economic dimension in Panchayati Raj has to understand these aspects to make it sustainable alive.

Success Parameters

Before we proceed ahead, it would be in the fitness of things to examine in detail the success parameters. It is a fact that a successful individual may not be successful for the society and the State. Success parameters codify evaluation, replication and need of holistic approach.

By generating internal resources, a successful programme has to become self-supporting. A parasite whether economically, physically and socially, cannot be termed as successful. Cost effectiveness is yet another point which vouches for the success of any programme. A programme which is not cost effective cannot survive the test of success. It is bound to be unsustainable. Cost can vary. But the total package of costing has to be done to ensure cost effectiveness in the longer run.

There is a general consensus that traditional quality of products from rural areas is considered to be below standard. This is a very important element which can partly be got over by utilising the quality infrastructure and experience of various institutions successfully working in the area. Also by involving existing marketing oriented institutions at low cost, the problem can be solved.

Need of Centre for inducing Enterprise in Rural Areas

Panchayati Raj institutions will definitely succeed in the long run in this regard. This is not a new concept for country like India. There are many evidence in the history to show how the village communes are run. They had their own culture, rules and regulations, practices, habits and the way of life. Various groups in the villages are supposed to contribute to village activities. They had their own systems to resolve conflicts and ensure harmonious environment for sustainability of life and the society.

Mahatma Gandhi deeply thought on it and wrote about constructive programmes which can be elaborated below:

All the 29 items are to be looked after, managed and funded by Panchayati Raj institutions. But can we adopt "Enterprise" concept, so that full justice could be done? Can there be different way of looking at many of these activities to spare the society from paucity of resources? There is definitely need for rethinking.

Following points need consideration:

1. Can there be cost effective basis?
2. Can there be Bank Finance?
3. Can there be backward and forward linkages?
4. Can there be value addition?
5. Can there be appropriate technology provision and ready availability of spares and services?
6. Can there be sharing of cost?
7. Can there be regular openness and interaction?

Some of these issues have to be understood with reference to the policy issues for sustainable employment generation.

In an unorganised society, the importance of pressure lobby need no over-emphasis. The Centre for inducing Enterprise in Rural Areas would precisely attend these aspects. There is a need to look into the following aspects:

1. The advantages of inducing enterprise concept in rural areas.
2. Linkages with self-employment and internal resource generation.
3. Linkages with communication, information sharing and effective technology development and dissemination.
4. Value addition and skill upgradation.

The enterprise development concept in rural areas needs change as also massive co-ordination and understanding of the transitional problems. It is essential particularly, when an agriculturist or an artist is to be converted into an entrepreneur.

A shift from agriculture to industry invariably calls for the following requirements:

1. Public policies, Planning and Tax Systems.
2. Regular flow of information.
3. Infrastructure—Roads,Godowns, Communication, Transport, Security, Electricity/Generators.
4. Raw material stocking.
5. Entrepreneurship development and training facilities.
6. Development of value addition items and ideal industrial climate and appropriate technologies.
7. Packaging and further value addition.
8. Finished or semi-finished stocking and marketing facilities.
9. Banking system.

The above points have to be considered in totality and Panchayati Raj institutions have to take additional responsibilities in this regard. They can also provide the following facilities:

1. Arrange land, water and training facilities to the enterprise.
2. Take up the policy issues with the Government and Zila Parishads.
3. Ensure backward and forward linkages.
4. Develop suitable local enterprises through self-supporting institutions.
5. Take up promotional and regulatory mechanism for sustainable growth of enterprise.

The Panchayati Raj institutions have to play a very important role with the growing emphasis on decentralised area planning approach.There is a need for clarity, commitment and willingness to learn from other's experiences and evolve implementable plan of action with local initiatives. The solution lies in area plans with better linkages and marketing approach. All activities have to become self-supporting and self-sustaining. Hence any amount of time spent on better plan formulation should be welcomed.

Training

Training has become so important and ever changing. Many opened training centres, but they face the problem of grant, stipend, subsidy etc. There are many issues to be considered in this. They include past experience, the effectiveness of linkages, success of vocationalisation, utilisation of infrastructure, privatisation possibility and so on and so forth.

Pre-requisites of Success

Hence it would be pertinent to mention the pre-requisites of success which are detailed below:

The privatisation of education taking place all over the world also calls for change in system. But there are some pre-requisites before the vocational education could be a successful endeavour in creating jobs in the industries, service and business sector. This pre-requisite would improve the following:

1. Make relevant infrastructure available either through State or private investments.
2. Have policy framework both of State Government and local governments. to involve organised institutions, philanthropic groups and ardent associations to mobilise students towards vocational education.
3. Develop in-built economics and suitable internal resources generation in each programme.
4. Imbibe entrepreneurship and risk taking capacity in the youth.
5. Lay greater stress on development of marketing skill and to learn from mistakes.

6. Develop multi-purpose skill with special emphasis on women and disabled.
7. Based on strengths, weaknesses, opportunities and threats of each activity, create conditions for economic linkage building and publicise success stories.

The role of teacher in successful implementation of the vocational educational programmes for employment generation needs no emphasis. In this connection, one may also look at the success parameters from the point of view of a government organisation, the self employed entrepreneur and the society at large and why as a concept it has failed?

Vital Points for Consideration

Various programmes relating to agriculture, rural development, forestry, employment and overall sustainable development including education etc., would be under their purview. Their success would depend on the following:

1. Capacity to give political, economic, social leadership to the members to create condition and pooling resources where self-employed could become the coveted member.
2. Integration of various theoretical and practical concepts for replicable model development with simple laws and minimum of reports and returns.
3. Creation of condition where all should reach their maximum level of efficiency.

Besides, we know how the power structure ensures continuation of the vested interest be it political, religious, social, bureaucratic or academic. The basic issue of exploitation of unorganised remains the same. Patternised approach, "*mai bap*" concept would work so long as leaders are not sensitised to adopt humanistic approach.

Panchayati Raj and Local Expertise

The society does not leave or die with generations. It is a historical process and with proper creation of conditions, enterprise development is possible. Hence the local expertise of arts, crafts, enterprise service, manufacturing, processing, selling and reserving should always be incorporated. It means the local bio-diversity, not only on biological factors but also on instructions and the individuals need appreciation and propagation.

Shri M. Gadgil of Centre of Ecological Sciences, Bangalore has brought out beautifully the bio-diversities prevailing in rural India and efforts are to be made to conserve and protect them. This pre-supposes acceptance of certain facts which have bearing on economic aspects of Panchayati Raj institutions. There are plethora of activities in rural hinterland which could improve the quality of life provided suitable policy incentives are given and checks and balances are ensured. While talking about the bio-diversity, we may also mention various types of employment generating possibilities which are available in the rural area.

Constructive Programmes

Constructive Programmes propounded by Gandhiji in early twenties have close relation with Panchayati Raj institutions. By construction we ordinarily understand engineering work. But Father of the Nation used this term for rebuilding India according to his vision of non-violence, non-exploitative social order. The constructive work is a unique concept.

The constructive work is a positive contribution in our time to win both socialist and capitalist models of development which are under dispute. However, we should not forget that the principle of constructive programme invariably follows decentralisation, building from below, moral and self-reliance and willing co-operation. The edifice of constructive programme of man is to stand on five pillars. They aim at decentralised development.

Decentralisation needs availability of trained, willing, competent managers, appropriate trainer of supervisors, servicing facilities at the affordable cost and binding factors accruing from income. The Sarvodaya social order is in fact based on these principles. But can it be selfless? In this connection, articles by Gandhiji published in *Young India* in 1924 makes an interesting reading. The Father of the Nation wrote: "I am a humble seeker after truth. I am impatient to realize myself, to attain *Moksha* in the very existence. My national service is part of my training for freeing my soul from the bondage of flesh. Thus considered, my service may be regarded as purely selfish. For me the road to salvation lies through incessant toil in the service of my country and through that of the humanity. I want to identify myself with every thing that lives. So my patriotism is for me a state in my journey to the Land of Eternal Freedom and Peace."

Thus we see that the framework of the constructive Programmes is Truth and Non-violence coupled with determination and dedication, *Vairagya* and *Tyaga*. Truth is the end. Non-violence is the means. The path to the goal on either side is guarded by virtue of *Vairagya* (determination) and *Tyaga* (dedication). Functioning within this well structured framework of constructive work is bound to yield the desired result.

In fact, Constructive Programmes aim at holistic

growth. They need gingerly implementation in the stage at which we are today. It is interesting to look at these problems holistically. The Father of the Nation in 1941 listed 13 items under his Constructive Programmes, they are:

1. Communal Unity, 2. Removal of Untouchability, 3. Prohibition, 4. Khadi, 5. Other Village Industries, 6. Village Sanitation, 7. Basic Education, 8. Adult Education, 9. Uplift of Women, 10. Education in Health and Hygiene, 11. Provincial Languages, 12. Propagation of Rashtra Bhasha (national Language) and 13. Promotion of Economic Equality.

Revising this list thoroughly in 1945, he added the following five items.

1. Kisans, 2. Labourers, 3. Adivasis, 4. Lepers and 5. Students.

As a matter of fact, after the sad demise of Gandhiji, additional 5 items such as (1) Cow Protection, (2) Nature Cure, (3) Bhoodan (4) Gramdan and (5) Shanti Sena were added to it to strengthen the constructive movement and march towards the realisation of Sarvodaya social order. But at least a few will not accept "Cow Protection" as a separate item. Bhoodan and Gramdan may be as a single item and other items such as Shramdan and Sampattidan also may be added to this. "Nature Cure" is yet to become a movement. Some would like to include peace and disarmament as a separate item. It is very interesting, enlightening and self-satisfying to go into the details of the various aspects as enshrined in the goal of constructive work to know why today the youth do not believe constructively in this concept.

In a nutshell, we may sum up that the Constructive Programmes comprise self reliance, self help, voluntarily sharing of what one has with others, co-operation, mutual aid, sacrifice, fellow feeling and giving due respect to other's feelings. Let us all march towards this goal with proper understanding and firm conviction.

Constructive Programmes had their framework, principles, concepts and also the organisational structure to ensure sustainability of life and society. It also ensures the changes required. Self unification has become the essential part of constructive programmes. Over a period of time, constructive programmes have become the part and parcel of the national life.

Conclusion

From all the above discussion, it will be clear that a good number of schemes on training, monitoring, funding, marketing, etc. will not help the sustainability of Panchayati Raj institutions unless economic aspects, policies, principles are suitably analysed. This calls for a holistic vision and deep commitment and conviction to the inherent quality of the masses. The commonsense approach will have to be blended with scientific approach to ensure the growth of self supporting systems of the village self sufficiency.

13

NGO's Voluntary Organisations : Need for Introspection

Today NGOs are working in diverse fields like health, family planning, rural development, education, social welfare, drinking water, forestry and plantation etc. On the one hand, the voluntary organisations are supposed to be low cost, closer to the public and manned by dedicated people, and hence more effective and successful but on the other hand, the experience of last forty years cause a serious doubt on their achievements and their replicability. There are many who feel that voluntary organisations like government departments have become expert in budget utilisation, non-accountable and are working devoid of linkages. Barring a few cases of dedicated voluntary efforts, others have not been able to replicate the so-called successes easily. There may be many reasons for their not coming up to expectation and specially in a system where inputs besides the success of the programme and not the outputs or a sustainability of the programme is taken into consideration. We may not fully blame only the NGOs. But one thing has to be accepted that in all our national planning, marketing approach to plans, concepts, technologies, ideas etc. have been missing. There had hardly been any efforts to improve internal resource generation capacity of the organisation. While one may not totally agree with the marketing approach to the extension agencies but it is worth considering how long can any organisation continue to work only on grants, rebates, charities or subsidies. Programmes like disease and other natural calamities like starvation etc. can well be understood for grant purposes since they will not be able to generate either self-employment or internal revenue but in many programmes like Khadi, tree plantation, nurseries, family planning, education or even social welfare, why cannot they after a certain period, be expected to generate additional funds. The entire attitude to developmental and commercial programmes must be made to deviate from regulatory programmes. Even in Government, various commercial activities are being run with rock bottom efficiency under the guise of social services. It is a pity that the work culture has not only disappeared from many government departments but also from the voluntary organisations while one can attribute this to overall deterioration in standards, one must also examine if there are some programmes which can now be funded on commercial lines. Obviously, there is a need because of the scarcity of resources. Even foreign funds are becoming scarcer and attitudinal changes are required not only in voluntary organisations but also in many governmental departments to be accountable for every penny which they spend.

It is needless to emphasise again that those who work in decentralised, unorganised, informal sector do have a case for certain amount of incentives but these incentives cannot be allowed to go on forever. The role of Cost Accountants and Chartered Accountants, apart from special auditors and planners, becomes very important in undertaking these unpleasant but very much warranted exercise. We also must examine how the grants, rebates, subsidies have contributed in the attitudinal deteriorations and moral fibre of the society. Have not only governmental organisations but also many other public spirited organisations become victims of conspiracy in spending public money? The growth of the tendency to depend excessively on public funds for every activity also must be probed thoroughly. The C.A.B. as an important tool also has examined this aspect, but probably because of mental reservations at every level, no effort has been made to increase the accountability of all those charged with spending public funds. Many voluntary organisations of repute have possibly accepted the need to have market approach to all developmental activities. Sri Karan Bhai of Gandhi Ashram, Lucknow and Sri Prem Bhai of Banbasi Seva Ashram have openly come out with this writer to adopt the market approach to the activities because of the need not only to conserve scarce resources but also to propagate self-employment. Various studies have also brought out that because of precisely absence of this concept, the self-employment programmes have not been catching on. Even the programmes like SEEYU or IRDP or even Sericulture have not been able to show expected success because of precisely this weakness. The need to have informal extension system for informal target group also needs close examination. Even here, the voluntary organisations with their informal way of working can be major tool of extension of developmental programmes for the target groups. But the real success will lie only in developing a market approach with the activities of voluntary organisations NABARD, CAPART, OXFAM and many other charitable organisations will have to carry out introspection whether they have been able to fulfil the objectives of their organisations.

NGO's have undergone radical changes in their outlook, funding system, accountability etc. But for the first time the compulsion to work with Panchayati Raj Institutions and community is becoming important and unavoidable. This is happening because of the following reasons:

1. Resource scarcity
2. Experience of the past
3. Need to optimise resources
4. Need of convergence
5. Compulsion of marketing
6. Need to reduce overhead
7. Transparency and Viability compulsion
8. To involve the beneficiaries

NGOs were traditionally in the field of pure charity like drinking water, Dharamshalas etc. Gandhiji was the first practical innovator who introduced business like approach by forming a very pertinent and timely institutions in All India Spinning Association and All India Village Industries Association at Wardha in 1920 and 1935 respectively. One may not easily comprehend the long term implication of these institutions but if we examine holistically we will see the multi-dimensional benefits of these Institutions. It is pity that both these organisations within the period of time faced with the problems of

1. Greed and Human Nature
2. Dependency of State rather than consumer
3. Bureaucrates like
4. Neglect to consumer
5. Excessive grant rebate subsidy
6. Vested interest creation
7. Overall discarding basic principles for which these organisations were created.
8. Periodical review from time to time
9. Inability to perceive changes
10. Overall decline in public institutions

11. Organisational weaknesses.

The above are only some of the reasons because of which an excellent NGOs became totally dependent on the State.

Today almost all departments of the government which encouraging NGOs, apart from CPAART (Council for Peoples Action and Appropriate Rural Technology), NABARD (National Agriculture Bank for Rural Development), SIDBI (Small Industrial Development Bank of India), even corporate sector, Chambers of Commerce have also realised the need for supporting NGOs in all walks of life. It is high time all the stake holders review their programmes, priorities, system to make NGOs sector relevant timely and futuristic.

NGOs have a very important role in awakening people community to explore their full potential. This is the challenge of our time. The following action plan may help in achieving these objectives of all total utility of the society:

1. Characteristics of good NGO
   * Good NGO run their programmes on the basis of people's participation.
   * Transparency in work.
   * Conscious about the welfare of their workers.
   * Access to all sections of the society through good work.
   * Adequate respect of all sections of society and representation.
   * Transparency in work account.
   * Good management system.
   * Availability of qualified and skilled workers.
   * Self-employment creation.
   * Emphasis on self reliance.

2. NGOs should commit to:
    * People's participation in Project.
    * Sustainability of project.
    * Replicable, bankable and viable project formulation.
    * Encouragement to non-farm sector.
    * Encouragement to local knowledge and technique.
    * Project based on local resources with an element of Swadeshi.
    * Identification of development possibilities.
    * Emphasis on marketing.
3. NGOs contribution in Panchayats empowerment:
    * Encourage people's participation.
    * Women's empowerment.
    * Youth awareness.
    * Transparent planning.
    * Self reliance and self respect in development process.
    * Encouragement to non-farm sector.
    * Bankable and viable project fomulation.
    * Encouragement to local knowledge and technique.
    * Encourage Swadeshi through projects based on local resources.
    * Publicity of duties and rights of Panchayats.
    * Identification of development possibilities.
4. Success Parameters:
    * Project based on local needs and resources.
    * People's participation in project formulation, implementation and monitoring.
    * Project execution at village Panchayat level by village entrepreneurs and government's role should be catalytic one.
    * Village people should participate in the project with faith and hope.

* Project should aim at balanced development, self reliance and sustainability.
* Decentralised permanent system for production and marketing.
* Active beneficiary participation in production and marketing.
* Quality work.
* Application of locally available technique.

14

Networking for Unorganised Sector

Introduction

The unorganised sector is represented by certain characteristic. The very fact that they are unorganised means that they are not able to present their case, their problems, their aspiration in an organised and forceful manner. As the systems policy makers and bureaucracy are not so much sensitised to the needs of the unorganised sector. It would respond only under pressure. The organised sector is able to corner the unorganised sector due to their strong network and effective lobbying capacity. The past experiences show us innumerable instances where public policy have been formed on the basis of lobbying by the organised, which have today become detrimental to the unorganised sector. Since unorganised cannot present their case and have no mechanism for lobbying, a lot of harm is done to them. Therefore, in this context, it is necessary to examine, how networking can be one of the way of solving the problems being faced by the unorganised sector.

Broadly speaking networking means coming together of group of people or organisations for realizing common goal and purposes by pooling their resources, expertise strengths for negotiating a better deal for themselves. Whatever may be the origin of this word but in common prevalence it indicate indirectly vested interest group coming together to achieve a common goal in an effective manner. Whatever may be the implication in the longer run the fact remains that networking for the unorganised has remained a missing link in the country like ours. Networking is an effective tool for joint action and ansure lobbying, therefore its principle has to be understood in totality.

How Networking works?

Before we examine this question we have to understand why people, institutions, groups come together, stay together and work together. Ultimately it is propagation of common interest for getting desired benefits for the group as well as individual in the group. Without self and the common interest it is difficult to stay together since each individual would like to see their own benefits and interest from other powerful groups or systems of associating themselves in any network, which they cannot nurture on their own. Networking helps in this process. But networking also means sacrificing something whether it is subscription, adhocism, arbitrariness. It has to be understood and recognised that something is to be sacrificed to gain, achieve and preserve something better whether it is competitive advantage over others or deriving extra mileage from State or society. This often requires the assistance of a catalyst who can bring various interest groups together, bind them and draw common advantages to be shared commonly by all. In this process the State also plays very important role as it provides various incentives, to accessibility lobbying and can even share various secrets, prescription, data and statistic, possible course of policy direction with this group rather than individuals. Networking of this group also provides forum for the State to interact with disperse people. Indirectly it also means involving the beneficiaries. Needless to say that organising comparatively well organised target groups is much easier than organising the unorganised hence by understanding the process how the networking works we may be able to understand why unorganised are hardly able to get organised on a common platform.

Effect of Poor Networking

If we understand how comparatively advantageous groups are developed and gain benefits through the process of networking, it will not be difficult to understand the effect of poor networking. Based on experience, we can face the following negative effects due to poor networking amongst the unorganised:

1. Poor communication with the policy makers.
2. Lack of opportunities for leadership development amongst them.
3. Losses on all fronts, procurement of raw material, marketing policy support, financing etc.
4. Lack of opportunities for future expansion potential.
5. Overall neglect of the disadvantageous groups.

Past Experiences of Networking in Unorganised Sector — Achievements and Pitfalls

In the field of village industries Shri Kummarappaji was the first to convince Gandhiji in 1920 the need for All India Village Industries Institution. With his superb organising capacity Gandhiji organised a number of voluntary institutions like :

1. All India Spinners Association.

2. **Hindustani Talimi Sangh.**
3. **Go-seva Sangh.**
4. **All India Village Industries Association**
5. **Harijan Sevak Sangh.**

Today when we look back at the experiences of these networking organisations registered under 1860 Act of Trust and Charitable Institutions we have to realise the superb intellectual planning which must have gone into organising its bodies. To what extent have these bodies served the original objectives may be the area for examination but we cannot forget that they had created fear in the Britishers and hope in the masses. It is also a difficult matter that so long as these bodies were not dependent solely on government, they had to derive their strength and remained real service oriented networks. As these bodies became over dependent on State, they lost their original stamina dynamism and effectiveness. What we find today in most of these networking institutions is as follows:

1. Over a period they have lost their direction.
2. They have become over dependent on the State.
3. They have huge infrastructure in land, building grossly underutilised.
4. They are serving mostly on their past and they hardly have any vision for future.
5. There are lot of dedicated workers but some how their energy have been hardly utilised.
6. With the passage of time these institutions have the potential to become useful tool for social and economical transformation with better technology, human resource development, policy direction, contributory financing, marketing approach.
7. Managing bodies have developed vested interest

which has resulted into hardly any new areas/ opportunities getting induced.

GDP versus Human Development Index — Implication for Networking of New and Old

The last century has seen excessive emphasis on Gross Domestic Product concept which has made money earning as the only indicator of development. More and more consumption of electricity, gas, fuel, wood, petrol, diesel have become the indicator of development. Money is an important thing in the materialistic world which enables these fulfilment of needs and creates conditions which will lead to realisation of these objectives of attainment and happiness, however, it was misdirected emphasis. But in the last decade sustainable human development concept has brought out need for looking at different concepts, approach and indicators of development. Sustainable human development concept has many more indicators. Only money and so called monetary wealth can never be the ultimate objective of life. It is happiness, attainment and principles thereof. This realisation makes it imperative to understand that unless all are happy nobody can be happy and therefore needs to appreciate the sustainable human development. For this reason, one has to do a critical analysis of SWOT (Strength, Weakness, Opportunities and Threats); HIPPOO (Hidden Investible Potential Power of Organisation); KIPPOO (Known Investible Potential Power of Organisation); TIPPOO (Threatening Investible Potential Power of Organisation). These analysis, namely SWOT, HIPPOO, KIPPOO and TIPPOO, would make our job much simpler by identifying the various key components of sustainable human development.

Networking of Institutions to Revitalizing the NGOs Movement in India

Biogas Network of NGO's — Experiences and achievement in brief. INSEDA experiences.

Critical Issues in Networking for Unorganised — Role of NGOs and Federations

As a first step, it is important to examine the critical issues in networking as well as to analysis of various aspects of working of NGOs and understand the linkages in networking.

Some of the Critical Issues in Networking

1. Why should unorganised sector come together?
2. How can they come together?
3. How can they stay together?
4. What will be sustenance parameters in the networking?
5. What is the experience of past in networking of NGOs specially in relation to the unorganised sector.

The above mentioned critical issues needs to be studied as opposed to networking of organised sector like CII, All India Manufacturers' Organisation, Federation of Exporters Association, Chamber of Commerce, Solvent Extractors Association etc., etc.

While examining these issues we should not overlook the nature of target groups, their poverty level, their ignorance level and their overall inability, to organize themselves into a network.

Another area for examination would be the vested interest of the organised sector and how they use them for the benefit of their members. This is where the self interest of the leaders matters to a great extent as they can use unorganised, ignorant, dispersed, target groups for their own selfish motives and gains and thus their exploitation continues.

KVIC Initiative in Supporting Financially, Administratively Organisation of the Beneficiaries and the Industry.

KVIC has a very bright past in the sense that it has its roots in the vast membership of voluntary organisations which had visionaries behind their formation with purpose and clear cut defined goals. It is great abrasion that over a period of time, post independence era, the traditional dedication spirit and public service and sympathy gave way to over dependence on State for everything.

However realising the need for organising regional and industry-wise Federation for future growth, as well as overcome foreseeable problems and short-comings in the existing approach, KVIC took a policy decision to give various administrative and financial support to Federation of industry-wise beneficiaries. Otherwise also in the field of Khadi, KVIC had always been encouraging the Federations of Khadi Institutions to take up new and new activities as a part of consolidation, expansion and developing marketing network but for Village Industry this initiative of KVIC was totally new. It is worth examining that over a period of last 4/5 years this initiative has been translated into action. Some of the salient features of that initiative included:

1. Making it compulsory for all recipients of the funds to be member of all the Regional Federations.
2. Incentive package to Federation by KVIC in terms

of financial and monitoring packages.

3. Utilisation of infrastructure of KVIC by these Federations.
4. Reward and incentive scheme based upon good graded Federations and beneficiaries of organisations.
5. Meeting of network Federation at various places to share experiences and widen further network to cover unserved and unrecognized members.
6. Identifying further new growth areas in terms of better technology packages, better returns on investments, raw material, States, marketing tie-ups including quality controls and product diversification, cost reduction, public involvement.
7. International exposures and cooperation. For example All India Hand Made Paper Federation sent about 20 of its members on cost sharing basis to various countries for training, marketing, survey etc.

Networking by Other Institutions

It is not understood as to why a national movement has not so far been launched though networking of various institutions of common objectives for reaching the unreached. Government machinery has proletariated in the last five decades with the result that even networking within their own organization is dire necessity, hence not only for government but also for NGOs networking becomes dire need of the day. The movement nothing short of a national movement and a proper analysis of SWOT, HIPPOO, KIPPOO, TIPPOO will open up opportunities to the groups to work with each other, could help the diverse groups to see the advantages of "To Learn To Work Together", as well as share experiences.

The networking within unorganized sector will have to be a national phenomenon so that a long term sustainability could be ensured by developing win win situation for all. In the development policies pursued in the last half a century majority has been loser while minority has been the gainer. The time has come to reverse this process by taking those policy initiatives which will help Win Win situation creation for majority. It is here the networking by all the well meaning in the unorganised sector becomes the crucial necessity of today.

Marketing as a Means for Networking

Technology, training, marketing, entrepreneurship development, exports, cost reduction, financing or any other field of specialised institutions have to diversify and develop long term linkages with each other. Natural institution linkages will become sustainable only through marketing approach. Marketing means not only risk taking but also developing sustainable business like mutually beneficial and gainful relations by give and take. The greed is controlled by egalitarian behaviour pattern to support each other.

Proposed Plan of Action for Networking for Unorganised Sector

(a) Identification of the target unorganised sector.

(b) Identification of external resource groups for guidance, awareness, training, specialist, inputs, follow-up and strengthening and stabling the network.

(c) Awareness of generation about the networking of the groups selected from the different unorganised sector.

(d) Exposing the groups to some of the existing networks.
(e) Explain them about the benefits and pitfalls, and accountability of each member and the various groups/sectors.
(f) Selection of a core group of leaders from the different organised groups.
(g) Training of core groups for effective functioning and lobbying.
(h) Servicing of unorganised sector by organised sector for mutual gains.
(i) Gradual movement from unorganised sector to organised sector.
(j) Use leaders in the unorganised group as an entry point.
(k) Identify SWOT, HIPPOO of each big institution and federation.
(l) Codify lessons learnt from the past.
(m) Direct communication with the target groups.
(n) Mechanism for reducing response time.
(o) For a success of any network some results have to be shown atleast in foreseeable time therefore the external facilitators should find some pressing problems of the unorganised group which requires lobbying to get results so that they develop confidence, benefits and strength of networking.
(p) Create an environment of democrative and participatory decision making, transparency in reporting, information sharing as well as overall transparency.
(q) Give regular feedback to the members on the achievements, results and impact of networking, till this concept is fully internalized and they can go on with no or very little external assistance.

Role, Responsibility and Vision of External Facilitating Individual/Groups.

— Awareness, functioning educations, skills upgradation, management and marketing training and overall capacity building of members of targeted unorganised sector, training in practical lobbying and negotiating with Government, donors and decision making.
— Develop appropriate promotional, campaign and publicity materials.
— Identification of right leaders and core groups from amongst the target unorganised sector who can be further used after appropriate training to strengthen the network.
— Follow up on regular basis and be a good listener and analyst of problems and possible solutions.
— Follow a participatory approach, as far as possible, getting views of all the participants.
— The facilitator should have a clear vision to match the aspiration of the group and play an inspirational role and true facilitators, should act as a philosopher friend and guide to the network rather than interfering in their affairs.
— The facilitator should give the feeling to the groups that the results achieved are due to their own efforts rather than his/her interventions.
— Collect good case studies and prepare them in simple language to be used further for training.
— Develop appropriate project proposals which would match the skills of unorganised sector, for enhancing their income and employment generation.
— Introduce participatory monitoring and evaluation methodologies along with network members, which should be used as a learning experience

and improves the qualitative aspects of the network.

- Organise workshops and seminars and dialogues with government officials, decision making etc.
- Providing regular information to the members as appropriate information flow at the right time will empower the group and enhance their lobbying and negotiating power.
- Develop a sound MIS system.
- The facilitator should work out a sound withdrawer strategy for himself/herself rather than keep on sticking and creating a power base for his/her own selfish gains.
- Identification of new appropriate technology for enhansive production and reducing drudgery.
- Developing new markets.
- Inculcating saving habits in the group.
- Assisting in organisation of corpus funds and risk and investment funds for groups (Network).
- Linkage with other network.
- Procurement of raw materials in whole-sale to cut down the cost.

Role of Other Inputs in Effective Networking of the Unorganised Sectors

- Role of incentive systems in organising the unorganised.
- Role of computers in monitoring the impact of organisation development.
- Role of low cost practical consultants.
- Role of marketing led development systems in organising the unorganised.
- Role of vocational education in developing low cost practical organisers.
- Role of effective and appropriate technology

transfer mechanism in organising the unorganised.

— Role of policies of Central, State, District and Panchayati Raj bodies in encouraging the unorganised to get organised.

— Role of mother in encouraging self employed unorganised encouragement.

— Role of Corporate Sector in helping the unorganised to get semi-organised for mutual benefit.

— Policy support in inviting the genuine organisations of the beneficiaries for monthly, quarterly and annually discussions.

— Role of financial institutions.

15

Introducing Industries in Rural Areas

While introducing industries in rural areas we have to keep the following things in mind:

1. Need, definition with reference to the specific location of the rural industry.
2. Linkages with various government and non-governmental organisations.
3. Mode and source of finance, and infrastructural availability.
4. Existing system of training, and nature of trainers.
5. Vocational training and other institutional support.
6. Essential components for future development patterns.
7. Low cost practical consultancy availability in that area.
8. Marketing, Production, Training, Concept (MPTC) acceptability.
9. Role of organised industry in training for rural industrialisation.
10. Strengths, Weaknesses, Opportunities and Threats (SWOT) of the people in those areas.

Most of the programmes in rural areas have historically been managed on a subsidised basis, that is on charity as opposed to merit. However, even those programmes have not percolated properly and the majority of artisans subsist on their own. While many pockets of rural areas are still the scene of poverty, destitution and exploitation, a few States and areas have been developed beyond expectation. In the States like Punjab and Haryana the countryside does not look like the rest of India. In this situation it is essential that a holistic developmental programme is evolved for industrialising rural areas.

By developing industries in rural areas the following advantages will accrue:

1. Fund flow to rural areas through industrial services.
2. Development of rural entrepreneurship.
3. Better communication and information sharing.
4. Development of appropriate technology.
5. Value addition to raw material.
6. Less pressure on urban areas and facilities.
7. Reverse flow of people from urban area to rural area.

Centre for Developing Rural Industries

Today we do not have any organised agency which could integrally coordinate the growth of industries in rural areas. Many of the schemes and subsidy incentives were available only so long as permission was available to start industries. Now, with openness and structural changes industries will have to become economically viable. Hence they would flow to those areas which offer the best terms and overall long-term advantages. The advantage of going to rural areas can be multiplied only when the strengths are projected and weaknesses are reduced. Thus there is a need for an organised body for planning, motivating, and propagating industries in rural area. This is basically required to develop linkages between agriculture and industry for overall development. It is essential that the products of agriculture, horticulture, sericulture, animal husbandry, minerals and all other fields are processed with value addition in non-city areas itself. To achieve the above objective the following chart will explain some of the essentials of plans and action required:

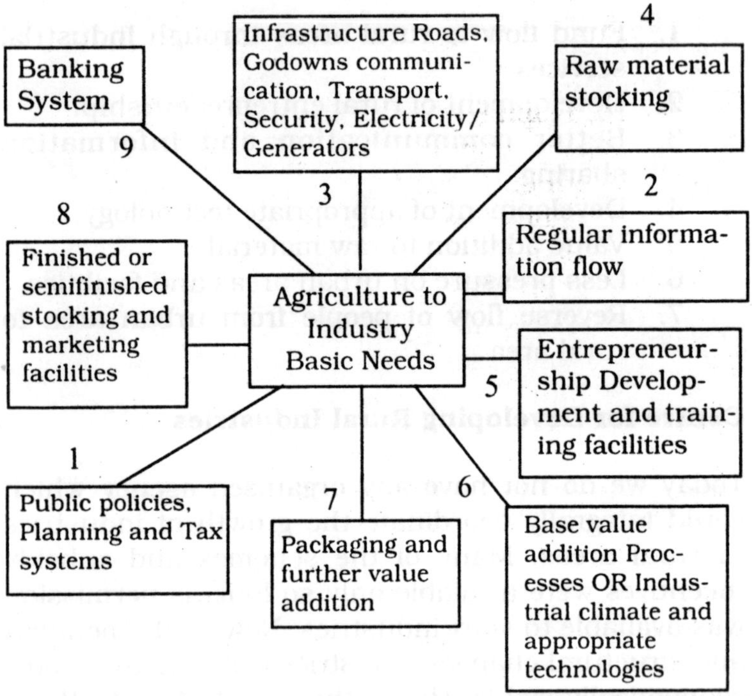

Problems Faced in Rural Industrialisation

It needs no mention that lot of problems would be faced when concerted efforts are made to take appropriate industries to appropriate non-urban areas. For some time the problems will be much more because these industries have been used to operate under shelter and protection. As competition increases, certain problems are bound to be faced by them. The answer lies in restructuring organisation, financing and monitoring and through other systems developed to attend to these problems.

Possible problem areas:

1. Infrastructure
2. Finance
3. Marketing
4. Skilled manpower
5. Motivation
6. Politics
7. Wrong policies
8. Inappropriate technologies and scale of operations
9. Local disturbances.

Apart from motivating industry to go to rural areas, there is also an urgent need to encourage local entrepreneurship. The following can be some of the selected enterprises invitation activity:

I. (1) Briefing session at a site for industrial use.
(2) Briefing session for enterprise groups, industrial associations, etc.
(3) Tours of inspection of sites for industrial use.
(4) Individual visits to the enterprises.
(5) Newspaper advertisements, public relations drive and video shows.
(6) Utilisation of bulletins of the related organisations.
(7) Distribution of documents of the site for industrial use.
(8) Investigation by means of questionnaires.
(9) Developing contacts through local people, schoolmates, business acquaintances and

affiliated companies of the enterprise which are located in that area, local seasonal workers etc.

(10) Computerised information sharing.

A tentative plan of introducing industries into agricultural areas is presented below:

1. To designate rural areas as target areas to improve the storage capacity of raw materials and also to provide employment through ISB sector.
2. Concerted efforts to develop rural areas into industrially cultured and clustered areas.
3. To involve Zilla Parishads as the nodal points for developing their own schemes, plans, monitoring system and infrastructural development agencies.
4. The local area has to develop its own potential industry; it must plan and act to provide incentives in rural areas, basically in terms of infrastructural support.
5. Administration at the level of the State as well as the Centre, must enable rural industrialisation to become an economically attractive proposition.
6. The central government has to take concerted policy, steps to encourage, plan, fund and monitor the implementation of schemes through Zilla Parishads. For this, positive incentives which should be at par or better than those available to urban industries must be mooted.
7. Linkages with educational institutions keeping in mind the problem of funds and cultural development of institutions. We should realise that it is only under pressure that better results

are obtained. The coordination required between educational institutions, farm and industry, planners and funding institution can be achieved only through coordinated efforts.

8. The Centre can act like a non-profit-making body consisting of major departments of government which are interested in rural industrialisation.
9. While organising this centre the following points will have to be kept in mind:
   (i) Area planning
   (ii) SWOT analysis of those areas
   (iii) Infrastructure and linkages with educational, developmental, and marketing institutions.
   (iv) Study of marketing potentials, both local and outside the rural area.
   (v) Institution and local finance.
   (vi) Identifying entrepreneurial capacities and institutionalising them.
   (vii) Linkages with on-going programmes.
   (viii) Learning lessons from past mistakes.

The above steps, if taken in right earnest, will go a long way in involving agriculture, rural development department, voluntary organisation and industrial houses, etc. for sustainable industrialisation.

The infrastructure of banks, which has multiplied enormously in the last two decades, has to be fully tapped in consultation with educational centres and with greater rapport with the Reserve Bank of India.

The following problems will need special attention:

1. Need for monitoring an appropriate communication,
2. Need for output-based incentives.
3. Need for tapping local resources for rural industries.

4. Increasing the different infrastructural facilities in remote areas and utilising the existing infrastructure to the maximum.

The experience of backward area development. IRDP. Small Scale Sector and Special Thrust Programme for SC/ST or women's groups will give us clear insight for future schemes.

Based on our experience of four decades of planning, implementation, monitoring, evaluation, funding and overall dichotomy of development the time has come to look into the need for an organisation to take overall charge of rural industrialising.

While talking about developing industries in rural areas in a vast country like ours, we must bear in mind some essential requirements from different regional authorities. This conceptual confusion has resulted in neglect of developing a suitable package for the growth, sustenance and overall equity of rural industry. The following analysis will help in understanding the concept better:

Village and Block Level Authority

Wherever these authorities have taken interest, the industries have found it expedient to shift to rural areas, as was the case around Bombay, Pune, Calcutta, Madras, Bangalore etc. Various villages did take initiative in inviting industries to their villages. This resulted in increasing the land value of that area on the one hand and provided job to rural youth on the other. The industrial culture which came to the villages and been the third indirect advantage. But it also resulted in better infrastructural development coming to the rural area. Our villages are not aware of the facilities which follow the coming of industrial houses. With the promotion of industries to rural areas the village and block level authorities will automatically get greater attention and will become the focal point of development. With the ongoing emphasis on decentralised planning, a conscious effort should be made to mobilise these authorities to realise the need for taking active interest.

The Zila Parishad

Apart from local taxes, training, linkages, water and basic educational facilities, the Zila Parishad can also take up with the State government the case for industrialisation of their area. With the initiative and active interest of the important decentralised statutory State authority, it should be possible to motivate the State governments to relax many of their tax burdens and to enhance incentives. The Zila Parishad can also act as a representative for industries of their area for financing and providing other package assistance.

The State Government

According to the Constitution, the village industries are the State governments' responsibility. But, as we all know, the State governments invariably go by the policies of the Central government. This is also understandable because the incentives, rebate, subsidy and other corporate policies of the Central government have great influence in shaping policies of State government. Another problem is that institutional finance is invariably governed by the policies of the Reserve Bank, which again follows Central government's policies. This in turn, results in State government not paying adequate attention to the sector which deserves maximum stress. Hence the States have to be made to understand the need for paying attention to the unorganised sector. This will automatically be reflected in the policies of the State governments if the Central government emphasises this aspect.

The Central Government

As mentioned above, the banks, excise, customs, financial institutions, exports and even television and radio are all guided by the policies of the Government of India. Unless an attitudinal change is reflected towards the Village Industries sector by the Planning Commission and other departments of the Central government, no attention by subordinate institutions would be paid.

In this connection the good work of city based, organised union leaders must be praised. In their enthusiasm and political expediency to maximise the benefits to organised workers, they have forced some of the industrialists to shift to rural area. This is a good development. Specially in industries for which the raw material comes from rural areas, it is also economical in the longer run to shift the processing base to the rural areas. Many of the industries based on agriculture, horticulture, fisheries, minerals etc. would find it much more expedient in the longer run to shift. The trade union and transport bottlenecks in cities, coupled with law and order problem will definitely help in giving a lasting blow to the urban based industrial development that we have witnessed so far. With focussed efforts by all in an organised manner, it can be possible to achieve the goal of shifting emphasis to rural industries.

16

Palaces of Arbitrariness

Palaces are the place where kings, rulers and high religious preachers live. These palaces act as forts and also places of authority. They are constructed to suit the purpose of the people who are going to live there. We have palaces of 'rajas' and 'maharajas' in abundance. Many of those old palaces have been converted into hotels and museums. Though they have lost their pristine glory, yet new palaces of authority have mushroomed. Centres of influential people and various activities are all around us.

Arbitrariness is the act of acting without judicious basis of action. Rational, legal basis cannot always be tolerated. There are factors which make arbitrariness inevitable. Normally, in our private life, arbitrariness may be tolerated, but in public life, act has to be justiceable.

Places of authority may be for legal or illegal power. The system of democracy pre-supposes checks and cross-checks. Independent institutions are created— both by statutes and conventions — to cross-check the exercises of power. Palaces of arbitrariness start flourishing and new change becomes inevitable. Change comes to herald newness. After some time, the change becomes the old and inertia is followed by arbitrariness. The will-entrenched interests look after only the vested interests. Any change is resisted tooth and nail by the will established. Adhocism, arbitrariness, indifference to complaints and change becomes order of the day. Any forced change becomes temporary and action pronouncements by judicial authorities gets confounded. Respect for palaces of authority tends to become common and physical forces tend to become power popular. Rationalism and logic along with commonsense become casualties and arbitrariness rules. Palaces of arbitrariness try to multiply. Organised, prepared to use force, ruthless can only develop new palaces. The following quotation about change would make the point clear:

> For every ailment under the Sun, there is remedy or there is none. If there is one try to find it. If there is none never mind it.

Solution to the acute problems lie in making systems work. Palaces must be made to work according to well-propounded principles of functioning, based on reasons and willingness to accept change. Understanding of reciprocal recognition and mutual back-scratching for the welfare of the members of the palaces needs careful check. Tendency to benefit mutually by arbitrary actions would take propriety nowhere.

The rules also come very handy to people who believe in *status quo*. No human ingenuity can propound rules for posterity, as time and tide wait for nobody. Same way, rules cannot be sacrosanct for all times to come. Arbitrariness cannot be for mutual gain. Occupants of legitimate palaces have to keep on looking for coming signals desiring change and accommodate whenever necessary. Growing feeling of discontentment and cynicism has to be countered with growing prosperity and inculcation of positivism. Changing times call for sagacity and calculated manoeuvres. Arbitrariness in democracy at top level tends to be misunderstood, especially, at lowest level. Religion can, to some extent, exercise control. With the fast expansion of means of communication, further difficulties arise. Palaces of arbitrariness tend to get criticised.

Only answer, if the palaces want to continue, is to shun arbitrariness and take measures to exercise sobering influence over changing aspirations.

17

SWOT of IAS

Sometimes, we do not know our strength, weaknesses, opportunities and threats. The constant analysis of SWOT is necessary for the development of not only individuals, society, organisations, but also for nations. As service also, we must carry out the analysis.

During the last few days, the question of SWOT of an I.A.S. has been coming very often in the papers. To discover more about this, I discussed this aspect with people from various walks of life and also those in the service. The summary is interesting:

Strength:

(a) Promoter of national integration.
(b) Linkages and historic tradition of service.
(c) Highest paid public services.
(d) Public confides trust even today.
(e) Closeness to power and role in policy making.
(f) Broader outlook and varied experience-diversity.

Weaknesses:

(a) Lack of cohesion.
(b) Individualistic attitude.
(c) Growing cynicism.
(d) Lack of expertise or opportunities for specialisation.
(e) Arrogance-egoist.
(f) Falling humility and tradition

bound, security oriented.

Opportunities: (a) Job variety available.
(b) Opportunity to do really good, especially in neglected sectors.
(c) Opportunities to influence decisions.

Threat: (a) Growing regionalism and opposition from other services.
(b) Growing undue political interference.
(c) Short-cuts for promotions.

When we consider the above SWOT, the very prestigious service, we should also keep in mind that in a country where more than 50% population lives below povertyline and more than 80% lives in rural areas, what do people expect? Again, to find the answer, I discussed the question of expectation of majority of rural population with various people. Depending on the background, perception and expectations, the priority can change. But, by and large, the following came as priorities in rural areas:

1. Irrigation.
2. Road.
3. Schools.
4. Electricity.
5. Drinking water.
6. Security, both economic and social.
7. Improved quality of life.

When we consider the SWOT and what the majority of population living in rural areas expect, the big question remains, 'Is the service really equipped, motivated and willing to fulfil this role?' There are no readymade answers to the mind boggling problems of our country but way has to be found out.

18

Thought Sharing

I have been thinking over the question of improvement of productivity culture in rural developmental sector. This issue was also partly discussed with various officers.

The main steps required for improving qualitative productivity in our system can be summarised in the following way:

1. We should put the right man for the right job.
2. Continuous study of our works, procedures and the environment for our working efficiency is required.
3. Training should be qualitative and the trainers should be symbol of proven track-record. They must follow up the utilisation of trained people.
4. Clear Recognition of:
   What is possible immediately? Insist on doing it.
   What is just not possible? Rethink about it.
   What is possible with little extra effort? Try it.
   What is impossible — today and tomorrow— discuss it.
5. No productivity culture can be developed in isolation but role of leader at every level is paramount. He can by 'will' and 'skill' develop 'conditions' and 'system' conducive to fulfilling of objectives of the organisation.
6. Importance of HRD — at every level — plan it.
7. Regular study and effective corrective steps on

'Demotivating' factors.

8. Development of open system — regular interaction with critical managers.
9. Regular monitoring of programmes/performance with emphasis on lessons both good and bad. Follow up on these lessons is must.
10. Identify and positively examine:
    What is in my hand?
    What is in the hand of my boss?
    What is in my organisation's hand?
    What is in the hands of the system as such?

Can I have your views please?

The thought sharing is that scientific communication which helps in opening up. I have been trying to regularly share my thought with myself and I am quite satisfied with the output.

The taste of the food is in eating. It is right time to explore, examine and analyse regularly as to how can we perform better and better.

19

Essentials for Success of the Programme

1. Adequate reports to all
2. Bankability of the project
3. Linkage/tie-up
4. Regular research
5. Dissemination of all information including marketing potential etc.
6. Lessons of the past
   (a) How programme has been run?
   (b) How funds have been spent?
   (c) How recruitments have been made?
   (d) How linkages broke down?
   (e) Whether coordination was minimal or Nil?
   (f) Was transparency absent?
   (g) Why achievement could not be spread?
   (h) What was the net result?
7. Importance of working together
   (a) All-round resource scarcity.
   (b) Falling standard of working culture.
   (c) Isolationist tendency.
   (d) Rising expectation and inefficient systems.
   (e) Back to nature.
8. Success parameters
   (i) Viability and transparency
   (ii) Cost effectiveness
   (iii) System for replication and dissemination
   (iv) Traditional goodness of programme and

attracting new entrepreneurs.

(v) Linking with masses

(vi) Hidden Investible Potential Power of Organisation (HIPPOO)

(vii) Involve youth and schools and colleges.

9. Scientific and rationalised conviction of the merit.
10. Value addition.
11. Strength of market force.
12. Codify lessons of both good and bad work.
13. Develop replicability and self-sufficiency in each programme and its component.
14. Areas of concern

(i) Habit by heart or human nature

(ii) Egoistic nature

(iii) Unorganised beneficiaries

(iv) Effective publicity and delivery system

(v) Neglect of youth and women

(vi) Developing system of coordination

(vii) Bringing diverse groups and holding them together

(viii) Fear from organised.

20

Gender Equality through Women's Empowerment : Key Issues

What are the Lessons of Past Efforts?

(a) What type of Programmes have been planned, implemented, monitored and coordinated in the past?
(b) What are the holistic lessons of the past experiences?
(c) What are the principles of the next plan of action?

What Should be Examined?

(a) Transparency, (b) Viability, (c) Marketing Approach, (d) Environment friendly development process, (e) Fairness and win-win situation for all, (f) Replicable model for development.

Key Issues

(1) Policy Issues
Policy issues include Policies related to financing, technology transfer, training, monitoring, rewards, publicity and vision for long term success of the mission, etc.

(2) Women have to be promoted as sensitizers, organizers, trainers, and financers in this process, New inter-disciplinary roles of women have to be properly churned and understood.

(3) There has to be a marked shift from charity to creativity, capacity and confidence building and the process involved.

(4) Issues relating to leadership and key decision makers.

(5) Issues in consultancy with special reference to low cost practicable consultancies.

(6) Issues relating to training in neglected programmes.

(7) Issues relating to modern industrialisation and contemporary policy and their implications for effective technology, entrepreneurship, marketing, brand image and overall competitive strength building.

(8) Issues relating to liberalisation and self-realisation.

(9) Issues concerning marketing of products.

21

Corporate Sector in Rural Development

(1) What is the Corporate Sector?

(2) What are its Strength, Weaknesses, Opportunities and Threats?

(3) What are the challenges of economic liberalisation, their relationship with Rural Development Programmes and how there is need to differ from charity to some commercial to full commercial gradual change?

(4) What are the issues in Rural Development and who are all players?

(5) How do we define the success in Rural Development Programme?

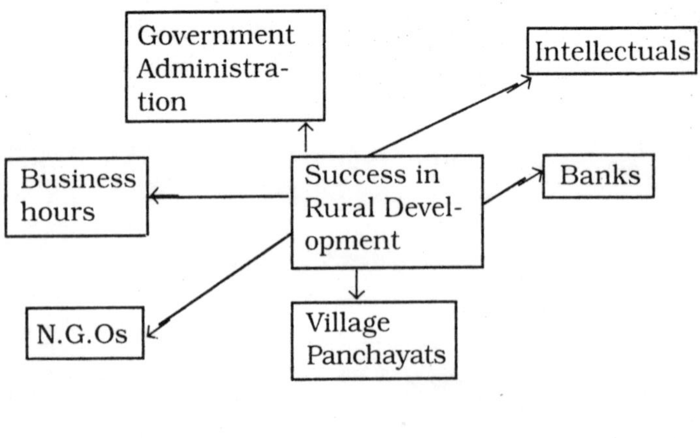

(6) What are the gradually emerging issues in the Rural Development and how Corporate Sector can influence the following:

(i) Policy issues at various levels
(ii) Financing Issues
(iii) Marketing Issues
(iv) Enterprise Development issues
(v) Science & Technology issues
(vi) Self Employment issues
(vii) Panchayati Raj linked sustainable development issues
(viii) Holistic Development and Rural Development
(ix) Lessons of implementing this programme in the last 4 decades and need for innovative bold approaches.
(x) Action plan to ensure:
   (a) Corporate Sector plays its judicious legitimate role without getting involved too much in charities.
   (b) Identifying selected areas and programmes.
   (c) Catalyst role — prioritisation — tactic for competitive àrea identification developing on the whole bankable project with fair amount of transparency to utilise local resort without too much dependencies on outside agency.

PART - II

TRAINING ATTITUDE

22

Need to Learn Lessons

In a diverse, vast and seemingly heterogeneous country like India, various, experiments have been done. These experiments are of varying nature. The targets groups have been different. The system of planning, action, research, codification, extension, loaning have already been different from time to time and place to place. The role of various role planners and stake-holders have also been different as per perception, appreciation and priority of the perceiver of the experiment.

However, a broad principled interaction with these varying groups bring out some common concern for further detailed examination. These include the following.

(1) Persistent neglect of marketing through self-sufficient emphasis.

- (a) Because of lack of marketing approach, there has been no compulsion to generate surplus or to make the experiment replicable, sustainable and thus widely acceptable.
- (b) Because of missing market approach, the mind sets of important role players have been conditioned to grant benefit, subsidy syndrome, leading to inefficiency and ultimate failure.
- (c) The innovations, bold steps, non-

accountability have been the results because of corruption, inefficiency, casteism and regionalism become the dominating factors.

(d) As opposed to business mentality, the system of nepotism, charity and "*bakshis*" syndrome spreads.

(e) The non-involvement and non-education of the masses results into one percent wasted educated class rule the unorganised masses.

(f) *The Need For Codification*
Due to lack of marketing culture, lot of harm has been done to the society. The insensitised system gets hardened and becomes indifferent and callous to the suffering of the masses. The marketing approach opens up vision of many stake-holders. The codification thus becomes very important analysis process of opening up.

Marketing and Codification

These words have many implications. Whether it is financing, training, technology, policy or any other socioeconomic, or biological science, there are lessons for everyone to learn. Marketing codification enables everybody to draw lessons for the welfare of all. By neglecting the welfare of masses, a few beneficiaries cannot be winners for a long time. The marketing codification helps us in training multi-dimensional lessons which have bearing on long term impact on the society. Why marketing codification? Marketing and codification both have been misunderstood. When combined both may face disaster unless action projected, presented, packaged, priced, delivered and serviced effectively. There has to be a taker and a seller. But there is one more word — coerced marketing also. How do we define and correlate all these seemingly heterogeneous words?

Are these irrelevant when taken for study in totality? Marketing if taken as an effective tool to service and fulfil a felt or a created and approached demand in a given situation, to felt or perceived target group at a given point of time or a place, then how do we correlate? Who will do this work? Why should he do it? Who will be the taker of these unheard terms, but timely notions? What is the role of a prominent civil servant, planner, financer, banker, professional, all leaders of society? Why should they expect to show willingness to be the takers of these incentives, but difficult changed process induces?

In a country like India and a State like Uttar Pradesh with massive, diversification of mind-set of conservatism and rigidities should be willing to accept these turnabout words which have been used to neglecting lessons in the past. No doubt neglect of past experiences compels us to commit same blunders with greater magnitude every time. This leads to collapse of hope. Every time this happens, one more stroke is given to the propagation of pessimism. The process of change visualise creation of conditionality and mentalities where resistance to change diminishes. How is this to be monitored, planned and visualised? There are no simple, straight answers. But with some commonsense, wisdom, practical approach to the identified problems and with properly marketed, codified experiences (PMCE), it should be possible to improve upon. The following are the essence in this process:

(1) Open mind (OM)
(2) Learning to work together (LTWT)
(3) Transparency, viability and contingency (TVC)
(4) Internal resource

(5) Emphasis on replicable related issues

(6) Issues of social integration like neglected groups, abled groups as opposed to disabled groups, women, children, etc.

(7) Emphasis

(8) Overall feeling of freedom, equity, win-win-win for all and spirit of win, risk taking and bold approaches to identified problems.

Marketing codification may be a new experiment for many. In a fast changing supersonic technological world makes this work important. Everything is possible in this exciting time. The marketing world would be a catch-word to competition, to usher in spirit of adventure, to make everyone a master of his destiny and to open up vistas for equity to all. There is need to broaden our vision. There is need to look at the hidden investible potential power of organisation (HIPPOO), known investible potential power of organisation (KIPPOO) and threatening investible potential power of organisation (TIPPOO). This is not only for the survival of an individual, but also a part of group-survival. By isolating ourselves we cannot ensure long term, sustainable development of anybody.

Marketing codification helps us in getting over these complexes which make us dependent, weak, dejected, despirited, disheartened and overall laughing stock in the eyes of others. Marketing codification helps us in avoiding past mistakes. It builds our confidence to perform better and better. It opens our vision by looking at past experiences with open mind. Market and marketing may be bad words for socialists, or capitalists, but to awaken humanism, we have no option. It is to be faced in a phased manner for the survival, growth and sustainable sensitised humanity.

Here lies the hope. Hence we should all pool our energy, resources and problems to learn to make the marketing of the codified experience. Let us not be ashamed of our mistakes, past experiences of marketing and marketing intelligence. This realisation itself need to be marketed in a codified manner.

23

Organisers Training for Self-Employment through Rural Industries Cluster

Our experience of planning for informal decentralised industries has been one of utter dismay. The very nature of dispersed industries shows that they do not have a self attracting power to invite and retain buyers, policy planners or even implementors. Thus the list of sympathisers and propagaters gets reduced. Even those who do admire the sector are pained to forget the distances and lack of regular interaction. The target group hardly has the capacity or resource to be constantly in touch with all those who matter. On the other hand, the organised urban based industries have the capacity to develop their observation and constantly interact with those who matter. They also inadvertently kill the surplus generating capacity of those which are not organised.

The lesson of world history has to be borne in mind to understand how the policy planning takes place. Due to utter faults of the system, they are unable to do anything for the unorganised. Induction of more and more sophisticated machines, pricing of government facilities in terms of telephone, railways, buses etc. in favour of urban and those organised the pressure of public demand on powers make a very sad analysis of the situation. The conclusions are clear that unless groups or cluster approach is adopted and suitable organisers are trained, their cases however powerful will always come out without success.

Role of Organisers

In any organisation, it is the organiser who acts as a catalyst. He ensures doing and undoing of various activities not only around the organisation but also far off areas in so far as they affect his organisation. Today we know of many good organisations which have performed well when organisers have organised them well. Over a period of time apart from other reasons lack of experienced organisers led to the organisations' failure. Organisers dealing with rural industries have to face additional handicaps, the urban based rural industries have everything available around them whether it is raw materials, facilities, technical problem, marketing or communication. They can manage all these at a very minimum cost while cluster of rural industries would mostly face all these essential requirements at a great disadvantage.

An organiser for rural industries will have to have training and practical experience which will equip him to take up this onerous task. Cluster approach in rural areas will succeed only if he is committed, motivated, trained and groomed through actual training. Thus he can shoulder this responsibility successfully. There is no short cut and no system. It is essential that the organisers are suitably equipped to be physically, mentally, motivationally, and commercially competent enough to take up this challenging opportunities.

What are the Organisers supposed to do?

The field of rural industrialisation is an essential part of rural development. Rural development encompasses health, hygiene, education, small savings, plantation, roads, electricity, living together, brotherhood and all that make quality of life best. This is the stage to let human being as animal to human being as human. The third stage of efforts — human being as super human being will come only through spirituality and tolerance. But the stage is far off when every human being aspires to rise to that level.

Rural industrialisation will be one of the important channels to stimulate rural development. This will be done by offering him sustained employment based on local raw materials and demand. Skills will not only be traditional, but will improve with demand and income. The greatest motivating force will be the surplus which it can generate. When rural industries are treated on par with organised industries and the tendency of buyers towards urban products etc. will definitely undergo a massive change.

Ecologically, considerable hygienic products would be sold at premium. Sustainment of developmental process is bound to take a practical shape. Emphasis on education for degrees and degrees being essential for better quality of life would evaporate. Internal resources generating capacity would become a guiding factor in the coming time. This can be easily understood. When surplus funds are available with every department, there is a competition in spending and those who can spend more get rewarded. This will lead to inefficiency, corruption and lethargy. This in turn will invariably breed inefficiency and ensure death of goodness. Sincerity, consciousness and hard work are bound to suffer under this situation. It is only the shortage of resources and dire need to generate surplus through internal resource generation and aggressive marketing that will change the attitude.

Marketing makes one dream, organise, considerate and result oriented. Output instead of input becomes parameter for evaluation. Coupled with this cost effectiveness competition makes it imperative to read, write, discuss and analyse. This has to be examined with reference to their acceptability and marketing. Consumer preference and acceptability of once professed views should be given all the more preference when funds are coming from various resources very easily, they make people irresponsive. This leads to a changed reaction. They also get organised, rather highly organised to protect their ill gotten powers and privileges. Under the situation those who can manage the facility extraction from them also have to surrender their pride. They become beggars and no wonder in this situation begging becomes an international culture.

An organiser has to understand all the cycles of thrust, reactions, theory and products. Many good ideas could not see the light of the day because of the incapacity of the originator. Practical views of things have to be always borne in mind alongwith their implication. Experience of those who are successful or unsuccessful have to be examined to improve things. All the problems of poverty, ignorance, population can be solved. Money is only one input. There are many more important things than money. Training itself is coupled with various misconcepts of stipend, longer duration and degree or certificate. The essential inputs of good training are very difficult and they often get totally neglected. These are left to the entrepreneur who in turn sets a very bad example by his failure. In the end remains a strong desire for a government job. This is how today's helpless situation have culminated. It is not one day's or one year's development. Many people, organisers, planners and implementors have contributed wholeheartedly to put an end to such a sorry state of past. Hence proper organisers training would be very essential to make any ray of hope visible.

Essential Training Requirement for Organisers

Once the above analysis is cleared, it is right time to have the specification of training components, i.e., (1) Conceptual clarity and (2) Physical fitness.

The basic requirement for any organisation in decentralised sector must be physical and mutual toughness. Unless both are present no means of other training can help him in becoming successful. This means, doing all that is needed to make a strong body including physical exercise, balanced diet, regular habits, awareness of hygiene, health and essentials of spirituality including yoga, meditation and all that which add to broaden the vision. Both these aspects will ultimately turn the organiser into a fully grown highly developed versatile personality which can in fact command the informal confidence.

Sound Technical and Organisation Knowledge

In today's competitive world, organisations are built and broken, competition of organisation clusters, leadership, motivation, good and bad workers are the essential part of research. Because of the induction of technology, various complications have developed and the capacity to use and manipulate appropriate technology in every field from production to distribution and monitoring got distorted. Technology may not be of the highest order, but capacity to use must be of the highest calibre. It is this capacity which will make the organisation fully competitive and superior.

It is here that the organiser will have to evaluate his performance regularly. Latest development in the field of technology and research and development will have to be constantly monitored. Technology does not mean, only machine, but techniques of managing things both in respect of man and material, raw material procurement, processing, storage, packaging, costing, accounting, transportation, marketing strategies. Other technologies, skills, distribution network relationship with cosumer, publicity through various media, product development etc. will have to be routine affairs. Some defences of COR, ICOR, social cost benefit will have to be redefined and they have to be defined by those who launch their institutions. This will also be part of the organiser to ensure this. When social values are undergoing vast changes, the organiser for decentralised sector will have to be more convinced logically and analytically to further disseminate his conviction to those who matter. This will be possible only when he knows the techniques and technologies of moving things, man, materials, ideas and problems.

Women Power

Because of their very nature, women are more conscious about responsibility and security. They are economically wiser and broadminded. Their capacity to pay attention to details, sensitivity, perseverance will have to be fully utilised by the organisers. The main issue is productivity. But there are no activities which cannot be performed by them. But conditions have to be created where blending of suitable aspirants and accepted roles can be possible to achieve the ultimate objective of overall sustainable development. The organiser has to take into account this aspect and takes suitable decision based on location, seasons, qualification, overall responsibility and long term benefit.

Quality to Look Ahead

Another important area which requires sustained training is the capacity to look ahead within the same situation. Even though one is surrounded by immediate problems and is hardly left with time and energy to look beyond one's immediate future, there is a need to look beyond. Organisers have to be risktakers, outward lookers and capable of foreseeing things, All these can be developed by practice and exercise.

Real situation like exposure can open up these hidden capacities. With proper guidance, motivation, probing of slipping capacity it is possible for every one to look beyond. Many of the good programmes, ideas, concepts and experiments could not be popular and useful to society because of this weakness to ensure that future holds promise for decentralised and well intentioned programme. It is essential for organisers to develop this quality. Through case studies and exploration, real situation will have to be developed to make organisers' training a grand success.

Follow-up and Monitoring

In today's competitive world no programme can succeed unless it is regularly monitored. This means, those who are trained should also take responsibility for follow-up. The follow-up and proper training have failed to a considerable extent because of insistence on pay stipend and extending period of training. To understand this vicious circle, one has to study the role of stipend, why training periods are extended, who are the trainers and how lopsided less useful non-marketing oriented training is imparted to students?

Stipend Oriented Training (SOT)

SOT become a big racket and big drag on public funds. This also multiplies due to the reasons of overflow of funds and incapacity of the systems to have inter-related cross check. The organisers' training must bear this point in mind. For this either the training stipend must be stopped fully and replaced by earning by learning to pay fees and meet other expenses or entire funds of stipend may be taken as loan with interest to be repaid over a period of time by the student or institution which sponsors. This point has wider repercussions and tomorrow all highly subsidised temples of learnings like medical colleges, IIM, IIT, and those printing out degrees and certificates would have to take extra care because students and parents will question their capacity.

Training institutions will have to devise groom their policies and attitudes for internal resource generation which will in turn help and expedite their overall capacity for the challenging task. There are no short cuts and easy solutions. If all-round steps are taken improvement can also come.

Easy solution is to make the training institutes also responsible for recovering this money over a period of time. This will help in establishing direct rapport with the students and teachers would have to be more open, committed, responsible and knowledgeable to ensure success of the training. Needless to say, the real success of training will not lie on imparting degree or marks, but on the capacity of the trainees to repay loan with interest. This means candidates have to be competitive and capable to deliver goods.

In so far as this relates to organisers for rural industries, entrepreneurship concept, which applies to the present situation, must be understood. The entrepreneurship today is not only to take risk but also to organise things. Organising is most difficult because of various complications and multiplicity of rules and regulations. What is required is the capacity to put all things round to the best use. This means understanding the psychology and programmes of multifarious departments and identifying useful activities. The clusters of rural industries will pave the way for development. Apart from employment generation, they will also help the organiser in developing his full potential by co-ordinated self-management.

The above analysis pre-suppose the competence of trainers. They are not theoreticians but actual doers. We had enough of research on the third world countries. What is required today is action research. There are enough of successful models which a good organiser will have to follow and copy. The need is to have open mind and strong commitment to the cause which ensures not only his growth but also sustainability of the activities. No programme can be successful unless it is widely acceptable. Concepts have to undergo vast changes and organisers will have to be the basic catalysts.

24

The Importance of Training for Rural Industrialisation

For a rapid and self-sustained development of rural areas, rural industrialisation is an essential ingredient which leads to the development of the entire economy. Since the economic activities in rural areas are exclusively in agriculture, while industries are located exclusively in urban areas, the linkages between rural-urban or agriculture industry are not strong and there is a wide gap between them. Rural industrialisation is only the effective means of reducing this imbalance and accelerating the process of rural development.

Need, Meaning and Definition of RI

In an economy where agriculture predominates as a means of livelihood and dependence for the greater part of the population, even a relatively rapid growth of agriculture is not likely to employ the entire rural labour force at reasonable levels of productivity and incomes. The pressure of population on land is already high and increasing and has already resulted in a large surplus of labour in rural areas. Therefore rural industrialisation is to be the only solution of the unemployment problem in such situations. It is believed that with very small amount of capital investment, it is possible to employ people in village industries provided that a market is assured for their products.

The growth of rural industries in India has been one of the most significant features of our planned economy. Our experience has demonstrated that rural industries are the powerful factor for the rapid and decentralised growth of a developing economy. Hence, the policies and programmes adopted by us should be to accelerate the growth of rural industrial sector. Rural industries should thus carry the message of industrialisation of the rural areas to the nooks and corners of the country through various traditional and non-traditional industries.

Rural industries have been making their due contribution to economic growth in terms of the contribution to national income, industrial production, employment and such other, factors. The achievements of this sector in terms of the diversification and sophistication of production is equally impressive. With this phenomenal growth has been raised various expectations that the benefits of economic development should accrue to the relatively less privileged classes of society and that there should be progressive reduction of concentration of incomes, wealth and economic power. Therefore a comprehensive programme has to be drawn up to strengthen and utilise the existing rural industrial sector and to attract new entrants into this field in large numbers. The programme should catch the imagination of the growing numbers of educated men and women at the middle and lower levels of society.

Need for Revising Training Modules

Rural industries in India suffer from various handicaps compared to their counterpart viz. large scale industries. One of the most important among these is the non-availability of technical and managerial personnel of the required calibre. Large industries can employ qualified staff specialised in different aspects of production and management. The rural industrialists cannot even enhance his technical efficiency through proper training. Besides, they do not have the required equipment and resources to train their workers. Unless and until this lacuna is removed by providing proper technical and management training, the development of rural industries is beyond imagination.

In rural areas, everyone appears to be involved in one or the other activities, but how gainful that involvement is not guessed by anybody, Lack of enthusiasm, illiteracy and shyness create a sense of withdrawal from the participation of various income generating activities in rural areas. It is in this context that development of the required skills and training assume prime importance. Existence of local resources, availability of market and matching production activities are to be studied carefully. Skills may be available to use local raw materials for production linked with market potential. To fulfil this training facilities and orientation course are needed: besides, credit at concessional rates of interest, priority in supply of raw materials, extension services and marketing assistance training are the most vital components.

The process of participation and decision making become crucial for the survival of any rural industry. Periodic training programmes which result in effective participation of people at all levels and in facilitating decision making are to be organised systematically. The innovative training methodology should try to involve them in learning and sharing of experiences, which would make them participate actively in various development programmes. The content of training should include organising skills, group dynamics and consciousness, communication skills and awareness raising.

Further, the people who are employed in some rural industries, need to upgrade their skills and learn new operational skills where they feel interested. They must be in a position to assess and control production and marketing. They must be imported minimum management and accounting skills. It may be worthwhile to have a relook and study of the existing industries in rural areas to evolve a suitable training mechanism. It is not for discovering something entirely new but only for redefining the existing problem and evolving an overall strategy for energising rural folk through skill development.

Existing System of Training

While there are no two opinions about the necessity of equipping rural people with new skills and upgrading the already available skills, attention has to be paid to both traditional activities and also the newly emerging non-traditional ones. The basic framework for imparting training and skills already exists though in a limited way. The KVIC through its Training Directorate has evolved a very comprehensive training infrastructure to train artisans and supervisors in various technologies developed in its R&D centres. The KVIC imparts training both in Khadi and V.Is. Recently, KVIC has expanded the coverage of industries to 96 product lines which includes electronics also. It is, however, necessary to identify these trades which provide large scope and employment opportunities in each village and to train them accordingly.

Essential Components for Future

Training of beneficiaries assumes considerable importance especially in the case of non-traditional trades promoted in rural areas. As the beneficiaries are from those families which are below the poverty line, training should be given in a detailed way so that these beneficiaries will comprehend the subject matter and gain confidence to practise them. One area which is common to both groups of beneficiaries selected for traditional and modern trades is acquisition of simple managerial skills to run the enterprise in an efficient way. Thus, for all entrepreneurs, skills needed for filling the forms, managing the enterprise, accountancy and book-keeping should be taught. Technical skills should be imparted to those beneficiaries who are selected to take up modern trades so that they will have a thorough knowledge of machines, simple tools and processes involved. Working in a similar unit or training centre will give confidence to such beneficiaries.

An important aspect of training is to develop training infrastructure wherever it has been found to be inadequate. New training centres have to be set up particularly in rural areas. It is also necessary to impart training in modern activities in addition to traditional trades. In this context, it is very important and essential to enlist the cooperation of many voluntary organisations, some of which are already doing commendable development work in rural areas. However, training should equip the individuals with modern skills to absorb improved technology so that productivity and earnings of artisans can be enhanced and in particular drudgery of operations has to be minimised.

It is suggested that a permanent training set-up be established at the district level to meet varied training requirements. If a composite training centre is set up at the district level with facilities for trades relevant for beneficiaries of different programmes, they can be trained effectively, nearer home in a comprehensive manner.

Linkages

There is also great need to undertake extension work to convince rural people the need to equip themselves with new skills and upgrade the already existing ones. Thus, the training input to be successful and productive has to be supplemented with a comprehensive strategy and supported by a lot of extension work through NGOs (non-governmental) organisations like Welfare Board and other voluntary agencies). The extension agent after identifying a group of persons should motivate them to undergo training, organise live demonstration of improved technology and also offer all supporting measures and guidance to ensure the success of the scheme.

Vocational Training

Vocational training is given importance for diversification of educational opportunities for unemployed youth and those persons who could not pursue higher education. For making vocational education more effective, the following steps are necessary:

(i) Identification of skills which will suit the needs of the local students in their particular area of training; (ii) giving them training, organising them into industries, societies or federation to provide backward/forward linkages; (iii) identifying the areas where the products of students trained in their vocation can be suitably marketed; and (iv) identifying good institutions working under KVI Sector to take up this work by providing linkages at a reasonable cost by the Education Department.

KVIC is conducting training courses in different industries under its purview through aided and departmental training centres. Those courses are highly suitable to rural youth especially in the field of soap-making, book-keeping, carpentry and blacksmithy, village leather, palmgur products, etc. It has also been considered necessary to ensure direct involvement of rural youth as self-employed entrepreneurs to take up programmes of rearing of silk cocoons, cotton ginning, etc. and supervising of construction of biogas plants.

The Commission has also decided to involve educational institutions and deemed universities in its training programmes. The programmes conducted by these bodies will be non-residential and non-stipendary. The students who are admitted will have to pay fees. Vocational education will infuse in the youth: (i) Work ethics and a sense of dignity of labour; (ii) enable both the individual and the society growth oriented, ultimately improving quality of life; and (iii) develop vocational and income generating skills in the student community and educated unemployed youth in rural and semi-urban areas for economic independence.

The main objectives of the programme are to provide diversification of educational opportunities so as to enhance individual employability, reduce the mismatch between demand and supply of skilled manpower and to provide an alternative for those pursuing higher education.

Marketing/Production Training Concept

The different methods by which internal resource could be generated are: (i) Production and Marketing; (ii) Low Cost Practical Consultancy (LCPC); (iii) tuition fees; (iv) consultancy fee; and (v) laboratory fee (in the case of training centres who have laboratory facilities). According to the present concept, the main thrust of the training programme is production and marketing. Assuming that a training centre has a complement of 40 trainees in a particular batch, the production per month is expected to be fairly good and, therefore, it should not be difficult for a training centre to earn a sizeable amount by production and marketing alone. It is not sufficient for the training centres to produce the same type and quality of goods. The earning by way of production and marketing could be further augmented by way of fees, etc. All this demands more dynamism on the part of the principles and staff members of the Training Centres.

It is, therefore, felt that a Training Centre should generate internal resource at least to the extent of 10 per cent of its annual recurring expenditure. This may be enhanced over a period of time.

LCPCs

From experience, it is seen that trades of certain village industries are concentrated in specific areas where the industries are doing well and over the years have developed expertised skills. For example palm gur is doing well in Tamil Nadu, Village Oil Industry in Maharashtra, Handmade Paper in U.P., Beekeeping in Kerala, and Tamil Nadu and Cane and Bamboo in North Eastern Region. There is a cadre of artisans and operators in these areas.

A practical concept would be to create a cadre of

trade-wise Low Cost Practical Consultants (LCPCs) who would be basically persons working in the particular trade for considerable length of time and would be operators/skilled workers in the particular disciplines having worked in areas of installation, erection, operation and manufacturing of various categories of products with their own hands. These categories of skilled artisans would be of utmost use for establishment of similar units in virgin areas where potentiality exists but technology is not available.

The salient features of the LCPC scheme are as under:

(1) The Industry directorates, Principals of Training Centres will in consultation with the institutions, State Boards and State Directors prepare a panel of LCPCs for each industry.

(2) Industry Director/Principal on receipt of need for deploying LCPCs would assess the number of LCPCs to be deputed depending upon the proximity of location. Therefore, the Industry Director will negotiate with the institution, etc. The terms of reference, cost involvement for deployment of LCPCs vis-a-vis additional incentive, to and fro travelling expenses, accommodation and other requirement to be met in respect of LCPCs and obtain the concurrence of the institution.

(3) Once the LCPCs reach the site of the implementing agencies, the concerned State director would deploy his Technical Officer to coordinate, deployment and utilisation of the services of LCPCs within a time-bound framework and the Technical Officer of the State Office or State Board would ensure that all requirements relating to machinery, equipments and tools, power, etc. are made

available to the LCPCs.

(4) The State Director or State Board would coordinate fixing up areas of work which the LCPC is required to attend to which may cover areas of installation, erection, power connection, raw material, procurement, preparation of jigs, fixtures, product development, production/manufacture, etc. Accordingly, the State Director and the Industry Director would determine the number of LCPCs for a particular work, duration etc.

Setting Up of Artisan Villages

With a view to encourage the artisans/craftsmen and promote the development of the industries under the purview of the Commission, it has been decided to establish Artisans Village in the training centres where adequate space is available on an experimental basis. The scheme for Artisan Villages is given in a nutshell:

(1) In the Training Centres, where space is available, talented artisans may be invited to work as self-employed craftsmen who will be provided with residential accommodation and worksheds at a nominal rent, initially for 9 months;

(2) In deserving cases, working capital will be given to the artisans with facilities to make use of the worksheds, implements and other available facilities;

(3) Display of the products of the Artisan Village in the Training Centre;

(4) The artisan will be required to give training to prospective artisans; and

(5) The artisans will be authorised to extend Low

Cost Practical Consultancy (LCPC) to untrained workers and others in the nearby villages.

The Scheme of Artisan Village is proposed to be introduced initially in training centres where land is readily available for construction of accommodation for the artisans. The scheme will be implemented on an experimental basis for 9 months.

The Artisan Village will have to be run on replicability concept. The house will have to be production unit which means change in the attitude of housing authority or HUDCO, marketing concept for internal resource generation and linkages building with cultural centres of Government of India, vocational education. Involvement of NGOs and industrial houses. Artisans can get recognition, incentive for self-employment only through marketing.

Training Organiser

While talking about developing replicable models for rural industries through traditional and non-traditional industries, we have to also consider the need to organise organiser's training today, organisers will have to attend to various problems connected with history, accounting, marketing, technology, human resource development, bankability and replicability of rural industries programme. The training has to cater for human force, appropriate technology, skill upgradation, linkages and coordination, along with self propelling motivation. The implications of technology helping in cornering of resources by few has to be substituted by trusteeship concept in practical shape. Need to constantly watch for new opportunities with sustainability and to modify them for appropriate conditioning of the concerned target group has to be appreciated and it is here that the role of the teacher and the Principal becomes paramount.

If training had assumed the role of preparing for facing the competition in an "opened up liberalised world", the training cannot be through closed institutions and trainers. Various on-going handicrafts, handloom, coir, KVI sector, special target group etc. have to be substituted by marketing production training (MPT) concept where the role of organisers will be of paramount importance. Learning from past mistakes it can be summed up the need for re-visiting the so-called acclaimed successes of the past. In terms of investment, employment, replicability, bankability, hope generation, how can the earlier "successes" help in multiplication? All trainers, evaluators, funders and overall sympathisers will have to answer this question.

Role of Organised Industry in Training

While the industrial houses possess various strengths, there are certain areas where rural industrialisation through traditional and non-traditional industries would have their own strength. While a separate exercise needs to be conducted for analysing SWOTs of each sector, there are certain interlink areas. Organised industries have good communication network, marketing strategy, transport, guest houses and other infrastructure, which, if passed on to hinterland of the industrial activity may help in self-employment being glamourised. Naturally, this "glamourisation" can come only through status, recognition, reward and adequate remuneration and sustained returns. While providing jobs in these industries can be one way of solving the problem, the more important is creating condition wherefrom "cultivation to multiplication through value addition" is possible based on local raw material, local demand, local skills and appropriately local co-ordination through in-built system. The very concept of "help" has to be substituted by creating condition for self-help. This is possible only when concept of charity, grant, rebate and subsidy is substituted by equitable growth with social justice by providing adequate source for marketing linked production. This is also basic requirement for infrastructure development, godowns, bio-gas linked power generation and use of existing resources in terms of educational institution, polytechnic, transport network and cost effective method of distribution. For this existing production centres may be ideally situated developing them with the collaboration of industrial houses for induction of PARTE concept. Even institutions like IIM, NPC, NIDR, SIRD, IRMA, etc. have to come forward by mobilising their faculty to take sustainable development experiment through replicable model. All these activities will need reorientation towards concept of self employment through selfhelp. The role of 80,000 banks which have multiplied from 8,000 in the 20 years has to be appreciated in this connection. With reference to area approach can better be utilised from "concept to concretisation" only with the help of industrial houses which again have to prove their own bonafides by taking up low cost high impact programme. Indo-Gulf at Jagdishpur and Lupin Laboratory at Bharatpur have done commendable work in this sector. Their experience without any grant or income tax exemption has to be properly evaluated, codified and conditions created for multiplication on a massive scale. The training input will be the centre with replicability.

25

Organiser's Training for Rural Industries Cluster Programme

Introduction

The biggest problem faced in the induction, implementation and managing of rural industries, programme is in the field of shortage of organisers. As appropriate technology is inducted and marketing becomes a crucial activity, it is essential that we groom/train/prepare organisers to guide, control, supervise, manage, finance, publicise etc. various activities. The ultimate aim is to train organisers, supervisory cadre of organisers to make nodal point for rural industries cluster programmes for employment generation on sustainable basis.

Duration

It is proposed that this training should be for about 6 months spread over in spiritual technical, manpower development centres. The programme should start at 03.30 hrs. in the morning to make the best use of the golden time and should continue upto 19.00 hrs. The idea of keeping such a heavy schedule is to ensure that the Boys and Girls who pass out after 6 months intensive 'firing' should be able to give the lead which is the basic need for the sector.

Course Content

After discussion with various experts, institutions, trainers and others who have worked in the Sector, it has been felt that the following areas should be covered to make these well groomed personalities of organisers, for rural industries.

1. Historical Development, Definition, Necessity of KVIC Sector

The historical background must be studied, codified and explained to the students because unless they know the past, the future will not be built on solid footing. The mistakes committed in the past, present policies, strategies, tactical requirements for this sector and the role of organiser are some of the crucial areas to be covered.

2. Funding, Accounting, Costing and General Economics including COR-ICOR -IRR-Social Cost Benefit Analysis etc.

Since financing from Banks will have to be restored on a very big scale, it is essential that Projects are bankable, backward forward linkages ensured and need for accounting, costing and their systematic maintenance etc. is sought.

3. Marketing including Packaging, Timely Supplies, BIS & Other Standardisation Methods

This has been one of the most neglected areas in the success of our programmes and now time has come to instil sense of marketing for not only products but also concepts, ideas, technology and other social advantages of buying rural industries products. This will also mean appropriate publicity, sustainability of products and development of low cost high impact marketing systems for products from rural areas.

4. Women Power

This is another area where potential has to be tapped with open mind and rationale reasoning. We may even have some trainings exclusively for women. Women have various roles and because of these different roles they have various powers and potentialities. For employment generation through rural industries, the qualities of perseverance, hard work, sensitivity etc. can be utilised. All programmes can naturally suit the women also. But some more than others. Hence suitable identification of programmes and industries will have to be done depending on location, season and qualification, beneficiaries.

5. Science & Technology

In today's highly competitive world no programme can succeed unless science and technology is blended with spiritual and day-to-day need of modern world. While science is not static, various new areas have to be constantly examined in the light of technological lessons. Use of appropriate technologies from production to marketing and product development will have to be studied in this field.

6. Spirituality

This may sound illogical, but the time has come also to include spirituality as essential ingredient in the training component of Organisers for rural industries clusters. Spirituality ensures broadening of vision. It also ensures linkages and wider appreciation of neglected areas. From meditation to Yoga, herbal medicines, age old traditional cultural values and sociological developments should also be calculated in this chapter.

7. Faith

No programme can succeed unless the Organiser learns to have faith and belief in his team, buyers, producers and dealers. While bureaucratic Organisers are notorious for lack of faith in every activity the world of business runs smoothly on faith. These difficult requirements have to be explained along with charts and graphs etc. to understand the proper ethos of business.

8. Group Behaviours, Motivation, H.R.D. etc.

The Organiser has to lead and motivate people around him to behave in a particular fashion. For this he has to understand the group psychology, their aspirations, traits etc. Host of literature has been developed in the last centuries and this has to be passed on to rural Organisers so that the known knowledge is available for effectiveness.

9. Computerised Monitoring M.I.S.

This is another area where decentralised industries have failed and the success in future will depend to a considerable extent on right type of monitoring at the right time by the right people. This will also include evaluation, inventory controls, feedbacks, role play and other hitherto neglected areas.

With the growth of multiplicity of Organisers, we will have to involve Rural Development Department,

Institutional Banks and many other on-going programmes and adopt area project. Keeping in mind the potential of export from ecologically pollutant free industries exports would be generated in a big way. For problem solving needs and appropriate informations, whom to contact has to be known. For the question of making success of cluster of rural industries in the interior/backward areas of the country, the Organiser will have to be multi-disciplined. For this, it is essential that the above activities are made essential part of the training for Organiser. Regarding skill to be imparted, we hope this will be multi-disciplinary and specialised differing from industry to industry. Specialised training will have to be imparted to workers but the Organiser will have to know about all the concerned industries.

Need for Coordinated Work

Apart from funds, monitoring, training linkages both forward and backward will have to be done by like minded organisations —NABARD, CAPART, KVIC, NGO's — will have to be involved in a very big way for success of these programmes.

Self Management

Taking a lesson or two from past experience, the best incentive for a Manager is Self-Management. An organiser will organise. The Producer will manage his own affairs. What cannot be managed by themselves at any stage is left to others to manage.

26

Organisers Training

Need of the Training

The point of philosophing, organisers, marketing, production, training, extension, codified training into, blend the harmonious business relationship between various aspects which make the sustainable like circle. The basic aim is to develop organisers for conceptualising to concretising the rural industrialisation clusters.

Rural industries are programmes of various aspects of storage, processing, packaging, branding quality testing and marketing of products both to cities and rural areas. The time has come when products from rural areas have to go to cities not in the raw form but value added for consumption. The need is now to maximise value addition in rural areas and send them to cities for consumption. A new concept has also come where products from rural area can also be directly exported in a big way. Simultaneously we have also to consider the problem of rural area which is not only of the uneducated but it is more of educated unemployed. In this situation rural industries become esential for rural area.

Selection of Students

It is proposed that in the first stage students from selected states should only be selected for this training. Since rural areas will mean regional language and Hindi as the base, it is proposed that instead of having a national training we may confine to regional so that maximum benefit is derived.

Best of Selection and Qualification

Though there should be no right qualification since students will be sponsored by selected NGOs, it is better that their IQ level, receptivity, analysis capacity is above average. They should be sponsored by institutions with the addition that subsequently they will be incharge of rural industries programme preferably to clusters. The salary etc. for those will have to be provided by the institutions. But training expenses, boarding, lodging should be borne by society. It may be a point for consideration whether 25 per cent of the total cost should be charged from the institutions. If that be so, what will be its implication?

During this training the objective will be to equip the students for undertaking organisational role for the programme of rural industries. Organisational capacity will have to be differentiated from that of managerial capacity. Organisation has to perform much more responsible active coordinating linkage building, public relation development role rather than manager in this programme the following syllabus is proposed to be taken up:

(i) Area planning what all goes into planning for rural industries clusters.
(ii) Involvement of local people.
(iii) Project making and giving it to banks
(iv) Linkage development
(v) While ensuring the sustainability, how to ensure the marketing concept for replicability of the

project. This can broadly be the part of planning process. Implementation process will involve actual implementation, coordination, problem solving, monitoring, reporting and fulfilling the condition of tax authority, local governments and bankers.

(vi) The difference between theory and practice, actual and perceived hypocratic behaviour, need for internal resource generation, performance based incentive output *vs.* inputs and human resource development etc. assume very important role. The historical lessons which effect unorganised sector, infrastructural problems to rural area are other points of exposure.

Communication

The importance of communication with reference to modern methods, use of hand communication, written *vs.* oral communication, costs, time factors and total impacts become some important elements of communication. Organisers have duties with reference to communication with subordinates, colleagues, customers, supplyers, policy-makers and press etc. is also important.

What are the qualities of organisers like openness, punctuality, timeliness, sense of humour, vision intuition, hard work? How are they developed and preserved? What are the functions of organiser as Manager, as communicator, as worker, as analyser, as accounts supervisor, as supplier and buyer, as diversifier, exporter and how these ideas and expectations to be matched with the life like situation? How workshop training codification can help him?

Orientation and Objectives of Courses on Basic Philosophy

What is an organiser and how it differs from management? What are the characteristics of Palmgur Organiser?

(1) Typical Indian senario and organisation in rural India.
(2) Facts and functions of good organiser.
(3) Decision making, how, when, what, where etc.
(4) Basic principles of economics, budget, accounting and market related activities.
(5) Marketing — creating demand, sustaining developing attitudes, advertising, pooling together and other related issues.

Extension and Codification: How does it matter if good thing do not spread or not codified properly. Need for codification. How Gandhiji mentioned by diary as an important tool of codification of experiences. How in this modern technological world codification work has simplified - V.C.R, Radio, Television, Cassette player, books, visits and even mouth to mouth. Need to codify too example and take steps to make them replicable. Need for replicable models for development. What all replications involved? Cost of replication are some other areas for training.

Human Relation in Extension of Good Programme

Examination of good models like Kelkar of Wardha, Lijjat, Ralegaon, Siddi, Tara and Kalbagh model at Pune. How these models were developed, structured and how can be useful in rural industries bankable programme?

government functionary, society and how things can be got done.

What the Course will achieve

As the name suggests, POMPTEC (Philosophy, Organisership, Management & Marketing Production & Process, Technology and Training Extenion and Codification) at the end of the course would try to achieve the following:

1. Confidence, knowledge and skill in the participation to plan implement, monitor and extend the rural industries cluster concept.
2. Keeping in mind the need for overall understanding of rural development, health, general conceptual, clarity and implementational programmes with reference to rural development programme.
3. Ideological induction concept to clarity project formulation with reference to infrastructure, raw material manpower machinery and the source along with financial requirement and maintenance will help in extending the programme and its replication. The programme will not give technical knowledge but organisational capacities which also include how to solve the technical problem connected with industries programme and accept the concept of appropriate technology.
4. To develop a coordinated approach by laying more stress on practical aspect of the theory. Hence what can be given in writing will not be spoken.
5. What can be shown and demonstrated will not be written and what cannot be sold will not be manufactured. Hence the faculty will

have to prepare special package literature which will meet the above tough requirements.

Whosoever comes to get exposed to the students must spend minimum whole day and one night with them. They should also give in writing their view of each student for record and results. The faculty has to consist of people who have proved their worth in the practical application of whichever field they are supposed to be expert. Hence they may not be missionary but experience, inquisitiveness, will and skill, spirit and hope has to be the essential components of their willingness to join in this effort.

Examination System

There will be no formal examination. But evaluation, monitoring, questioning and learning, developing, all round personality has to be an essential to will and skill upgradation. Hence there has to be daily evaluation by the faculty teacher. Weekly summary of what they have seen, felt, learnt, analysed and its practical relevance — a group report can be prepared.

2. Visit to Ralegaon, Siddi, Pune, Wardha and actual implementing with the institution concerned and writing their aspirations and vision.

3. After three months and subsequently again after 3 or 6 months, the experience sharing with students of actual performance will be done. This will keep them in contact for minimum one year and even teaching the institution of their perception of the difficulties for this problem. To achieve this, first one month will be here; 15 days at Wardha and 15 days at Ralegaon Siddi, Pune and third month again at Bombay. 70 to 80 percent time, attention, follow up will be on practical aspect of the objective and

every day minimum exposure time will be 12 hours with only one day holiday in a week. The Sunday concept has to be substituted. Hence problem solving, practical application can group behaviour will receive special attention in all programmes.

Faculty

Since the objective is ultimately to achieve dream of glamourisation of rural areas, it is essential that the organisers develop a versatile personality based on historical lessons, SWOT of rural India, changing horizon of developmental planning, encompassing sustainability to meet the challenges of liberalisation and opening up. Hence faculty has to be of people who have done proved track record work in their own field. NABARD, SIDBI, IDBI, KVIC, NGOs, spiritual institutions and experts of industry, communication, man-management would be involved. Since they have to spare one full day and night with the students, it is essential that they pay full time attention during the period of 24 hours in helping them broadening the vision. Hence faculty will have to represent the following 5 areas.

The following will be the plan of action to achieve the above:

1. Financial tie-ups and arrange advertisements in the local newspapers of Maharashtra.
2. Tie-up with faculty
3. Finalise detailed programme and objective of each day's interaction.
4. Having established liaison with Wardha institution or Dategaon, Ralegaon Siddi. A meeting will have to be held jointly for concretising the entire concept.
5. The students may have to be selected after the

nominations are received to see that they will be able to derive maximum benefit out of this.

Since it is a joint effort, coordinating role will be completed by the organising institution. But weekly meeting will be proposed for the funding institution. The aim is to involve the funding institution also in maximising the effectiveness of the programme.

It is hoped that by pooling the resources of all, this programme will be able to generate a national interest.

27

Relevance of Teaching Public Administration

The process of decision-making in the present modern, complex scientific world has become equally complex and difficult. The administrative system is so complex, inter-related that conflicts between polycentricity, planning and control, autonomy are often subtle questions of degree. Today, the decisions can be made either by adhoc resolutions or by imposing a plan of action or by full integration of many of the organisations concerned to a single agency. This is because organisational theory has become enormously complex and secondly, lack of effective coordination has come to stay because of hetrogeneity of demand-interests. This becomes more difficult when, as R.J.S. Baker says, "In relatively few instances can I recollect my own authority or that of my colleague — equal senior or junior—being defined by formal rules. Most of the time it was not precisely defined at all. It was nevertheless implicit and well understood."

The administrative training programmes deal with problems precisely enumerated above. Basic human nature and its problems are same everywhere. Lessons learnt at one place can be suitably useful at other places. The time, location factors would effect, but basic lessons can be fixed to draw up plans. As Bertrand Russel has said, "The trouble with the world is that the stupid are cocksure and the intelligent, full of doubt." The administrative training forum programme can be a useful one to bridge this gap. The interaction between various hierarchy operating at different levels and conditions of government may help in part-bridging. Administrative training time is also a most appropriate time for a serving civil servant to relax and coolly ponder over the conditions in which he is operating. The grass looks greener on the other side, but try to look at it from the other side too. There lies the reality. This is the important aspect of any training programme especially one for the administrators.

Government Policies

Political system is that system of interaction in any society through which binding authoritative allocations are made. This has inputs from various environment and these are converted into decisions. There are various regulatory machanisms to control demand and minimise overloading. They include pressure groups etc., etc.

Aristotle has said that the end of politics is not knowledge but action. The relation between academic knowledge and practical political activity has to be acknowledged. Political power is the capacity to effect another's behaviour by threat of some form of action. The sanction may be negative or positive. It is also a relationship. Though, usually, in a power relationship situation, it is very difficult to discover why a change within individual's or group's behaviour has been affected.

Regarding government, it is very very difficult to draw a hard and fast line between the policy making and implementation of these policies by the government and its professional administrators. The regulatory fields of health, police, land revenue, collection have been joined by welfare social and other developmental functions concerned with economic regulations and control. In some states, the direct control of training, electricity, gas, railways, road, air transport, etc. have necessitated a large expansion of public service. In states like USSR, state control of economic aspects of society is absolute and bureaucratic control extends to the cultural spheres. This is not to seize on some new aspect of human organisation and relate it to modern political developments. Public administration is a continuing feature of all political structure but the size and capabilities of modern bureaucracies present differences in degree. Even in the states like U.S.A. where federal government interference in the economic field is comparatively low, there are much more civil servants now than they were earlier. Same phenomenon is also visible in other states like U.K.

Professional administrators usually have a degree of performance denied to politicians in most political systems. Their expertise, career specialisation, ability to control resources, group solidarity, hierarchical structure, etc. can create additional obstacles to political will. In some political systems, the bureaucracy presents a degree of stability, coherence and continuity that is absent from political structure. It is claimed that economic development of France in 1950s was the result of excellence of permanent bureaucrats. In West Germany, the administration inspires greater trust than the politicians.

As Richard Rose has demonstrated, the roles of politicians are numerous and diverse, and cannot easily be summarised. Another difficulty is that political contributions are often divided between those made by members of the legislature and members of the executive. The executive, legislative distinction if often more significant for analysis of decision making. Apart from the above, there is always some degree of conflict between the politician's role and interest in helping his supporters and the administrators concerned with so called impartial rules and procedures. In modern democracies, the capacity to secure special favours has dwindled as public services have been purged of patronage and nepotism.

The crudest form of political discrimination consists at the procurements of job, business concession, welfare payments or other special services for supporters in exchange of their votes. An important and accredited role of politician is to bring individual claims and grievances to the attention of the relevant public agency. A Member of Parliament is supposed to assist equally any constituent and not just his supporter and he will not expect administrative rules to be broken solely for reasons of political pressure or expediency and he can exercise his own judgement about the strength of the case. Conversely, administrators give careful and prompt attention to all cases which M.P. brings to their notice, but they should not easily waive rules because of political pressure.

Politicians are the ultimate controllers of administrative systems and one of their chief problems is to maintain and demonstrate the reality of their control. It also means establishing an atmosphere in which administrator would continually be aware of political guidelines and constraints. It also means that administrator, while giving plans of action, must give a set of alternatives. The meaningfulness of these final decisions will naturally be increased to the extent that their options are kept open.

The management consultancy group which reported to Fulton Committee in U.K. defined the total management tasks of the civil services as:

(a) Formulation of policy under political direction.
(b) Creating a machinery for implementation of policy.
(c) Operation of the administrative machinery.
(d) Accountability of parliament and to the public.

Policy direction makes itself frequent and sometimes radical changes in the content of emphasis of policy. Civil servants are expected to be able to adopt to radical rapid changes at the time to change of government and to implement entirely new policies without any break in continuity. Chief Ministers frequently reshuffle not only their cabinet colleagues but also whole departments and agencies, so that civil service has to cope almost overnight with the creation and dissolution of substantial organisations. These decisions are sometimes on political basis which may have hardly taken managerial considerations into account. Public accountability requires meticulous attention to the maintenance of equity in implementing decisions and in dealing with specific cases. It requires elaborate arrangements to ensure consistency in the application of policy within and between departments.

The constraints of managing a political dimension inevitably have an effect on management style. Sir Derek Rayner, a businessman, brought into government early in 1970s as an adviser in management in U.K., has said, "Efficiency in civil service is dependent as in business on motivation, and whereas in business, one is judged by overall success, in my experience, the civil service tends to be judged by failures. This inevitably conditions his approach to his work." Similarly, the objectives of a civil service manager may be less tangible and are usually less quantifiable than those of a manager in a commercial organisation.

From the discussion above, it would be clear that an administrator has to understand the surrounding in which he has to work to become efficient and successful. Government and politics are moving realities of life. The administrative training programme tends to make the training better administrator. The role of government today has undergone vast changes. In the fast moving world, administrator has to adjust with very fast changing facts of life. Politics and government, their functioning, unless known properly, may fail a person.

To sum up, let us remember what Bertrand Russel has said about the conflicting requirements of democracy:

> "One of the peculiarities of the English speaking world is its immense interest and belief in political parties. A very large percentage of English speaking people really believe that ills from which they suffer would be cured if a certain political party were in power. That is a reason for the swing of the pendulum. A man votes for one party and remains miserable; he concludes that it was the other party that was to bring the millennium. By the time he is disenchanted with all parties, he is an old man on the verge of death; his sons retain the belief of his youth, and the see-saw goes on."
>
> "I want to suggest that, If we are to do any good in politics, we must view political questions in quite a different way. A party, which is to obtain power, must, in a democracy, make an appeal to which the majority of the nation responds. For reasons

> which will appear in the course of the argument, an appeal which is widely successful, with the existing democracy, can hardly fail to be harmful. Therefore, no important political party is likely to have a useful programme, and if useful measures are to be passed, it must be by means of some other machinery than party government. How to combine any such machinery with democracy is one of the most urgent problems of our time."

With the above analysis in mind, we should be able to appreciate the relevance of teaching public administration not only to politicians and practising administrators, but also to all those interested in the well-being of the nation.

28

Training Needs of Rural Development Sector

Before we go into the question of training needs of rural development sector, we must be clear about some basic issues being raised in this chapter. Training is basically to inculcate will and skill for some specific jobs. The days of general training are over. Same way, technique tried and applied successfully, at a place may not be applicable for other places. In the fast developing sector every day changes are taking place. Knowledge is reaching even the remotest areas much faster than even one could imagine. In this age of nationalization, even the training needs have to cope up to specific requirements. Keeping in mind the job requirement area of operation, and the calibre of the person, training syllabus will have to be prepared. It is sometimes said that today training has also become a big racketeer industry. While giving emphasis on training more and more funds being made available, the emphasis on quality seems to be getting lost.

When it comes to training of functionaries working in the field of rural development, one has to know the socio, economic, political system in which the functionary is working. The functionary is required not only to adjust, stable but deliver results in the same system. Hence, when it comes to training needs for rural development sector, one must bear this in mind. For our purpose, we can take the counterpart of rural, i.e. urban. For functionaries in urban sector, their orientation, work systems, inspections, facilities, etc. would be very different. To make the comparison very simple, it would suffice to say for a person working in urban areas that life is much simpler, facilities are in abundance compared to rural life. The ignorance, casteism, difference in languages, conservatism prevails considerably in rural life. Despite various measures, the major chunk of resources have also been cornered by urban sector. It is stills common sight to see uncompleted and badly completed roads, buildings, schools, panchayat houses and rural houses. The problems of land ceiling, water management, shortage of electricity need no mention. No wonder even a resident of village given the job of village development wants to stay in city and sometimes goes to village for the job for which he has been employed. It is a tragedy. But when one goes into the reasons, one leads to sympathise. As the massive multi-dimensions of the problems with the rural side become clear, no wonder even the propagator total prosperity of rural areas wants to settle in cities. Migration to semi-cities has created many new problems. People, who could afford, have shifted to towns and notified areas and left their agricultural activities etc. to servants. They have taken some or the other jobs in these semi-cities and made agriculture unproductive.

If the massive plan outlays are being earmarked for rural development sector, it is essential to develop panel of managers and administrators who are prepared to devote their career to rural development sector. They would require not only proper planning and giving suitable working conditions but also incentives and proper motivation. In our present day system, people are more attracted by glamour and facilities. Rural development sector cannot think of providing those facilities for atleast few decades.

Somebody has said that if you cannot convince, confuse. Same way, when it comes to people working in the rural development sector, if we cannot provide them with minimum facilities which are otherwise available in urban and industrial sector, we must at least rationalize the need for good people to specialize in this sector. People with resources, intelligence and dynamism can manage to remain away from this sector. Does it mean that, in villages only the worst sufferers would stay and people and functionaries working in government departments would only be frustrated and discarded lot? I think the best way of getting good results in short time is to make the best of all the strength and reduce the areas of weakness. Hence, it is best to think of areas of strength and weaknesses of rural development sector.

Areas of Strength

(1) Being with nature.
(2) Away from crowd.
(3) Comparatively plain
(4) Less tensions.
(5) Tremendous scope for work and possibility of recognition.
(6) Neglected sector.
(7) Challenges possible.

Weaknesses of the Sector

(1) Lack of facilities in terms of electricity roads, water, sanitation, houses and entertainment.
(2) Difficult people, tradition bound, ignorant.

(3) Very difficult to show results.
(4) Decentralised areas.
(5) Full of politics.

As explained earlier, due to lack of facilities, even people interested in village life want to stay in city. This way, the vicious circle of poverty, ignorance, lack of education, migration of intelligentia, insecurity, poverty continues. To break the circle, the following strategy can be thought of:

(1) Massive dose of investment in the integrated programmes of villages;
(2) Direct programmes to attack poverty;
(3) Systematic efforts to induct good brain in the field of rural development;
(4) Constant monitoring, evaluation and follow up of the programmes;
(5) Reducing total dependence on agriculture and diversifying surplus man-power into ISB sector; encouraging youths to take up various promotional and developmental activities in rural areas; these activities must generate a monthly assured income of about 1,000 to 1,500 rupees.
(6) State should give preference in purchasing items produced in rural areas. This way, not only small industries will be encouraged to move to rural areas but basic facilities would also become available in rural areas.

When we talk of all these different strategies for rural development, we must bear in mind the role of change agent. All functionaries including teachers, Pradhans, functionaries like Tubewell Operators, Village Development Officers, Lekhpals, Medical ANM are acting as change agents. The major difference in their role being that some are paid exclusively to act as change agents while others have that role implied in their jobs.

We can broadly classify the following types of functionaries as rural development functionaries:

(i) Development Officers;
(ii) Panchayat Officers;
(iii) Teachers;
(iv) Medical Representatives;
(v) Ganna Kisan Sewaks;
(vi) Tubewell Operators;
(vii) Electricity Linemen;
(viii) Cooperative Banks and RRBs staff;
(ix) Revenue officers;

Their Training Needs

Basically, their training needs can be divided into two parts. One is the professional or technical training and the second is general or environmental training. This will also include man and time management, psychology, human as a resource, group behaviour, leadership qualities, change agent, history, society, State democracy — strength and weakness etc. In short, these are the training needs to make any person keen and willing to shoulder extra responsibilities and to develop skill to handle job successfully. This helps in exploiting his full potential. This brings out the hidden strength which every human being possesses in abundance. What is required is its realisation. This also means motivation to do job better and better. People working in field of difficult areas of rural development have to be more motivated. Where no worldly gains can be had, conviction and motivation would be more important. Even the style of functioning would become more relevant in the field of rural areas than cities. The demotivating factors are in abundance in rural areas. The glitter and light of city attract every one. Having attracted, it dehumanises. It tends to make him perfect mechanical toy. Hence the training requirements for working in rural areas have to consider these harsh realities and modify training contents to suit these requirements.

The second portion of training would have to equip him professionally. Here, the aim will be to extend him knowledge of the linkage both backward and forward, rules and regulations, documents and documentation. Knowledge without ability to convince is equally barren. We all know that in rural areas health, nutrition, adequate remuneration and above all avenues for promotion play, very important role. These factors also motivate a worker. The importance of awareness, perception and attitude needs no emphasis. Here, ability to get things done becomes most important. This ability can come either through force or compulsion which is not possible in a democratic society. Then, in the field of rural development, force just cannot be applied. Hence other alternative of motivation only remains. This can come only by self-conviction, hard work, development of skill and ability to communicate effectively. This also implies developing working equation in the present-day system. Ability to deliver goods even in the present system can be and should be developed. This implies analysing the strength and weaknesses of the system and suitably modifying work culture.

From the above analysis, it will be clear that the training syllabus for functionaries working in the rural areas has to be very carefully designed. But designing a plan of action is not the end in itself. The trainer has to be self-motivated and a man of conviction. His experience, proven track record, capacity to learn and to assimilate knowledge along with effective communication method can only meet the need of meaningful training in rural development sector.

PART - III

SOME POLICY ISSUES

29

Environment, Development and Law

Before we proceed, let us have some conceptual clarity of the three words to be used as mentioned above.

Environment

It is a surrounding, external conditions influencing the growth of people, animals or plants or component affecting the development of living or working condition. Environment also, according to Indian thinking, consists of earth, light, nature, air and space which is the basis for sustenance.

Development

It is an act or process of developing and thus gradually unfolding of growth or evolution, elaboration of theme or that part of a movement in which new situations emerge. Development is also to help to move forward. We may also put it as reaching to full blooming capacity of individual or society which will in turn make backward and forward linked coordinated process of growing possible. Needless to say that development has to be of the whole body politic and cannot be of any limited portion or organ. Hence, it must be sustainable, self-supporting, environmentally friendly and unexploitative in the longer run. That means those neglected should also have full opportunity to prove their worth.

"The recent UNCTAD Report states forthrightly, "Development means industrialisation and industrialisation entails the systematic application of controlled mechanical energy to an ever widening range of productive activities. Although other sources of power undoubtedly have a role to play, a large proportion of this energy must come in the foreseeable future from fossil fuels."

The use of fossil fuels means accelerating global warming and although opinions may vary in details about the danger of this, there is no doubt that if temperatures rise sufficiently to melt the Tundra permafrost and release its methane (methane is 20-30 times as powerful as carbon-dioxide as a greenhouse gas) the results could be catastrophic, so catastrophic that it is imperative that action is taken now to check global warming. To act effectively will require the end of further industrialisation as we know it. The end of promoting economic growth, the end of production for profit distinct from meeting need, the end of the accepted values of the mammon-worshipping consumer culture being spread rapidly "world wide".

(Extract from Science for Villages January 1993 issue)

Law

A rule of action established by authority, a statute, the rules of a community or state, jurisprudence, established usage, that which is lawful, the whole body of persons connected professionally with the law, litigation, a rule or code in any department of action as morality, art, honour, arms (including heraldry), a game, a theoretical principal educed from practice or observation, a statement or formula expressing the constant order of certain phenomena.

Obviously law cannot be something static indifferent, insensitive or standard and uniform for diversities.

Environment has also another concept where earth, water, light/radiation, air and space are taken as '*panchbhoot*' and worshipped. There are the basic concepts of environment. These five elements constitute the entire vision of cosmos.

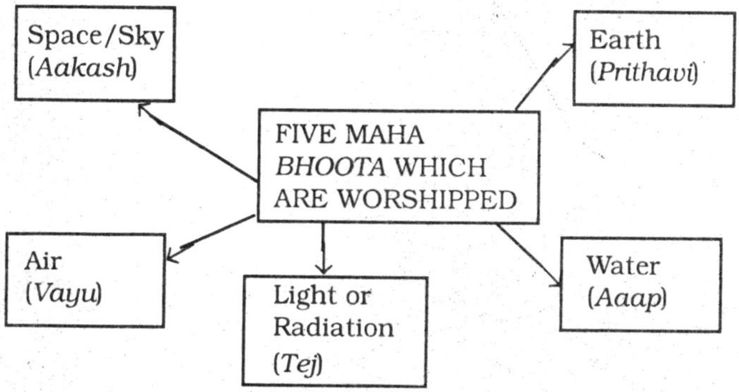

Attitude Development

There is no gain saying that no amount of law can help in preserving environment and ensuring sustainable development. Hence what is required is attitudinal development which comes through education both of formal and informal, inbuilt system, development of checks and balances, social controls and convictions, Here law becomes a tool. To give illustration, the following examples might help:

> We are told that trees should not be cut because ghost reside in them and if we cut the trees the ghost will not spare us. This is to create a pyschological inbuilt fear so that the tree is protected. Viewed against this background the importance of *pepul*, *neem* and various other

socially useful trees has to be understood.

Another example can be given where in the river and ponds urination was prohibited. This was an example of inbuilt automatic conviction that overtakes the people. The idea was that the land should be able to get manure both of human excreta and urine.

Need to Curb Urbanisation

Many thinkers have started feeling that the civilisation of urbanisation has played a real havoc. Not only the compulsion of day to day living and working but the very places of living make it imperative that environmental development and law enforcement are bound to suffer. Hence it is worth considering how the civilisation or urbanisation can be replaced by civilisation of sustainable development.

Role of Five Powers

The woman power, policy power, technology power, economics power and power of faith and spirituality have to be understood in the right perspective since they were always in isolation but powerful. But it is for the first time in the history of humanity and civilisation their togetherness would help exploit the full potential for the sustainable development.

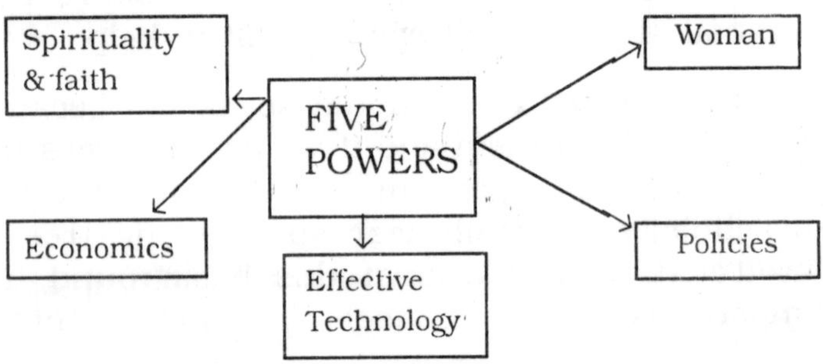

Are these Different or the Same?

In an isolated fashion if one looks at environment development and law, they may seem to be totally opposed to each other. This is ascribed precisely to the way we have been taught and nurtured to look at things in fragmentation. But if you look it in totality, we find an inseparableness. The salient characteristics of environmental development and law enjoin upon us the basic necessity of broadening visions and shifting man from animal to enlightened stage of development. This is possible with food security, informal education through family and broadening of vision through spiritual contents.

Areas of inter-linkage

Areas	*Environment*	*Development*	*Law*
Natural resources	Must be sustainably used	Cannot be over exploited	Must take holistic vision
Human nature	Exploitative	Monopolistic	Needs checks and balances
Economics	Distorted definitions	Need for holistic definitions	Broad vision needed.
Sensitivity	Neglected	Materialistically harmful	Basic necessity to guide
Methods of production	Can be exploitative	Must be with equality and justice	Must be appropriate
Products	Must be environment friendly	Must not be exploitative	Must ensure judicial distribution.
Lessons of history	Slow and steady exploitation	Changing concepts	Basic lessons remain the same.
Attitude formation	Depends on Training	May vary	Must be self-supporting
Role of Police	Exploitative	*Status quo*	Regularity

There may be more such points. But it needs to be understood clearly that in the long run the environment, development and law should be taken together and treated as an inseparable part for sustainable development.

Plan of Action for Ensuring Inter-dependence of Environment, Development and Law.

Before we proceed to analyse line of action, it is essential to accept certain limitation they are:

(1) Principles rather than people should be the basis of action plan.
(2) Output as opposed to inputs should be the parameters of judging of the performance.
(3) Truth, non-violence, tolerance, equity, openness and philosophy have to be the centre of any plan of action without compromise.
(4) Lessons of history should be the guiding principle.
(5) Action, Research and Codification (ARC) should be inbuilt in any plan of action.
(6) Multi-disciplinary approach is a must.
(7) Upgradation from animal stage to discretionary stage and further to enlightened stage should be the guide.
(8) Materialistic growth can never lead to the stage of happiness which is the ultimate aim. Hence parochial vision, perverted value system and multiplicity of organisation working in isolation can never solve the problem.
(9) Need to encourage talent, objectivity and hard work.

Based on the above selected principles, it should be possible to think of a plan of action.

1. Identify success models which fit into justify their replication. This is basically to ensure that scarce resources are not squandered again in locating

replicable models.

2. Identify marketable models and try to market them for internal resource generation.
3. Programmes and policies which have helped the society in developing and sustaining itself through local laws and customs should be publicised and honoured.
4. Multi-disciplinary team should go with their specialised knowledge to attend areas of chaos and confusion.
5. Role of non-producing group of exploitative class must be analysed and it should be employed to production related activities.
6. The role of education and its efficacy with reference to communication and conviction ought to be made public.
7. Laws which have worked to the detriment of sustainable development and those which have outlived their utility must be annulled.
8. Hipocracy, greed, utter selfishness both of individuals or society or professionals should be exposed.
9. Role of professionals and importance of professionalism from all walks of life must be constantly analysed preferably by the concerned professional bodies.
10. The prevalent value system of 'might is right', failure of accountability, falling work-culture and despondency ought to be substituted by Hope generation models discernible in various fields of life.
11. There is no short-cut and the five powers of woman, technology, economics, policies and spiritual development may be accepted for sustainable Hope for the future.

Areas of concern for all

1. Greed of powerful.
2. Insensitivity of power.
3. Changing consumer preferences.
4. Local institutional problems.
5. Glamourisation of state services.
6. Regular linkage, monitoring and developing.
7. Cost effectiveness of system.

Areas requiring changes

1. Change in laws on selective basis.
2. Change in funding pattern to encourage self help.
3. Change in attitudes — of organisation and funders.
4. Change in policies at all levels.
5. Change in priorities of projects/programmes.
6. Change in monitoring system to encourage results.
7. Change in totality with historical lessons and mind set.

Essential Components in a successful model

1. Validity in terms of some parameters.
2. Replicability in terms of diversity.
3. Sustainability in terms of time and cost.
4. Rural base as opposed to urban base.
5. Value addition — cost of machines versus man.
6. Linkages both backward and forward.
7. Involvement of neglected but powerful in terms of population, gender, education and skills.
8. Internal resource generation with special reference to market approach.
9. Overall glamourisation for all.
10. Sensitivity and possibility of involving youth.

11. Capacity to compete with multi-nationals and environmental upgradation both in short and long run.

Special areas for attention

- Complementary relationship with centralised industry.
- Internal distribution of government support.
- Dispensability of government support.
- Role of political organisation of the masses.
- Role in containment of bureaucratic tyranny.
- Assistance in evolution of holistic development through effective laws.

In short environment development and law has to take a holistic look at all levels. Not only with reference to marketing up, the above views may be useful but an action take off, may be necessary at the earliest.

30

Constructive Programme of the Father of the Nation

By construction we ordinarily understand engineering work. But Father of the Nation used this term for rebuilding. India according to his vision is non-violent, non-exploitative social order. The constructive work is a unique concept. The constructive work is a positive contribution in our time to win both socialist and capitalist models of development which are under dispute. However, we should not forget that the principle of constructive programme invariably follows decentralisation, building from below, moral and self-reliance and willing cooperation. The edifice of constructive programme of man is to stand on five pillars. They feel to have invariably for the decentralisation as a basis. Decentralisation needs availability of trained, willing, competent managers, appropriate trainer or supervisor, servicing facilities at the affordable cost and binding factors like income to the service provided. The Sarvodaya Social order indirectly had developments based on these principles. But can it be selfless[1]. In this connection, recently I had an opportunity of reading the articles of Gandhiji published in *Young India* in 1924. The Father of the Nation wrote "I am a humble seeker after truth. I am impatient to realise myself, to attain *moksha* in the very existence. My national service is part of my training for freeing my soul from the bondage of flesh.

Thus considered, my service may be regarded as purely selfish. For me the road to salvation lies through incessant toil in the service of my country and through that of the humanity. I want to identify myself with every thing that lives. So my patriotism is for me a state in my journey to the Land of Eternal Freedom and Peace". Thus we see that the framework of the Constructive Programme is Truth and Non-violence supported by determination and dedication, *vairagya* and *tyaga*. Truth is the end. Non-violence is the means. The path to the goal on either side is guarded by virtue of *vairagya* (determination) and *tyaga* (dedication). Functioning within this well structured framework constructive work is bound to yield the desired result.

I am too small to understand the holistic meaning of this sense. But when I tried to look at the constructive programmes they are rigid codification, implementation in the stage at which we are today. It is interesting to venture, looking at these problems holistically. The Father of the Nation in 1941 listed 13 items under the constructive programmes.

1. Communal Unity
2. Removal of Untouchability
3. Prohibition
4. Khadi
5. Other Village Industries
6. Village Sanitation
7. New or Basic Education
8. Adult Education
9. Uplift of Women
10. Education of Health and Hygiene
11. Provincial Languages
12. Propagation of Rashtra Bhasha (National Language)
13. Promotion of Economic Equality

Revising this list thoroughly in 1945, he added the following five items.

1. Kisans
2. Labourers
3. Adivasis
4. Lepers
5. Students

As a matter of fact after the passing away of Gandhiji, additional items such as (1) Cow Protection, (2) Nature Cure, (3) Bhoodan, (4) Gramdan, (5) Shanti Sena were added by his followers to strengthen the movement and march towards the realisation of Sarvodaya's Social Order. But at least a few will not accept "Cow Protection" as a separate item. Bhoodan and Gramdan may be as a single item and other items such as Shramdan and Sampathidan also may be added to this, "Nature Cure" is yet to become a movement. Some would like to include peace and Disarmament movement as a separate item.

It is very interesting, and enlightening and self-satisfying to go through the various aspects of goal of constructive work and how and why today the youths do not believe constructively in this concept.

In a nutshell we may sum up that the Constructive Programme comprises self reliance, self help voluntariness sharing of what one has, with others, cooperation, mutual aid, sacrifice, fellow feelings and giving due respect to other's feelings. Let us all march towards this goal unilaterally with a proper understanding and firm conviction.

Need for Centre for inducing Enterprise to Rural Areas

Panchayat Raj Institution to be successful in the longer run have to learn from past. This is not a new concept for country like India. There is enough evidence in the history to show how the village communes were run. They had their own culture, rules and regulations, practices, habits and obey of life. Various groups in the village were supposed to be performing inter-locutory activities. They had their own systems to resolve conflicts and ensure harmonious fraternity sustainability of life and the society.

Father of the Nation Mahatma Gandhi elaborately thought and wrote on constructive programmes and developed various live areas of constructive programme. These can be enunciated in the following way:

Life Areas of Constructive Programme

Religious 1, 2	Spiritual 19
Health 4, 8, 20, 17	Cultural 3
Economical 11, 12, 13	Educational 5, 6, 9, 10, 18
Political 21, 22, 23	Social 7, 4, 15, 16

Constructive Programme Items

1. Communal Unity
2. Removal of Untouchability
3. Prohibition
4. Village Sanitation
5. Basic Education
6. Adult Education
7. Uplift of Women
8. Health and Hygiene

9. Provincial Language
10. National Language
11. Khadi
12. Village Industries
13. Economic Equality
14. Kisans
15. Labourers
16. Adivasis
17. Lepers
18. Students
19. Cow protection
20. Nature Cure
21. Bhoodan
22. Gramdan
23. Shanti Sena

The constructive programme had their frame-work principles, concepts and also the organisational structure to ensure sustainability of life and society. It also ensured the changed required as per time and the duty and the rights are self unification became the essential part of this constructive programme. Over a period of time, this constructive programme became the part and parcel of the national life.

Today, the Eleventh schedule of the Constitution Seventy Third Amendments Act 1972 on Panchayat Raj mentioned about 29 additional items. All these 29 additional items have to be understood with reference to the economic development which is inseparable from employment generation.

These items have to be looked after, managed and funded by Panchayat Raj Institution. But can we adopt "Enterprise" concept, so that full justice is done? Can there be different way of looking at many of these activities, so that due to paucity of funds these are not neglected by society or they get relegated to background. All these activities have capacity to generate self employment. The following may indicate some of the areas to be considered:

1. Can be there on cost effective basis?
2. Can there be Bank finance?
3. Can there be backward forward linkages?
4. Can there be value addition?
5. Can there be appropriate technology provision with ready availability of spares and services?
6. Can there be sharing of cost?
7. Can there be regular openness and interaction?

Some of these issues have to be understood with reference to the policy issues for Sustainable Employment Generation.

In an unorganized society, the importance of pressure lobby need no over emphasis. The Centre floor inducing enterprise to rural areas would precisely attend to these aspects as mentioned in rural industrialization, a plan for the future by the author there is a need to look into the following aspects:

1. The advantages of inducing enterprise concept in rural areas.
2. Linkages with self employment and internal resource generation.
3. Linkages with communication, information, sharing and effective technology development and dissemination.
4. Value addition and skill upgradation.

The enterprise development concept in rural areas need not only change but also massive coordination and understanding of the transitional problems when agriculturist or an artist is to be converted to an entrepreneurs. The following are some of the points which need attention:

Agriculture to Industry Basic Needs

1. Public policies, Planning and Tax systems.
2. Regular information flow
3. Infrastructure Roads, Godowns, Communication, Transport, Security Electricity/Generators.
4. Raw material stocking
5. Entrepreneurship Development and training facilities.
6. Base value addition, Processes or Industrial climate and appropriate technologies.
7. Packaging and further value addition
8. Finished or semi-finished stocking and marketing facilities.
9. Banking system.

The above points have to be considered in totality and Panchayat Raj Institution have to take additional responsibilities. They can also provide the following facilities:

1. Land, Water, Training facilities to the enterprise.
2. Take up the policy issues with the Government and Zila Parishad.
3. Ensuring backward forward linkages.
4. Develop suitable local enterprises through self supporting institution.
5. Take up promotional developmental and regulatory mechanism for sustaining and developing enterprises.

The Panchayat Raj institution have to play very important role and with the growing emphasis on decentralise area planning approach it is possible and pertinent to accept that the areas of strategic competitive advantage is fully in favour of Panchayati Raj Institution. What is needed, is clarity, commitment, willingness to learn from other experiences and develop implementable plan of action with local initiatives to face the challenges of competition with compatible competitive addition, these they enjoy. The solution lines in local area plans with better linkages and marketing approaches. All activities have to become self supporting and self sustaining. Hence any amount of time spent on better plan formulation should be welcome. In this exercise the following guidelines may be of some help.

Success Yardsticks for Programmes

The success parameters of programmes are those by which we judge whether a particular programme or project has been successful or not. The success has to be with preference to certain issues to be studied with wider aspects of society, individual and the state. Those which are successful for individuals, may not be successful for the society or the state. Somebody's short-term gain may be other's long term loss. Success parameters invariably need planning, coordination, implementation, evaluation and on the whole a holistic area related replicable model. In this again, we may be reminded of the story where five blind people are trying to decipher that this can be an elephant by mere touch. Naturally unless all share their experiences and draw a holistic conclusion, any analysis of one's experience in isolation would remain far away from the truth. In some way, we may all have our own experiences and firm convictions based on our awareness. This does not mean that is the only truth. Ultimately howsoever the experiences of a person or institution be, unless it is prepared to examine its/their experiences with all others, the truth may be far away. But there is a catch. If all blind people touch only leg or only tail, then again their experiences sharing will be as parochial and away from truth as people from some background and condition may be undergoing experience-sharing.

Therefore for the purpose of being widely accepted, fully sustainable and broadly practicable, the following may be considered.

1. Replicability

Any success must be replicable which means widely acceptable, implementable and understandable. Any success which remains confined to four walls cannot spread for wider acceptance.

2. Self-supporting

Any successful programme has to be self-supporting. Standing one somebody's shoulder either economically, physically or socially, cannot be a success syndrome. Success must support itself which is to be universally acceptable.

3. Internal Resource Generation

This means that there has to be, from within the enterprise or organisation or institution or activity certain amount of funding from within. This ensures marketing of the expertise. This aspect keeps the organisations fully geared to the fuller satisfaction of the consumers by charging them for the services or facility rendered. The attitudinal developments which come with I.R.G. (Internal resources generation) change the whole structure approach. Hence success has to be judged with reference to I.R.G.

4. Cost Effectiveness

Any programme which cannot be cost effective cannot

survive the test of success. It is bound to be unsustainable. Cost can be varied. Total package of costing has to be done to ensure cost effectiveness in the longer run.

5. Inbuilt Marketing System

There has to be an inbuilt marketing system of programmes in the project to see that the programmes are successful.

6. Hope Generation

Without going into definition part of "Hope Generation", we would like to say a success parameter has to have hope generating capacity in the programme. People must see, admire and talk about the programme and for its good aspects. It should not lead to despondency or loss of faith either in the approach itself or in the institutions who have supported the so-called success. When we analyse, Gandhi, Vinoba, Kumarappa or Ralegaonsidhi model of development, we find some of them are even fit in the test of "Hope Generation". What are these factors?

7. Bankability

Banking institution has come to stay and even for small project, funds have to be obtained. It is a pity that even when private funding can be arranged, the systems of financial incentives or success parameters do not accept it as a legal method of funding. However, there is a hope sign that even what problem of bank finance becomes a clear policy issue, private funding should be permitted and encouraged as much as possible.

8. Test of Special Components

Any programme if it is not socially acceptable in the longer run will meet resistance. Trusty shape concept might have failed but social components of the programme do assume very important roles. Social marketing of difficulty programmes, social accountability, social marketing, social advertising all become important. Hence while judging the success parameters, those also become relevant and important.

9. Constructive programmes have to be maintained for success of any replicable parameters

In the end, it is safe to conclude that unless success parameters are widely disseminated, from very beginning and level plain field is provided to all competing enterprises, "long term success or so called success" would only be a short-lived publicity stunt.

SWOT Analysis of Gandhian Thoughts

As we know very well, Strengths, Weaknesses Opportunities and Threat (SWOT) Analysis is time specific. It is also of indepth, fruitful, perspective, analysis of the integrated nature. It is based on indepth study of past, present and future. It presents total picture. There are no prejudices or double talk or of irrelevancy in useful exercise.

Strengths

(1) Gandhi is not a person, a vision, a philosophy, but a practical doer, a frank, free, fearless, God-fearing, idealist and also marketing expert, a follower of golden middle path but he was also, at times,

ruthless, after convictions in implementation and usually, he started with himself, a solution.

(2) There is power, truth, simplicity, humility, democratic approach with integrative principles of sustainable and contented development.

(3) The very fact that sometimes he is remembered by all is itself is a strength. Mahatma Gandhi is still remembered all over the world, alongwith Eienstein, Roosevelt, Churchill, Lenin etc.

(4) His warnings have come true. Today, organised textile industry is in shambles and it was his vision that the so-called urbanised industrialisation development scenario is bound to be economically uncompetitive and hence decentralised cottage and home based, dispersed, humanised, processing and manufacturing process would rule.

Weaknesses

(1) Difficult to follow his philosophy by commoners both in habits, perceptions, behaviour and vision. Hence, it is not hope-generating in places where he worked ceaselessly that is, even in Gujarat and Wardha.

(2) Marketed by wrong followers for their selfish vested interest. Hence very few living successes are seen and heard. Those who swears by name of Gandhi, do not practice the high ethical standards in accordance with Gandhiji's teachings.

(3) Lack of transparency in the institutions, organisations which directly claim their descendancy from the Father of the Nation.

Opportunities

(1) Time has come to understand his ideas anew, because his various prophecies are coming true.

(2) As materialism grows one has to look for happiness through time tested formulation.

(3) The hypocracies or duplicacies cannot sustain for long. Hence, eternal truth, convictions would ultimately surface up. It is only a matter of time.

(4) Richard Attenborough, maker of Gandhi film cashed the opportunity and reminded the people about the noble soul. But as somebody has said "First we misunderstood him and murdered him and when we understood him we idealised him".

(5) Frustrated youth and old have accepted him.

(6) Time is right for back to basics or back to nature and the real solution lies in the properly developing packages to implement his philosophy and vision.

(7) World moving from West to East is also a pointer.

(8) Economic compulsion and need to link up with spiritual dimensions on true non-violence.

(9) Opening up of new opportunities not through government or salaried classes, but through competition, economic failures, need for decentralised democratic planning and implementation process and overall disenchantment with the policies perceived all over the world.

Threats

(1) The hold of those with fraudulent intentions may continue over organisations and places of experimentation, capitalisation of these principles may be delayed.

(2) The co-ordination of truthful, non-violent, well-meaning, God fearing becomes difficult. The fearless, violent, untruthful and untransparent may sway the show.

(3) The indifference of professionals goes beyond their limit.

(4) There is a need to induct new rational, scientific analysis, otherwise the water flow to fresh concepts may remain stagnant and become dreary and polluted.

(5) The constructive programmes have come in for wider capacities through new names and the policies are nearer to the people.

1. Defining Success

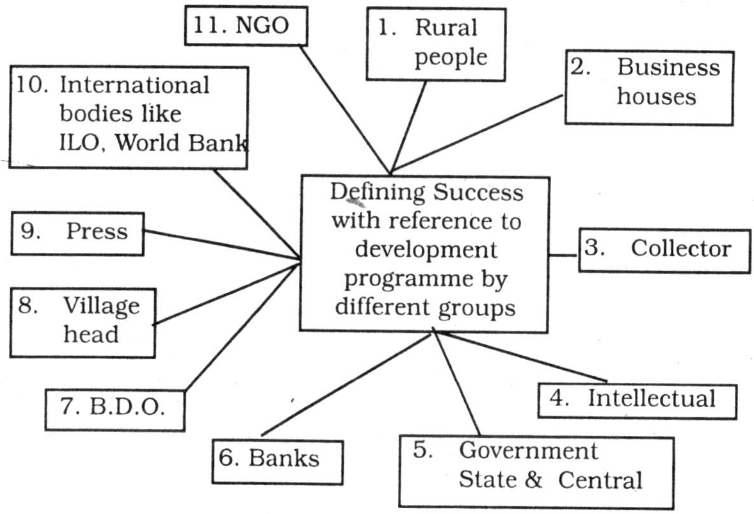

2. Basic Issues

(1) Whose Plan is it?
(2) For whom it is being managed by whom?
(3) Who are the evaluaters?
(4) Is it individual development or rural development?
(5) What are the common agreement points? Or common complaint points like corruption, delay,

marketing problem, less stipends, wrong selection, lack of involvement etc.

(6) Role of 'marketing as concept'.

(7) Need for convergence points and effective communication, students and need for precautions while defining success multidimensionally.

(8) What are the conflicting interests? Like business, philosophy versus mission or idealism philosophy-Mission or Commission. Are they contradictory?

(9) Enlightened self-interest through material harmonised interest—need for G.O. and NGO co-ordination—binding powers or convergence points in people philosophy, purpose, projects, profit or workable practices.

(10) *Fate accompli* aspect like zones and realistic plan of action excepting certainties of change top down-bottom up economic indicaters to development—demonstration impact—openness transparency and harmonising conflicting interests—back to basic and role of values for long term serviceable versus short term commercial concerns. Hence role of students and need for basic value orientation.

Conclusion

Defining success with reference to rural development is holistic concept and certain common parameters need identification for a hopeful widely acceptable economic generation.

Implication of Market Approach

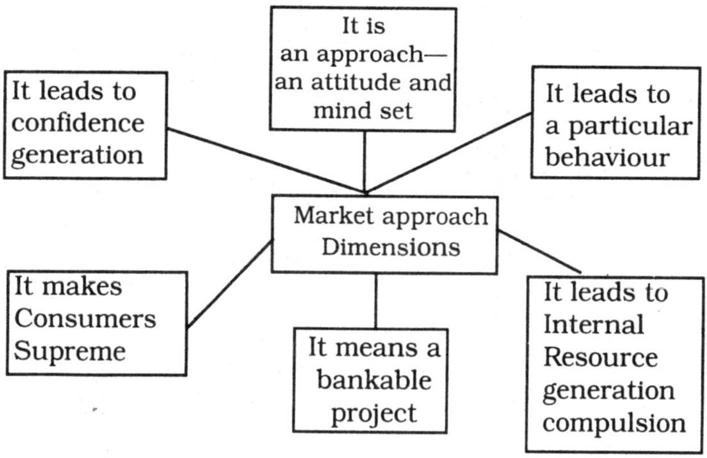

SWOT of Handicapped

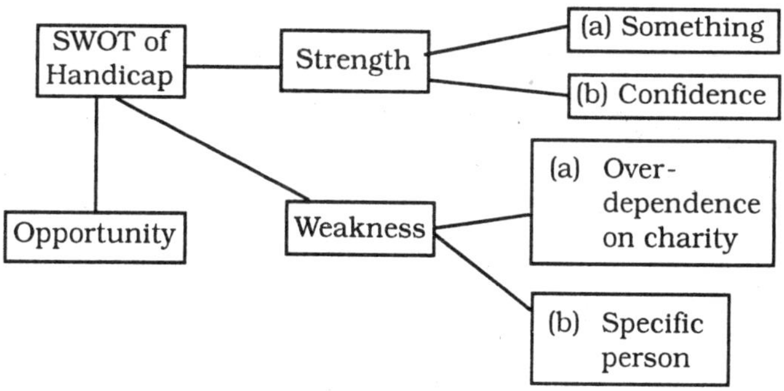

This needs proper understanding because each individual handicap would have different Strength, Weaknesses, Opportunities and Threat. While analysing plan of action for his usefulness we have to consider this aspect in detail.

3. Essentials for Self-employment of Handicaps

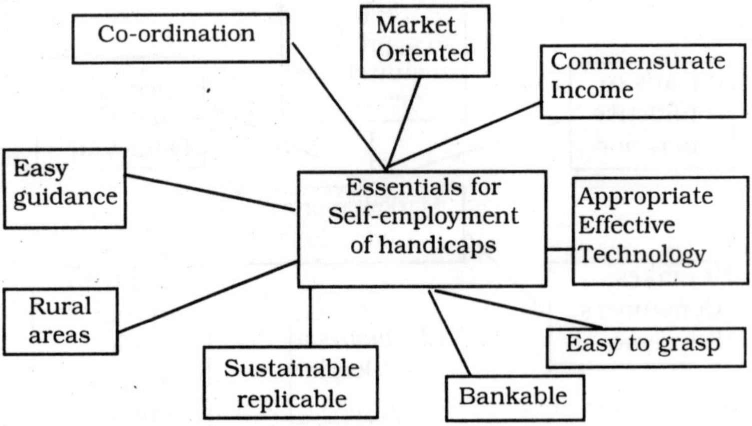

4. Types of Programme which can be undertaken

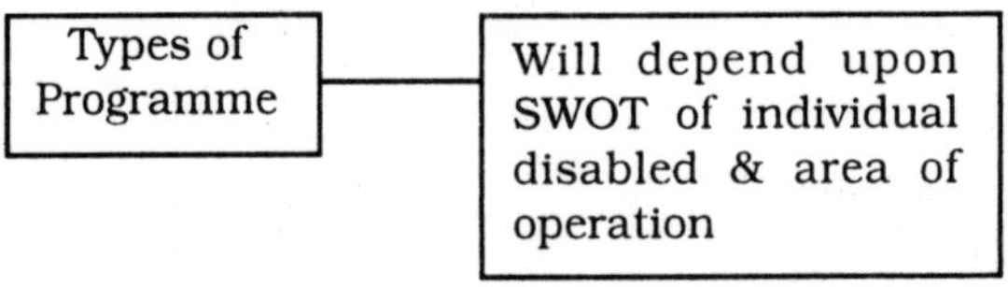

31

Gist of the Discussions on Eighth Five Year Plan

The strategies mentioned under Chapter-III on page 21 in the report of the Working Group on Khadi and Village Industries for Eighth Plan were discussed by C.E.O., Jt. C.E.O. etc. in the presence of Chairman and the gist of the discussion is as follows:

Strategies as mentioned in the report for Eighth Plan	Action Plan discussed
1	2
1. Systematic identification of rural artisans from non-farm sector who are potential to KVI fold	(i) For systematic identification of rural artisans from non-farm sector, we have to take help of DRDA, VLW and institutions. (ii) The Khadi institutions may be motivated to undertake the work of identifications, if necessary some incentives may be provided to them for doing this work.
2. Selective approach in the expansion programmes assigning priority to industrially backward areas, high unemployment index areas	(i) For expanding the progress in backward areas etc. we have to again take the help of institutions which are ready to

1	2
and growth centres identified by the Government.	take the responsibility of implementation of the programme. (ii) Need for identification of the organisations/Federations which are of traditional nature and which constitute a particular community or caste from times inmemorial. (1) i.e. collection of medicinal plants and herbs - this can be successfully undertaken with less cost and with best expertise by "Vaidyas" who are the best expertise in the line and have knowledge. (2) Processing them into medicines with the knowledge they inherited from their fathers and forefathers. (3) Identification of "Kagazis" who are doing the Handmade paper work for centuries and form their Federation or Association. (iii) The Commission may do the co-ordination work and hand over the rest to these types of organisations/Federations. Since they are directly affected, if work is not

1	2
	done, they will take utmost care to see that things are immediately attended to in their own interest. (iv) The Commission may procure orders for marketing. The Federation/ Organisations will produce the required quality and specification and utilise the demand so procured. (v) By direct involvement of institutions/Federations/Organisations in implementations of programme there will be better impact as these programmes cannot be done by KVIC's officers because they are not directly affected if the things are not implemented.
3. Promote and strengthen the infrastructural facilities for training of artisans, procurement and storage and processing of raw material, manufacture and supply of improved tools and equipment and marketing arrangements through the Marketing Development Corporation.	(i) For securing Bank Finance loan for training of artisans we can take the resources from the Banks. **Construction of Godowns** (i) The Commission may avail the facility of 50 per cent finance available from Rural Development Departments for construction of godowns in

1	2
	rural areas, which will solve the problems of procurement and storage and processing of raw materials. **Storing of Raw Materials** (ii) The Commission may also avail the facility of hiring the godowns from Warehousing Corporations on rent for storing raw materials for rural industries. (iii) For storing of oil-seeds and also finished products like oil we may take help of Warehousing Department. **Laboratory Testing** (i) Commission may strictly follow Agmarking etc. wherever feasible for KVI finished products. (ii) KVIC's Laboratories may be equipped fully to attend to this type of work. They should be so equipped that the laboratories meant for oil and soap may also attend to the work pertaining to Handmade Paper. The Commission should also make optimum utility of the existing facilities available with it.

1	2
	Supply of improved Tools and Equipments The Commission may entrust this work of supply of improved tools and equipments to some Federations. **Marketing** (i) The Commission may have its own Federation for marketing of finished products which may be called as Joint Marketing Federation/Corporation and the Chairman, KVIC may be the Chairman of such Corporation. (ii) If necessary Statewise Joint Marketing Corporations can be set up. (iii) The work of implementation of KVI programmes may be entrusted to these Joint Marketing Federation and different Federations for Village Industries products. This programme cannot be taken directly by KVIC. **Tapping of Potentiality** (i) Looking to the vast potentiality there is immediate need to take up the Fruit Preservation Industry in a big way.

1	2
	(ii) Commission may try to cover as many fruits as possible in the rural areas for processing them as it is commonly observed that huge quantity of fruits and vegitables are spoils during their seasons in rural areas due to lack of cold storage facilities and also processing facilities. (iii) By setting up of number of fruit preservation centres in rural areas will not only solve the problem of unemployment but it will also give an additional income to the producer by way of marketing of products in cities and thereby flowing money back from cities.
4. Setting up of a strong infrastructure for research and development in appropriate technology, undertaking research and development in production and processing technology, product development, diversification of raw materials and processes, designing, improvements in packaging etc., with a view to reducing the drudgery of work without reducing employment and quality control	**Research and Development** (i) Units like Carpentry and Blacksmithy may take up the work of Research and Development also. (ii) Instrumentation units may also form their own Federations and the Federations may take up Research and Development work. (iii) Federations may do the work of transfer of technology to KVIC's training centres. By this way

1	2
and improving the quality of product and also increasing the productivity and earnings of artisans and to make arrangements for transfer of the improved techniques to the beneficiaries.	they will be marketing Research and Development to our units. (iv) Some schemes have to be evolved by means of which the best potters or the work of the best research work done will be given some "AWARD". (v) Potters Research Federation may not only be involved in Research and Development but also in transfer of technology to training centres thereby improving the products. (vi) There will also be some incentives in the form of rewards for doing the research work for reducing drudgery. Even the universities may also be asked to participate in this Scheme. **Dyeing** (i) The Commission may encourage natural colours and not artificial colours. In other words, vegetable colours are preferred compared to chemical based colours.

1	2
5. Revamping the patterns of assistance for various industries and programmes introducing adequate flexibility to accommodate regional variations in costs.	**Patterns Advisory Committee** (i) The Patterns Advisory Committee is already taking care of the need of flexibility to accommodate regional variations in costs. (ii) Further, the Patterns Advisory Committee may consider 10 to 15 per cent flexibility in the patterns.
6. Organising production centres in areas where local entrepreneurship is not forthcoming, with the idea of transferring the centres to artisans in due course.	**Organising Production Centres** The idea is well, this may be achieved with the help of Federations/Local Bodies with the marketing schemes and LCPC.
7. Giving priority to deprived sections of the society, especially SC/ST.	**Priority to deprived Sections** Under this item the following may be added. (i) Minority Community (ii) Disabled (iii) Weaker Sections etc.
8. While selecting new industries, emphasis will be laid on high income generating activities and higher coverage of women in such activities in order to increase the income and earning capacity of women.	**Identification of Women** While selecting new industries, women may be identified and necessary steps may be taken to increase their income and earnings.

1	2
9. All women institutions/ co-operatives (run by 100 per cent women) should be provided with some incentives such as higher dose of management subsidy etc. in order to promote the growth of more and more all-women organisations.	**All Women Institutions/Co-operatives** (i) In order to encourage women to form women (cent percent women) co-operatives/organisations some special assistance like salaries to women secretaries on honorarium basis for a period of 3 to 4 years may be provided. (ii) The advantages by organising cent percent women organisation are: (1) Women takes things more seriously than men. (2) Women cooperatives are bound to be more successful. (3) Cost of products may also be fairly low. (4) There is no likelihood of increasing losses.
10. Achieving greater co-ordination with similar other agencies engaged in rural development as well as with the organised large, medium and small sectors wherever necessary.	: This suggestion is accepted.

Tactical Strategies

1. While agreeing fully that pressure groups must be developed for bringing problems to the authorities and also to ensure that programmes move systematically and policies and procedures remain conducive to the objective possible. For this it is proposed to take the following steps.

- (i) Institutions having various strengths will be identified regionwise, industrywise, districtwise and they will be organised to look after their members' interest and also to extend various programmes to the eligible target groups.
- (ii) While agreeing that in the democratic systems pressure groups can have impact over longer duration, efforts will be made to allow these pressure groups to be merged in the systems. For this in the various committees and study groups the representatives of these pressure groups will be associated and given due representation.
- (iii) Various activities like studies, project development service and seminars would be organised through these pressure groups.
- (iv) Keeping in mind the strength of our traditional Indian society, it is proposed to analyse the strengths of various heirarchical structures and also castes and communities depending upon their suitability for various industries both traditional and new. Their cooperation will be solicited specially in the field of identification of beneficiaries, organising them into some structures and most important of all, marketing, training and production.

(v) While talking of pressure groups it is proposed to organise the lovers of KVIs who have not only sacrificed their youth, energies for achieving the freedom of this country, but even today continue to love nature, ecology, pollution free industries, villager's life, simplicity and hold unabiding and unflinching faith in our roots. The number of these people is increasing. From educated to urbanites to villagers, they have to be organised and suitably motivated to form a group which may be termed broadly as LOKVI.

(vi) These also include intelligentia, opinion makers, writers, poets, artists etc. to form pressure groups for the sector.

While talking about pressure groups and tactical need to organise them we must bear in mind that howsoever good and ideal policies and programmes and pioneers may be, unless the systems are attuned and are kept to translate in reality, no purpose will be served. Our experience of almost four decades proves beyond doubt where we have gone wrong. Hence at every stage it must be regularly realised how the best of wishes expressed in the Planning Commission document, Industrial policies and other policy statements of government states and VIPs are translated into action. Even the role of people's representatives in and out of the government has to be properly appreciated specially with regard to decentralised, dispersed heterogeneous and at times conflicting industries. Here again a systematic effort has to be made to expose these important segments of the society to the importance of this sector by showing them demonstration and models, examining the validity and relevance of this sector in relation to various problems being faced by the society and keeping in mind the scarcity of funds, the available resources must be optimally utilised.

Tactics Part

We fully agree with the recommendation about the need for proper management information system and build up a suitable data base. For this purpose the available computer facilities and testing data retrieval systems must be developed. We are all aware of the decentralised dispersed unorganised nature of our target group and more the decentralised sector the more is the need to intensively and timely monitor and give feedback to it. We need not recapitulate here how the organised delivery systems done to expedite development of unorganised target group has fared so far. Once the basic flow of the system is cleared the management information system must be insisted upon by the topmost person in the organisation. The tendency to leave monitoring work to lowest functionaries is often seen. Computers are hardly used and if at all used, they are for preparation of salary bills. While accepting that on first of every month salary will invariably be disbursed to the organised of the lot it is surprising why computer should be utilised to duplicate effort. It is nothing, but misplaced priority and shows the dire need for attitudinal, change for realising right priorities. If we accept the realities of the system then Science i.e. computer must be utilised through right aptitude of the top people of the organisation. This also means putting the monitoring system as an integral part of the system which is otherwise not always conducive to unpleasant feedbacks. The quality of implementation and provision of linkages both backward and forward can be ensured only when the feedback system is developed. This also means clear responsibilities and persistent emphasis on performance of duties. The feedback while going down must inform all those involved in improvement of performance. While reducing the paper work the downward movement of performance report enjoining upon all touring officers to sit down with the concerned institutions and ensure improvement. Instead of sending letters of these efforts to all points and showing its best to wait for computer report of the next month where improvement, if any, will be automatically reflected in terms of performance.

There is also need to open up our system. While monitoring within the organisation is important other groups are also have access to the information, this would also mean publication of list of beneficiaries, regular interaction with villagers, scientists, academicians and policy planners. Indirectly this would point to the need of social audio which is of paramount importance today.

The overlapping and duplication which is often seen in the decentralised programme also make it imperative that the data of various organisations working in the same field are also compiled and collected properly to ensure quality implementation. With the scarcity of resources it is imperative that every penny is utilised optimally. This action means areawise identification of the efforts made and results achieved by different organisations working for the same target groups. This also becomes important as and when organisations funding directly or indirectly from scarce funds get into these difficult areas with their special programme, but for the same target group.

It is agreed that the State KVIBs with their expertise and experience be involved to develop particular select village industries through consultancy, exchange of personnel marketing etc. While agreeing with many KVIBs institutions, societies have done exceptionally well within the resources available, it would be pertinent to mention that many State Boards have been devoid of any resources or work culture. Fund is one of the problems. The type of extension work, technology and other infrastructures which are available may generate hope and confidence. But still as per the recommendation of the Ramakrishanayya Committee the following steps are proposed to be taken.

1. Start a monthly competition evaluation of the working of all KVIBs depending on their performance in select items based on well laid down criteria.
2. Some KVIBs have already been involved to prepare action plan for village industries based on availability of raw materials, skills and linkages with marketing.
3. In KVIC headquarters one officer has been nominated to coordinate KVI activities within the State. This will ensure coordination and redressal of grievances and availability of data base and package of information with senior official.
4. To develop the spirit, monitoring examining and competitions are proposed to be taken up on All India basis.
5. Essay competition, publicity and innovation. Boards will be requested to come up with specific suggestions for overall improvement of KVI sector.
6. Specialisation in the field of appropriate technology attention to backward and tribal areas low cost delivery system, consultancy and marketing services, product development would also be fully utilised depending upon the availability of these Boards.

7. To fully tap the potential and strength of KVI sector it is proposed to start system of deputation within all good institutions, even entrepreneurs expansion agents and staff would be suitably motivate to take up difficult assignment like marketing, taking over sick unit, project formulation for new industries etc. It is also proposed to suitably link up and integrate the training facilities available within the KVI sector to provide holistic approach to this sector.

While agreeing that various departments are working in the field of village industries and village development will have to so develop systems to fully tap various resources available with each of them. For this it is proposed to start a cell in the KVIC to keep watch on new projects and programmes being initiated by various State Governments and local bodies. It is also proposed to involve the KVI sector personnel in a big way to identify the best work done in and around its centre disseminating regularly the success and failure stories alongwith resume to involve all those who have the potential to work in this sector. The communication gap will be broken and system would be developed to make people accountable, responsible, punctual and work culture conducive to overall development of the target group. This also means developing a culture of working together through scientific analysis of apparatus tools at the headquarters level and studying in depth the work styles of people at the field level. The training, marketing, R&D, funding and product development will be suitably interlinked to reduce cost and make our products competitive and self-sustainable and acceptable to larger buyer groups. Instead of depending on captive market through coordination with various field agencies and monitoring systems effort will be made to produce products worth competing in the open market. This means developing marketing organisations and maintaining close regular interaction between various organisations which will be veering around KVI sector. This means KVIC will basically be catalyst and will endeavour to develop institutions, people, training centres and take place of learning and marketing to develop a strong chain to ensure rural industrialisation with minimum of funds and through ecological sustainable development.

Tasks ahead are difficult and will need people with strong determination, clarity of thought, physical fitness and openness to the core. The Commission may consider the strategies and tactical approach outlined in the note, the steps crystallised and take appropriate decision.

32

Economic Offences

Economic offence, broadly defined, are violation of laws enacted by the government in persuance of its economic policies and programmes. These crimes are mostly committed with the connivance of or in collusion with the public servants charged with the enforcement of the relevant laws. Unlike the crimes of passion such as murder or rioting, these offences are committed with deliberation and are the result solely of expected gains. The offenders generally come from the wealthier sections of the society who have acquired sufficient influence in right quarters to continue their nefarious activities without detection. Even if detected, they manage to escape punishment, taking advantage of legal processes, delays etc.

2. The economic offences may be broadly categorised are as follows:

(a) Misuse of or trafficking in licenses and permits;

(b) Hoarding of scarce commodities and selling them higher than the statutory price;

(c) Adulterating food-stuffs, drugs and such other essential commodities of common use;

(d) Evasion of taxes lawfully imposed;

(e) Over or under utilization of industrial capacities to evade payment of taxes/to create artificial scarcities;

(f) Supplying goods/services below the contracted specifications;

(g) Making of contracts, disposal of public property etc. by public servants and issue of licenses/permits by them even with the prior knowledge that they are not in the best public interest; and

(h) Theft and misappropriation of public funds/property.

3. The above crimes, if allowed to go on unchecked threaten the economic health of the nation and hamper its growth. With the generation of vast unaccounted funds, they disrupt the moral fibre of the society and pollute the public life by corrupting the individuals in high positions. They also frustrate the efforts to secure equitable distribution of commodities essential for human existence at prices within the reach of common man and this cause misery and disillusionment on a wide scale. The existence of a parallel economy financed by black money also blunts all efforts to fight inflation and distorts the image of the administration and the government despite programmes/policies carefully evolved and implemented for the welfare of the people.

4. With the advancement of science and technology and the resultant complexity of the modern economic life, active participation of the government in the economic activity has become inescapable. The modern taxation is also fairly complicated process as through this instrument the government seeks to optimize the use of national resources with long-range objectives and to secure an equitable distribution of wealth in order to reduce the gulf between the rich and the poor, besides raising adequate resources for its own functioning. A large number of departments deal with economic activities

e.g. ensuring balanced growth of industry and agriculture, regulating and monitoring the use of scare resources, mobilization of public savings and channelizing them into productive use, acquisition and distribution of essential commodities including regulation of private trade in such commodities, promotion of cooperative etc., etc., as also to administer the tax laws. The Government have also set up a number of corporations to participate directly in the industrial and commercial ventures in vital sectors or in order to promote multi-dimensional growth and healthy competition.

5. In the mixed pattern of our economy the private and public sectors function side by side, but the direction of economy rests with the government. A private entrepreneur comes into close contact with public servants in a large number of government departments to secure the necessary licenses/permits etc. or to enter into contracts for supply of goods and services. Such contacts are sometimes utilized by the unscrupulous to promote their interests by resorting to all sorts of dubious tactics. Advantage is taken of any loopholes in the procedure or by persuading the public servant to do or not to do something which he as a public servant has a duty to do. Quite often, a number of departments are concerned in a single venture and the unscrupulous businessman manages to exploit the tendency of public servants to look into matters pertaining to their own respective departments, to his own advantage. It is in such circumstances that economic offences are committed. It is significant to note that an economic offence once committed has tendency to lead to commission of a series of such offences down the line. To illustrate, power-theft by industrial units in which production is related to the running time of machines, leads to excess production which is

concealed from taxation, and public distribution system and thus enables the management to multiply it ill-gotten gains. Similarly trafficking in licenses/ permits for scarce raw material leads to use of such resources for production either in prohibited or non-priority area or in production totally concealed from the taxation and official supply systems. It thus generates black money and distorts priorities carefully devised. Marketing and supply systems devised for essential commodities are similarly subverted with a view to making large profits out of human wants. The existing social system, with a large army of young unemployed persons is also contributing towards aggravation of economic offences. Such persons find it very easy to obtain permits for scarce commodities which are subsequently disposed of at a premium.

6. With the growing complexity of economic activities, the economic crimes have assumed alarming proportions and threaten the very vitals of our economic system. They have defied all organisational efforts, elaborate rules and procedures devised for, primarily because the offenders command large resources and manage to corrupt or hoodwink the authorities entrusted with the task of administering the departments dealing with them. While it is not possible to make and uptodate assessment of the demage caused, there can be no difference of opinion on the existence on a vast scale in practically all the departments dealing with economic affairs. There is therefore need for (i) streamlining procedures and removing legal lacunea wherever found making penal provisions more deterrent and quick, and (ii) setting up an agency to (a) collect intelligence about these crimes, (b) oversee enforcement of rules and procedures, (c) exercise vigilance on the departmental machinery, and (d) organize investigation and prosecution of offenders

according to law.

7. The various departments of the government have been regularly releasing statistics regarding the action taken by them to prevent and detect economic offences and such other malpractices. Whereas a large number of raids have been conducted to discipline the trade and create a climate of strictness on the part of the administration such raids only have a temporary and limited effect because persons prosecuted are often let off with light punishment or the cases drag on, first, at the investigation stage and later in the courts. Such periodic drives are also often used as opportunities by racalcitrant staff to indulge in corruption and to harass the trading community. The provision in respect of summary trials in the Essential Commodities Act are inadequate in the first place and there is urgent need to amend the Act in this regard. There is also a persistent feeling that punishment involving only a fine is seldom an adequate deterrent since most of the offenders never find it difficult to pay. Administrative procedure should also provide for preparation of history sheets as in the case of offences under the Indian Penal Code. The Judicial machinery available for disposing cases of illegal economic activity also needs to be updated, special executive magistrates for trying cases in this regard is essential.

8. Mere amendment in law, arming the existing enforcement machinery with more stringent powers is unlikely to achieve the objective. Strict laws serve public good only if they are used to catch the big sharks operating on a large scale. These very laws can become instruments of oppression if their enforcement is entrusted to the present machinery without providing for expert supervision and direction.

9. Establishment of the agency so suggested in para 6 above does not in any way dilute the

responsibility of the Head of the Department to ensure proper functioning of his charge. In fact, vigilance cells on the lines of UPSEB, Food & Civil supplies etc. need to be set up in other departments dealing with economic affairs and also in corporations participating in industry and commerce. Some of the existing Cells need strengthening in order to make them more effective and useful. The agency when set up will help coordination of the activities of these cells. giving them direction wherever necessary will ensure proper follow-up action. It will also develop, in addition to these cells, its own sources of intelligence and advise the government matters of policy. It will also provide the government with an objective picture of the state of enforcement of economic laws.

10. The problem of economic crimes has many facets and requires to be dealt with at all levels and on all fronts. In sensitive sectors, gradual replacement of private trader by a cooperative agency would perhaps be desirable. Committees of public-spirited individuals known for their honesty and integrity could be set up at the local levels to oversee the functioning of various economic departments and to point out distortions of policy or dishonest actions if any. Above all, a well-sustained effort to create an awareness of the dangers posed by economic offenders is called for to achieve social participation in the eradication of economic crime. Strict adherence to a high standard of ethical behaviour at all levels, particularly at the higher once is necessary for the ever and honest functioning of modern economic, social and such other processes and no efforts should be spared to make the various sections of the society to appreciate this need.

33

Need for Close Linkage in Rural Development

There is a close inter-link relationship between Agriculture, Rural Development and Rural Industrialisation. All these three sectors have specialised requirement and depending upon the level of Agriculture Development, Rural Industrialisation needs proper attention. This means analysing the prevailing state of economy in the Agriculture Sector and to ensure proper and smooth linkages for co-existence and gradual upgradation of harmonious switch over the Rural sustainable development stage. This will become clear from the following areas of activity.

Linkage of Agriculture, Rural Development and Rural Industrialisation for Integrated Self-Supporting Sustainable Development Models

Major Activities

Agriculture	Rural Development	Rural Industries
(1)	(2)	(3)
Agriculture	Health	Rural Industrialisation means:
Horticulture Forestry Sericulture etc. Animal husbandry Fisheries etc.	Small savings Pollution Environment Ecology Drinking	Value addition on local raw material like agriculture, forest, horticulture,

(1)	(2)	(3)
	Water Education IRDP Roads Housing Tourism S & T (Science & Technology) and many other programmes.	chemical etc. which are either demand based industries- thus making marketable products and marketing in either (a) Village (b) and/or Cities or Export etc. For holistic view of rural development- all these are must

Programme Needs

1. Extension
2. Godowns and cold storage
3. Standardisation and quality controls
4. Agmarking
5. Systematic regulated market
6. Funding and bankable projects
7. Computerised monitoring
8. Appropriate S & T and feed-back
9. Development of system for linkages
10. Publicity
11. Rural Entrepreneurship
12. Attitudes of extension supports.

Target Group for Rural Development

All those who stay in villages:

(a) Farmers
(b) Labourers
(c) Artisans and support service providers
(d) Women groups

(e) Unemployed educated
(f) Retired senior citizen groups.

Policy Support for Rural Industrialisation because of Educational Needs

With the induction of 10+2 educational system and opening up of various educational institutions, time has come to link up self-employment programmes, vocationalisation, economics and marketability of products to provide attractive remuneration in Rural Areas. This means good institutions from all sectors in Rural Areas should be involved with the educational institution for developing confidence in students and employed to earn honest reasonable income. This means analysing the SWOT and ensuring coordinated extension systems for achieving the objectives of self-employment. This can be done only by ensuring adequate income which will discourage from trying his best for government job. This also means linking up programmes like SUPW, teacher's training, multiplication of basic and secondary educational institutions as mere certificate issues and ensuring their resources in the field of self-employment are generated through various vocational activities.

G.V.K.R.V. Rao Committee had suggested an apex organisation at state level headed by a senior-most officer of the rank of Chief Secretary to ensure availability of all services, facilities and extension of agencies in the field of education, minor irrigation, rural industries, primary health, forestry, rural tourism, rural housing, rural roads etc. in a compact package. While many states have not still ensured this integrated system of administration, time has come to optimise the resources available with various different agencies to give maximum service in Rural Areas in a time bound manner. G.V.K.R.V. Rao

Committee had also recommended a holistic approach for rural development which will, in turn, help stopping migration of people from rural areas to cities thus solving many problems related to urbanisation.

Ramakrishnaiya Committee

As far as Rural Industries are concerned, Ramakrishnaiya Committee can be taken as milestone which recommended various policy supports to make the KVI sector an effective instrument of Rural Development. This policy change involves competition with small scale sector which is based basically in urban areas industries. If Rural Industry have to be accepted as major force for Rural Development, naturally policy issues which many times do directly confront and come in conflict with so called small scale have to be projected in their right respective. This can be done only by understanding the nature of village industries and decentralised sector. Even the policy support was originally justified on the following grounds:

"(a) Rural industrial activities have an important role to play in generating employment at low cost among the socially and economically backward strata of rural society, particularly in remote areas,

(b) Rural Non-farm activities, if developed properly, can arrest the exodus of population from Rural Areas to Urban Areas to some extent and thus reduce social costs of urbanisation,

(c) Rural Non-farm objects being labour intensive and short question should be viewed as a corrective to inflationary pressures in a situation where a large chunk of National

Resources is required to be invested in the establishment of capital intensive projects of long question, and

(d) Rural Non-farm, which are desirable in terms of (a), (b) and (c) and above are not in a position to withstand competition from the organised sector and should, therefore, be protected."

Apart from various other policy issues which Ramakrishnaiya Committee recommended, to understand the real personality of village industries/ decentralised products. It is essential the psychology of distribution of government funds is understood and unless the integration of village industries takes place with Rural Development as a whole, no proper appreciation will ever materialise.

If you look into the various industries falling within the purview of Non-farm, we will find that many of them have direct relationship with the skills, infrastructures, raw material availability in the Rural Areas. What is needed is appropriate technology, standardisation, agmarking, quality standards and marketing with appropriate pricing policy. This can be done when decentralised production processes and value addition activities coupled with rural entrepreneurship development are suitably developed. This is the crux of the problem. Because of the lack of appreciation, it does not cater adequately these requirements for Rural Industry. Hence wherever Rural Development processes are taking place, rural industries activities have to be made an integral part of this. Hence time has come to take Non-farm sectors as an integrated part of Rural Development process otherwise it would result in duplication and frittering away of scarce resource when it comes to Rural Development.

Product Reservation

Decentralised unorganised informal sector have their own peculiarities. Their products should also be competitive. But they are only given some or other preferential treatment. This cannot compete with the products from heavy, medium or over small scale sector — whether it is cotton to garment, or wheat flour and bakery products or oil seeds to oil or carcass to finished leather, clay to bricks, fruits to jams and jellies and various other activities. The host of unemployed students can be groomed to understand the intricacies of these value additions through right rural entrepreneurship and adequate bankability of projects. This means holistic approach for solving this multifarious problems which otherwise rural entrepreneur can never be expected to solve.

Rural Development for poverty alleviation has been the major thrust of government strategies in the plans. But added thrust of employment guarantee and right to work will need organisational realignment keeping in mind the new flow of knowledge. Giving dole for right to work can never be the solution to the problem. Ultimate answer to host of our problems of urbanisation, unemployment, imports, foreign exchange, shortage is to be develop Rural Areas to attract and hold the people from migration. This can be done only by having maximum "percolation activities" in the Rural Areas. With the various types of infrastructures including computerised monitoring initiated by Rural Development Department, it is time to link up village industries sector as inseparable part by linking up agricultural marketing with Rural Industries marketing. The primary rural products should through adequate storage capacity value addition and processing capacity be turned into sample finished products and transported to cities and other consuming areas.

This may seem difficult, but that is the need of the day and any programme whose time has come cannot be delayed. With the growing realisation of nuisance of western model of industrialisation and resources scarcity all rounds. This linkage can very well be established today.

34

Non-Residential Indians and Rural Development

The involvement of non Residential Indians in taking up Rural Development Projects can be a very good idea. Before we think of areas and the activities in which they can take up Rural Development Projects we must keep in mind the assets of N.R.I.'s. These N.R.I.'s have initiative, adventure, knowledge and resources. Because of their excellence, they have done well otherwise but when it comes to doing something in the Rural Developments areas they suffer from certain weaknesses. These include ignorance of rural conditions, and other problems connected with socio economic environment prevailing in the villages.

2. Keeping the above in mind, they can supplement the efforts of Government in the Field of rural development. Their resources can be channelised in the following ways:

1. By forming voluntary organisation to act as catalyst of change. Because of their financial resourcefulness, they can do this work in a much better, organised way.
2. In the field of imparting vocational training.
3. In the field of hospitals and other medical and sanitary works.
4. In the field of generation of electricity which is key to all other developments.
5. In the field of developing activity points. This can

be done by selecting right type of Graduates from Agricultural Universities, imparting them training, arranging for their funds and expecting them to take up various agricultural activities on custom and other basis. This way the activity generating person should be able to earn at least Rs. 1500 per month by taking up various activities. These may include Waste Land Development, Horticulture, Custom services of tractors, agencies of fertilisers, pasticides etc. and acting as technical resource person for rural development sector.

6. By participating actively in villages industrialisation programmes and its various dimension. This may for example include provision of improved type of sheep rearing to development of piggeries.
7. The rural life is not only very difficult but equally fraught with risks. The drudgery and lack of resources for entertainment make life very difficult. To tap it all the problems of basic necessities of life make people migrate to cities. Here NRI's with their expertise can make appropriate technology useful to rural scene. Some devices can reduce fatigue elements from day to day life. Here some time and motion studies would also enlighten the rural people about the way, quality of life can be improved.
8. When we talk of involving NRI's in the rural development sector we must remember that rural development is a very difficult sector. The glamour associated with city and five star culture is just not available. Not only this, but working condition are very very tough and results are often difficult to see. Hence NRI's have to be suitably motivated to take this onerous job without expecting much of results in short period.

9. Marketing of village industries products. Because of the strength of village industries products they can be very good source of providing additional income to rural people. Village products possess the following plus points:

    1. Decentralised production.
    2. Value adding possible in rural areas.
    3. Avoidance of pollution in over polluted cities.
    4. Saving in transport of material service only finished products would come to city.
    5. Less migration of people to city from villages.
    6. Putting life into villages possible.
    7. Heavy reduction possible in overheads in cities.

10. Export possibilities can be tapped—facilities, information centre, exchange of ideas.
11. Giving designs, facilities to rural products.

Non-residential Indians and those people who stay away from the State of their origin can contribute immensely a revitalising the dormant rural areas. In fully utilising their resources and desire we must keep in mind the need to integrate with Panchayati Raj Institutions. By not fully exploring the potential of this integration a lot of harm has been done to explore in full capacity of rural development.

With resource scarcity all around it is high time that a new bold imaginative, initiative is launched by one and all. Some of the important areas of action in these directions would include the following:

1. Can we have villages, blocks and communities survey to find out the origins of NRIs.
2. Can we have selected study to explore the potential area of the investment.
3. How do the NRIs perceive the villages, the Panchayati Raj, the State?

4. The existing infrastructure of training institutions can be very useful in exploring area of investment with NRIs participation.
5. NRIs can contribute substantial in training, education, consultancy, plantation, fisheries, rural technologies experts provided suitable policy packages are developed.
6. The role of Commissioner NRI Investment become very crucial as resource scarcity live limited options.
7. NRIs can also invite some Panchayati Raj Institutions on cost sharing basis to open up mind vision.

Unorganised sector whether in decentralised, non-formal, ISB sector is the sector of the future. It is the high time adequate attention is paid for convergence and optimisation of efforts.

One of the reasons of China all-round development is active involvement of NRIs. The spiritual dimension in the investment, consultancy will definitely open up more and more powerful avenues in making life of masses qualitatively better and affordable. This is the challenge.

35

Challenges of 21st Century : Need to Examine Gandhi for Organisational Effectiveness

Introduction

The world in which we are living presents picture of contradiction, perverted priorities and unthinkable change in the definitions. The Human Development Report, 1994 mentioned following:

> "Poverty is no longer contained within national boundaries. It has become globalized. It travels across borders, without a passport, in the form of drugs, diseases, pollution, migration terrorism and political instability."

But before we proceed further let us try to understand the challenges of 21st Century.

Thus the analysis of problem would not be over unless one also ventures to understand some commonalities required to venture in the next step i.e. steps to solve the problem.

Gandhi and 21st Century

This knowledge is free for all. Anybody can use it freely by quoting author but the aim is to disseminate

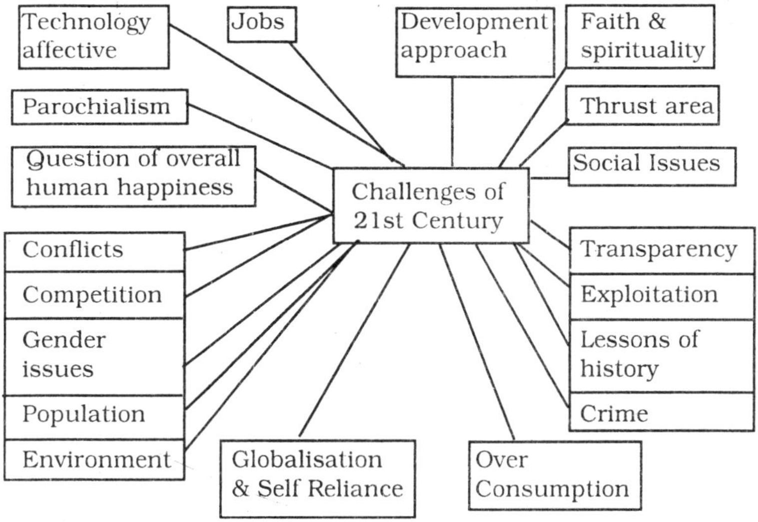

and propagate areas for exploration further scientific, rational, analytical benefits of systems development. The author claim no originality to any views or conclusions or patterns. He has observed, analysed, concluded and written. If there are better conclusions they have to be shared and examined further. There can be no end to this reasoned analysis and scientific tests.

Author was born at Wardha on 1.8.1946 and had the experiences of how Gandhi's philosophy, avowed principles, all those thoughts for which we lived being butchered. Today when at the age nearing 50 when we looks back, there is a mixed feeling. Has a excellent product been marketed very badly? Has it failed? Has hope generating model been sacrificed at the altar of expediency of various nature, man's over-ambition, neglect of historical lessons and overall greed of leaders! The author does not know as yet but as 'student' he would like to explore further as to what went wrong and would be grateful if examination of following could be initiated:

1. Was Gandhi projected properly through action research marketing models?
2. What was wrong with Gandhi and why did we have so many critics even during his life time.
3. Has strength, weaknesses, opportunities, threats (SWOT) analysis of this 'great man' has been properly done from time to time and improved upon to ensure wider acceptability and reasons analysis?
4. How present time makes his thought, action, propagation more relevant — why and how they have to be marketed internationally to realise India its rightful value?
5. What are the criticalities in this holistic examination of Gandhiji?
6. How Action Plan with Planning Action Research Codification Extension and Loaning components in it be formulated, marketed and implemented? By whom? At what cost? Where? When? How?

There may be many more questions if 'holistic sustainable human development models' have to be developed for future of world. After all mankind is only one component of the world and hence planning has to be for the world and not only human beings.

Under these situations here are some articles, thoughts, views which may permit a wider discussions for action. As Gandhiji said, "One step forward is enough for me".

These are challenging times of different magnitude. The spirit of entrepreneurship and desire to do improve economic lot by masses opens up whole new challenges. This may be the unique period in human history. I do not know if ever in the past following phenomenon of our time occurred simultaneously:

Challenges of Our Time

(a) Mass awakening.
(b) Pressure to perform on systems.
(c) Effective technology.
(d) High cost low cost performance systems.
(e) Emphasis of women.
(f) Study of policy powers and its use to masses, failure of economic models.
(g) Machines at doorsteps in all activities.

In such a challenging time those who claim to have studied or drawn patterns have a logical duty to carry out field experiments. The field is ready. Only little enthusiasm, faith, clarity and will is required to jump.

The time for these is ripe. Let us pray to that Nature, our Creator, God or Supreme Being

"Let noble thoughts come to us from all directions"

Human Race and Organisations

Even if the problems is proposed to be studied with reference to human races, again like global polity it cannot be studied in isolation. Human race is one of the creations of environment or nature. To study the human races in isolation would not repeat, would not solve the long term problem of human race both to survive and thrive. Without holistic approach the analysis would be short lived and hence time has come to understand nature of linkage.

Since our immediate concern is to focus not on solving this problem but on testing how far the current organisation of society provides means for managing each problem and finding ways to remedy deficiencies. Current policy as mentioned includes national and regional States, International diplomacy, multilateral diplomacy and International law. The discussions has to be around interrelationship of the problems and to forge links with commerce, education, governments, industry, non-governmental institutions, researchers and religious groups. The above discussion and focus become very important in the context of experience both of East and West. The policy of defining development, growth and systems of administration, commerce, education, research — identifying roles of non-governmental institutions and religious groups— all are known generally to solve problem. The interesting aspect is that the discussions focus not on solving problem but on testing how the current organisation of society provides the means for managing each problem and finding ways to remedy deficiencies. The above focus helps in drawing some interesting conclusions for discussion:

(I) Why are we not interested in solving problem? This has following dimensions:
   (a) finding solution is dependent on many variables of society and hence difficult
   (b) cost may differ for each problem solution
   (c) parameters of problem or method would be different
   (d) difficulty in uniformity is major aspect of social values systems
   (e) national scientific analysis is difficult to apply everywhere
   (f) laws are different.

(II) Principles of testing — how far the current organisation of society provides means for managing each problem and finding ways to remedy deficiencies.
   (a) what the current organisation of society to provide means?
   (b) implications of managing each problem and

finding ways to remedy deficiencies.

(c) current policy of regional and national States

(d) international diplomacy implications

(e) multilateral diplomacy and institution role

(f) treaties and International Law and their impact specially on the unorganised

The break-up of above into the following sub-sector, sub-related aspect, has to be thoroughly understood to address:

how institutions are formed?
how do they perform?
what makes coordination?
what are lessons of human behaviour?
how to sensitise?

Can Gandhi offer some solutions?

Gandhiji is not only a person but a philosophy and phenomenon which offer hope for the future. He can be examined rationally, scientifically and analytically since he was always after certain principles which were not consistent all the time. Mahatma Gandhi said about himself :

> "I am a humble seeker after truth. I am impatient to realise myself to attain *moksha* in very existence. My national service is part of my training for freeing my soul from the bondage of flesh. Thus considered, my service may be regarded as purely selfish. For me the road to salvation lies through incessant toil in the service of my country and through that of the humanity. I want to identify myself with every thing that lives. So my patriotism is for me a state in my journey to the land of Eternal freedom and peace."

Since the above quotation brings out the essentialities in his behaviour pattern it is worthwhile to examine it from different angles. This may include some of the following:

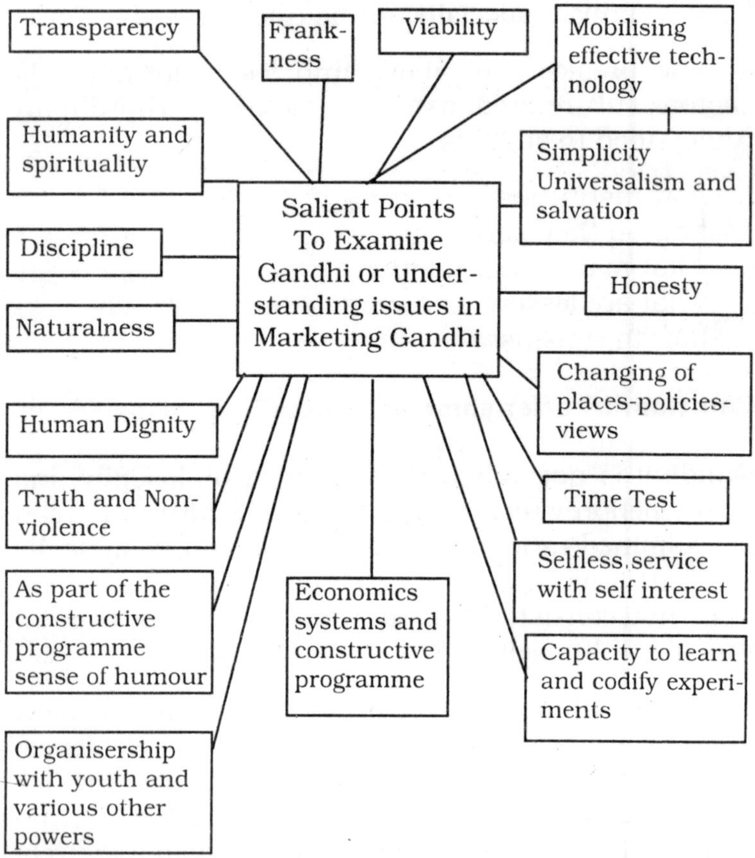

Criticalities of Our Time and Areas of Examination

Some are universal while others are location specific. Hence we have to adopt both local and universal principles for application and understanding the problems.

Inter-relationship of the Problems — How?

What are common issues of principles?

How will sensitization affect the behaviour pattern of all institutions?

Greed and creed issues.

Hence, need to forge links with commerce, education, government, industry, non-governmental institutions and religious group—their roles — target group — principles versus personalities — system of functioning — system and method of evaluation — monitoring, follow-up and dissemination.

The seemingly conflicting or complementary institutions have to be understood to make a conference, easily understandable plan of action.

Human resource development — equilibrium of forces guiding environment — behaviour pattern and role of the following spirits or powers:

Policy power
Humanism issues as spirit and power
Effective technologies as power
Economics as power
Women and youth power

Let us examine how commerce, education, government, industry, non-governmental institutions, research and religious group have been misdirected from their original intention of doing good to society.

How human behaviour shifted them from original path?

How have philosophers, scientists observers, researchers examined these aspects in totality and come to inseparableness of all.

How system of East looks as interrelationship, forging of links with various activities of life and how the present institution will not stand the test of capacity to solve the problem unless common principled corrective lessons are integrated to make things clear. Once this clarity emerges through focusing, the solution to problems could be found without any major problems.

In order to survive or thrive, the global policy needed for human race has to encompass the global thrust and then leave each society and its functionaries to find a holistic hope generating solution to suit their problem and environment.

As the globalisation becomes reality and self reliance becomes essential for sustainability, many issues emerge. Whether these are with reference to technology, market compulsion, economics, demystification, or various changes take place. This is the time when institutions and organisations have to prove their worth. Are they market oriented? Do they have enough potential to absorb changes. What is the new value system? These are the some of the areas which needs to be examined multi-dimensionally, holistically and through multi-disciplinary approach with sensitised mind-sets. Are we ready to learn to work together is the main question.

36

Approaches to Rural Development

Rural development may be defined as development of rural area, so that the ruralite are uplifted. It is not only growth but growth with equity for all. The best way to describe the objective of rural development is perhaps "no longer means agricultural developments alone. It is not a social welfare case of pumping money into rural areas to provide for basic human needs. It encompasses a spectrum of activities and human mobilisation to make people stand on their own feet and break away from all the structural disabilities which chain them to the condition in which they may live."

Rural poverty can be removed only by transforming and taking up programme for the majority of the people based on self-supporting, replicable low cost development models. This area become very important because agriculture and allied activities cannot alone help income generation on sustained basis. Hence in a situation where economic and social inequalities are built in protecting the interest of the week until such time that inequalities are considerably narrowed down.

Minimum Intervention by Governments

Granting that a positive intervention by Government is desirable a combination of basic needs approach, its variance of Integrated Rural Development, as also industrialisation and growth centre approach would be ideal for combating poverty which is the nerve centre of rural development.

But in our case, growth has not been commensurate with its percolation. Growth has been for those organised, well to do who were aware of the developments taking place around them. For the unorganised living in backward and tribal areas, growth has meant more difficulties and exploitations. Here again most exploited has been the women and disabled.

Self Employment is the only Solution

Self-employment is the only alternative as wage employment/impossible. The State has created wage employment in the last 30 years and how the recruitments were made, however, staffing has been done and how today they are mostly a liability on the State. Hence, the only solution that is now widely recommended is the self-employment.

This calls for not only the attitudinal change but also to understand the imperatives of the solution in our situation. We will have to find in all Departments of the Government and outside the areas in which self-employment can be propagated through cost effectiveness. Rural Industrialisation would be one of the major themes to achieve this objective. We must consider the various related issues including subsidised land, water, electricity, housing, transport and other related expenses like law and order, sanitation and long-term impact of urbanisation. Those unemployed will need the dole might take place through big industry, but the percolation would be only to a very limited employed people. If the same product could come from rural areas through decentralised units, then scenario would be totally different. But the entire planning today is oriented towards encouraging big unit in the city rather than decentralised units giving more employment in rural areas.

It is only with awareness that appropriate technology, skill upgradation and marketing oriented organised activities that can really help. Varl Mark, Adam Smith, Keynes have not visited the tribal areas of India. Even in Africa, the stark realities are becoming abundantly clear today. The borrowed fund, imported capital oriented model cannot solve the problem of unemployment and sustainable development. There are no short cuts and on many counts we may not have cases of success from other countries. Korea, Singapore, Japan, model do not really fit in to our condition and we have to develop our own model of development.

Tactics for Informal Sector for Areas of Disputes

It is well known that the formal bureaucratic organisation with all its various disadvantages would not able to help the informal sector. While the growth potential lies primarily in informal sector, the policies and technical weaknesses have made the situation worst. The policies which lay down the principles for organised sector are technically manipulated to suit right timings whether it is organised small scale neglecting the informal Traditional Industries (incidentally which are apart of small scale) or the organised lobby of big kulaks leaving aside the vast majority of unorganised small and landless farmers. These organisational capacity contacts with city dwellers force rural population to remain with the problem all the time i.e. big exploiting the poor the organised exploiting the unorganised. Here the role of motivated formal organisations can be useful only to certain extent. In the longer run, it is the organisation of the beneficiaries themselves that will solve the problem. Despite our tall talk on all these points, little has been achieved. The policies have spelt repeatedly on all these points but the problem has been of technical weakness. The action plan for changing the situation must look into the following:

(1) The cost of delivery through organised bureaucracy must be reduced and the delivery system must be able to generate income for itself. The NDBB experiment should be replicable in all extension programmes, especially in those catering to informal sector.

(2) Well conceived programmes like IRDP, TRYSEM, DWACRA, Social Forestry, Minor Irrigation, Animal Husbandry, Wool Improvement, Goat Rearing, Charkha, Handloom and many more must have umbrella covers of local institutions linked with marketing wherever marketing has been left to charity, rebate, grant, subsidy, results have been catastrophic. Needless to say, formal efforts have left informal groups devoid of confidence in themselves. The entire cooperatives have failed because of funding at input level and not output level. The money should have been given in phases depending on the self-propelling fund generation. The cost had no relationship with income or output.

(3) The need to have zero based money programme must be tactically implemented.

(4) The abundance of local skills, marketing and fund should not be substituted with the imported funds, machinery or even concepts. The local of everything must be fully utilised to suit the modern demand.

(5) The low cost, high impact concept must be built in all programmes for informal sector. This also calls for low cost practical consultancy as a substitute for high cost extension bureaucratic machinery. The lessons of history bring out clearly the need to keep the system of its own all the time. Too much of security makes the system inefficient. What a pity that in many rural areas where the worker earns only Rs. 2 or 3 a day by doing part time work seven to eight hours wants to send his child to private school where the private teacher charges anything from Rs. 15 to 25 per month. This becomes astonishing when the primary school teacher hardly goes to teach. Incidentally, the concept of free education has become redundant in the rural areas, so feel many.

(6) The need for integrated approach to decentralised programme got informal groups needs close monitoring from top. A water tank catering for drinking water does not take into consideration the drainage or mosquito problem created by this new project. Brick and mortar school or Panchayat Bhawan constructed in a muddy rural area does not cater for the utilisation of local resources or even for planting trees. This shows the heartening indifference for integrated plan. The problem of looking at only single area calls for a total integrated package in all development activities. In the longer run, this means having single worker extension project rather than multiplicity of formalised groups to attend to informal groups. The number of duplicacy in extension can be studied in various governmental activities and it is only with

informal extension machinery that self supporting informal sector can be made a vibrant growth centre for absorption of millions of our rural unemployment of both men and women. This calls for attitudinal change the technical manoeuvring of not only the policies but also the implementation in which marketing and internal generation of resources would play very key role. The low cost, high impact and sustainability and replicability of the programmes especially for the informal sector would be the watchword. Is it possible?

While we are talking about informal sector and formal delivery organisations, we should not forget the middle class mentality of postal clerks. Development economics needs a new approach. While low cost high impact replicability and self-sustainability of the programme will be must, the linkages must be suitably identified and parameters for success be pre-determined. The zero based budgets, computerised monitoring, regular inspections, openness and involvement would go a long way to bridge the gap between informal sector and formal organisation. While we have to learn to live and accept dichotomy and heterogeneity, technical maneuvres are must to understand the practical modalities to make the best in a given situation. While experts of African affairs and foreign loaning have thought out the ill effects of this dichotomy they are not at all unanimously clear about the modalities to be followed in solving the problem. It is here our decentralised entrepreneurs, voluntary organisations and lower level functionaries may be able to offer concrete practical suggestion or improvement.

Weaknesses noticed in Rural Development Programme

One of the major weaknesses noticed in the existing on-going programmes a part from their multiplicity is its excessive dependence on bureaucratic machinery. Though in theory, elected representatives at every level are involved in the formation, implementation and even intensive monitoring, the success of 20 points committees, in reality the picture is dismal. Most of the funds for the infrastructure comes as grant and loan comes as subsidised amount. Coordination required between banks, Government machinery, beneficiaries and elected representatives is often missing and mostly it is a question of mutual back scratch. Intensive monitoring system through computer hardly touched upon to include the aspect of backward-forward linkages, marketing tie-up, self supporting nature of programmes and their replicability. No wonder despite impressive records of the performance in reality much is yet to be achieved.

Privatisation for Rural Development

It is only in the late sixties that sporadic efforts of rural development model were codified into systemic action plan. Following are the major land-mark in the rural development scenario:

The basic thrust of the Fifth Plan (1974-75 to 1977-78) was to arrest the displacement of traditional artisans from existing crafts, providing further work opportunities, widening the employment base in backward areas and ensuring a level of earning adequate enough to meet the basic needs of life. Thus, Fifth Plan envisaged a substantial higher outlays for the development programmes in cottage and small industries. During the second-half of the Fifth Plan.

The Planning Commission began to show marked preference to the beneficiary oriented approach and self employment.

During 1977-78, some of the State Governments reviewed the Antodaya Scheme and accordingly the Sixth Five Year Plan set the target of providing gainful employment to sizeable sections of the unemployed. The basic thrust of the Sixth Five Year Plan was creation of employment opportunities as quickly as possible. In the Sixth Plan, Village Industries have been given a central place in rural development programmes. The Sixth Plan approved the Gandhi Strategy for Rural Industrialisation and observed that rapid development of small industries including cottage, household and small scale was one of the major objectives of the plan as a part of the primary goals of rendering employment and reducing unemployment.

During the Seventh Plan (1985-90) period, the total amount spent on major poverty alleviation programmes in rural areas viz. self employment programmes of IRDP, and wage employment programmes of NREP, RLEGP/TRY Programmes was Rs. 1,126 crores.

In the Eighth Plan (1990-95) the basic thrust is on poverty alleviation. Alleviation of poverty through overall economic growth and direct programme generation in rural and urban areas would be one of the thrust areas during the Eighth Plan.

37

Soldiers and Rural Development

We must remember that every group of person possesses some strength and weakness. When it comes to people from Defence Services, they possess certain sterling qualities. These include discipline, competence, willingness to learn, humanness and toughness along with experience. These qualities coupled with their integrity, capacity and willingness to work hard, make them real asset for any organization, but they have some weaknesses also like lack of inflexibility and intolerant attitude. Actually, given proper training and motivation, they can be very useful for any organization. Needless to say, when it comes to training them for suitable self-employment, these qualities must be kept in mind.

Basically, people from any wing of Defence Services would fall in one of the following categories:—

(1) Infantry type;
(2) EME, Artillery, Engineers type;
(3) Educational type;
(4) Armed Service Corps, Army Ordinance Corps type;
(5) Intelligent type.

Keeping above in mind, when it comes to inculcate skill for vocation, we will have to select right type of industry or activity for their rehabilitation. The following can be the type of activities in which they can be gainfully employed:

(1) Law and order activities. This can take different forms. Apart from direct employment in law and order forces, they can also be great asset for information collection and other voluntary organizations to be deployed for problem areas;
(2) In skilful vocations, they can be utilised in raw materials processing, repairs of machines and plants connected with rural life and operation installation, maintenance of schemes like Minor Irrigation projects, radios, T.Vs., etc.;
(3) In the educational field also, they can be useful for various activities connected with education in the rural areas;
(4) In the field of supply, packaging and marketing, they can be utilised in rural areas by organizing their societies and shops, etc.;
(5) They can be encouraged and trained to organise voluntary organizations to undertake different activities in rural sector. Detailed note, highlighting the various features of voluntary organizations have been separately prepared.
(6) In the field of horticulture, social forestry, user reclamation also, they can be directly involved.
(7) In the field of survey, introduction of appropriate technology and training, the trained and motivated person can be readily used.

Regarding the activities connected with KVI programme, the following would give detailed information as to the activities which they can be asked to undertake successfully.

Khadi & Village Industries Programme as enunciated by Mahatma Gandhi plays a pivotal role in restructuring rural economy and is aimed at providing adequate employment opportunities at a lower investment rate. Much emphasis is laid under this programme on the importance of human values and areawise self-sufficiency. The main thrust of this sector is to provide gainful employment opportunities at the doorstep of the entrepreneur, assisting him in the process of easy flow of finances and technical expertise besides marketing of goods produced.

U.P. Khadi & Village Industries Board is the recognized forum for implementation of Khadi and 23 village industries in the State of Uttar Pradesh. Dedicated to the cause of promoting and developing KVI programme, the Board happens to be a statutory body having its own network of District Village Industries Officer/Manager (KVI) in all district offices besides its own departmental commercial factories Training-cum-Production Centre and Raw-material Sales Depots (details appear in Annexure). Apart from promotional and extension activities, the Board extends financial assistance to individual entrepreneurs, industrial cooperative societies and charitable institutions as per pattern in vogue for respective industries under its purview, renders technical know-how besides marketing assistance. Thus KVI forum, by and large may safely be used to promote and assist in rehabilitation of ex-Army personnels in the manner detailed below:

(i) Scattered ex-Army personnel who rejoin their families to engage themselves in agriculture and allied sector may be persuaded to opt for Khadi & Village Industries Programme as per their aptitude and set up their individual unit.

(ii) Group of ex-Army personnel residing in a particular vicinity may be organised into co-operative fold or charitable institution to set up industrial co-operative society or multifold connected village industries.

(iii) Places where concentration of ex-Army personnel is available, chain of Khadi & Village Industries be set up which may be manned by a charitable institution formed and registered under the Societies Registration Act 1860 with ex-Army personnel constituting its membership.

(iv) An apex body in the shape of Federation be formed at provincial level with all Industrial Cooperative Societies of KVI of ex-Army personnel becoming its primary members.

The massive programme of resettlement of ex-Army personnel through KVI sector as envisaged earlier, needs ample financial support which is proposed to be met through sources detailed below:

(i) KVI Commission and State KVI Boards;
(ii) Funds sanctioned to District Soldiers Board and allied institutions;
(iii) Nationalised Banks and District Cooperative Banks;
(iv) Benevolent Fund created for the welfare and rehabilitation of ex-Army personnel.

Necessary basic ingredient for the success of any programme is proper and practical training of persons engaged in the programme. State KVI Board proposes to arrange training of artisans, instructors and supervisors at sources given below:

(i) Training Centres run by KVIC;
(ii) Training-cum-Production Centres run by KVIB;
(iii) Commercial/Departmental Centres run by State KVI Boards;
(iv) KVI units financed by KVI Boards;

(v) Technical staff of the Board;
(vi) TRYSEM Training Centres run by DRDA.

The key to success of KVI sector lies essentially in adequate and well knit marketing structure. This aspect should invariably be given necessary attention and much spade work will have to be done. Audio-visual propaganda and publicity will have to be undertaken on wide scale to achieve success on this vital score. Marketing structure is proposed to be based on certain assumptions which arc enumerated hereunder.

(i) Army units all over India are the largest consumer of goods and products of KVI units managed by ex-Army personnel should invariably be given preference;
(ii) Army canteens established in all Army units should display the products of KVI units and should act as the major outlet of marketing;
(iii) District Soldiers Boards should open their own sale depots to cater the sale of products of ex-Army personnel units;
(iv) KVI Boards own departmental Sale Depots set up in almost all districts of Uttar Pradesh will also manage sale of products of such Army units connected with KVI sector.
(v) Secretary of District Soldiers Board be also nominated in District Purchase Committees headed by ADM (P) to thrust sale of ex-Army personnel units on priority basis as this Committee finalises yearly purchases by Government Departments of the district;
(vi) Exhibitions, fairs and seminars be also organised to inculcate and boost sale of products;
(vii) Should funds so permit, the appex body of

ex-Army personnel rehabilitation unit may also arrange for mobile sale shops to popularise products of KVI units managed by ex-Army personnel.

It is necessary that proper links and liaison are maintained at district and Army units level to monitor, vindicate the shortcomings and adequate exchange of informations deemed beneficial for the rehabilitation of ex-Army personnel. It is, therefore, proposed that:

(i) District Village Industries Officer/Manager (KVI) of U.P. Khadi and Village Industries Board be nominated to District Soldiers Board;

(ii) Officers incharge of rehabilitation of ex-Army personnel at Army unit should act as liaison officer to discuss plan and finalise schemes of KVI sector in consultation with Chief Executive Officer of U.P. Khadi & Village Industries Board and monitor progress of the scheme.

Soldiers are not only disciplined a lot but also receiving pension. They retire at a young age. In the field of total rural development this category can play a very important role. The following are important components of attitude.

1. Mindsetting, 2. Right experience, 3. Marketing culture, 4. Convergence, 5. Discipline, 6. Learning to working together with civil institutions.

If country has to develop in totality it is high time various issues are properly explored.

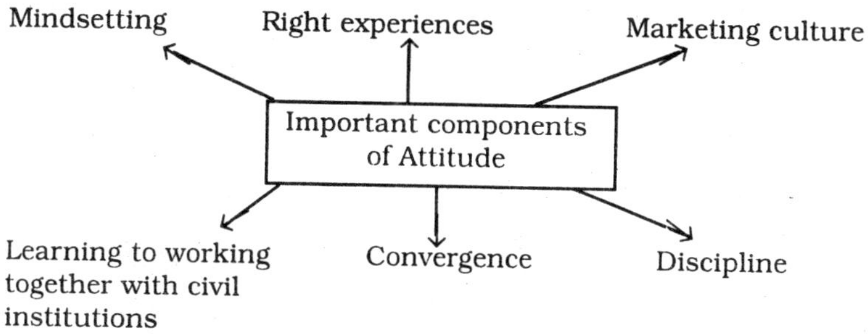
Mindsetting
Right experiences
Marketing culture
Important components of Attitude
Learning to working together with civil institutions
Convergence
Discipline

38

Rural Development and Self Employment

While privatisation or institutionalisation has been accepted as an essential component of any economic activity, it needs to be examined as to what extent the component of rural development can be privatised. Privatisation is not only for any individual's game, it is for the benefit of the group of organisation to derive returns while ensuring internal resource generation.

The strategy for poverty alleviation in India has always laid stress on growth (e.g. investment in agriculture and allied activities) as also re-distribution of income and wealth. The magnitude of poverty in the country, however, is too vast for growth and the legal process of redistribution to make its course in a significant manner within a short span of time. The slow 'trickle down' would be no consolation for the hungry millions. This problem of poverty is not unique to India. More than one-third of the developing world, and more than half of the low income countries, lived in absolute poverty even a decade ago. On present trends, the poor may still be around 60 million in 2000 A.D. More than three-fourth of these poor live in rural areas and about 40 per cent of rural people in all developing countries live in abject poverty (IBRD: 1978).

The vast majority of the rural poor are farmers,

tenants, share croppers, artisans and landless workers. They have limited access to natural resources, modern technology and services; they lack support from institutions which would sustain higher levels of productivity and they are usually found living alongside a relatively prosperous privileged minority.

Rural Development Defined

How does a country define rural development? It is development so that rural poor cease to be so, or mere growth of rural income, with no consideration of equity? The best way to describe the objective of rural development is perhaps "(It) no longer means agricultural development alone. It is also not a social welfare case of pumping money into rural areas to provide for basic human needs. It encompasses a spectrum of activities and human mobilisation to make people stand of their own feet and break away from all the structural disabilities which chain them to the condition in which they may live" (UNCRD 1985, Vol. I, p. 2).

Rural poverty can be removed only by transforming and taking up programme for the majority of the people based on self-supporting, replicable, low cost development models. This area becomes very important because agriculture and allied activities cannot alone help income generation on sustained basis. Hence "in a situation where economic and social inequalities are built in the system, the official agencies have to play a crucial role in protecting the interest of the weak until such a time that inequities are considerably narrowed down" (UNCRD: 1985, p. 26)

A Combination

Granting that a positive intervention by Government

is desirable, a combination of basic needs approach, its variance of IRD, as also industrialisation and growth centre approach would be ideal for combating poverty with the nerve centre of rural development. But in our case growth has not been commensurate with its percolation. Growth has been for those organised, well-to-do who were aware of the developments taking place around them. For the unorganised living in backward and tribal areas, growth has meant more difficulties and exploitations. Here again most exploited has been the women and disabled. For them somebody's growth has meant more work load, more fatigue and more distances to collect the basic necessities. The tribals who were allowed to collect basic necessities of life from the forest are helpless spectators to collection of these minor forest produce by contractors. The growth of law enforcing machinery, both of police and forest department, the utter exploitation by the powerful has given rise to various anomalies. One has to visit those areas to see and feel how growth has made them more poor. Hence growth may be a very powerful economic theory for some economists, but for country like ours it puts heaviest burden on the weakest. The theories of CORE, ICORE, GDP, saving rate are all redundant for those who have to struggle for the basic necessities of life. For them every day is toughest day. Let us not judge their performance from Metropolitan cities or even district headquarters. Let us get away from the cities and you will find the harsh realities perpetuated by the growth models.

The peculiar dichotomy in India is one of poverty amidst plenty. The problem is one of creating purchasing power among the poor, for generations cannot survive on doles nor are doles desirable and feasible for any country.

Components of Rural Development

Over a period of 20 years, all over the Third World countries, a clear picture of components of rural development has emerged. Earlier it was linked up only with agricultural development, then with animal husbandry, fisheries and the like sectors were included. In last 15 years, a very clear picture has emerged which encompassed rural development to include the following:

Agriculture	Rural Development	Rural Industries	Holistic self supporting development
Agriculture, Horticulture, Forestry, Sericulture, Animal Husbandry, Fisheries etc.	Health, Small, savings, Pollution, Environment, Ecology, Drinking Water, Education, Roads, Housing, Tourism, Sanitation, Science and Technology, and many other programmes.	Rural industrialisation means value addition on local raw material like agricultural, forest, horticulture, chemical etc. or demand based industries- thus making marketable products & marketing either in villages and/ or cities or export etc.	This pre-suppose the development of closely related systems and linkages where exploitationless holistically developed systems becomes acceptable and possible. This should be the ultimate aim of not only rural employment generation but in planning for quality of life.

While privatisation or institutionalisation of masses has been accepted as an essential component of any economic activity — today it is important to examine as to what extent the component of rural development can be privatised. We may make here one point very clear that privatisation is not only for any individual's game but it is for the benefit of the group or organisation to derive returns while ensuring internal resource generation. Indirectly it means gradually reducing dependence on State resources of budgetary allocations. While traditionally all components of rural development have been funded only by governmental grants or institutional subsidised loan, they have hardly been conducive to overall self supporting growth of rural development. Ultimate test of rural development will be attraction which holds people to either *stay back or to migrate from cities to rural areas.* This is possible only when life has incentive and facilities commensurate with those available in cities. The following are some of the areas which can be considered for privatisation on internal resources generation basis.

Animal Husbandry

The entire programme may be taken up under private sector and the role of Animal Husbandry Department may be restricted upto supervision and guidance level. The village community particularly progressive farmers, Yadavas, Kurmis, shepherds, educated unemployed and even retired experts can be involved in a large scale in different activities including dairying, poultry farming and sheep rearing.

Privatisation may work in this field because in the last few decades, various infrastructure have been created in the rural areas — all at government cost. This infrastructure has created a big vested interest of government employees who are comparatively well paid and working with minimum accountability. They also have problems of future promotions and further growth in income. They have no incentives if some workers perform better in terms of output. Hence, they have mostly started their private practice and attend to only those clients who pay extra fees. The free services are available only for the people who matter or indirectly those who possess nuisance value. Here is a fit case for maximising internal resource through encouraging them to either share the extra income which they will earn through personalised service or to hand over the entire activity to the above mentioned classes. The biggest opposition will come from hierarchy of headquarters staff and *babus* who have tremendous vested interest in perpetuation of inefficiency and grant related budgetary system. The problem between co-operative and regulatory government departments can also be partly got over by handing over these government departments to co-operatives on the basis of their capacity to generate resources. Gradually they can totally be self supporting. Another point is involvement of traditional goodness of caste structure to fully utilise the infrastructure both of men and material. There are other issues relating to costing of various facilities which are provided by these centres. But all these will be taken up only when basic change in the attitude is accepted with their capacity which must be utilised fully for making them self-sufficient units.

Village and Cottage Industries

Village and Cottage Industries can be grouped into traditional and non-traditional industries. Traditional group of industries can also attend to the problems of traditional communities/classes which have a rich heritage of expertise coming from generation to generation. What is required is their skill upgradation, technological changes and marketing support. Many of the problems of unemployment can be sorted out if we may pay attention to this aspect.

Following is an indicative list (not exhaustive) of industries under which traditional communities still have an edge over others:

Industry		*Traditional communities/classes*
Carpentry and Blacksmithy	:	Lohar, Vishwakarma, Barhai
Pottery	:	Kumhar, Kasgarh, Tribes
Leather	:	Chamar, Chikwa, Qureshi
Edible Oil	:	Teli, Sahu
Beekeeping	:	Nut, Mushar, Kanjar, Saunkh, Aadiwasis
Betel nut making	:	Barai, Chaurasia, Tamoli
Tailoring	:	Darji, Women

In the field of non-traditional industries, any industry which can be started in rural area with a given investment should be allowed to come on liberal incentive. In Japan there is a Centre called Centre for Inducement of Industries to Rural Areas. This acts as catalyst for rural industrialisation. All industries including transport, tourism, housing should be developed through private entrepreneurs and their initiative. For this infrastructural support should be made available liberally.

The role of existing on-going programme and organisation should be clubbed with openness and internal resource generation to make this programme economically viable.

Silk as a Promising Item

There is enough literature available to identify further

linking areas, but the biggest problem is abundance of funds available with organisations like Central Silk Board and State Directors of Sericulture. The private initiative can be inducted in this area by privatising many sick sericulture farms of State Government and Central Silk Board.

Soil Conservation

While Soil Conservation Department has been traditionally known for inefficiency, high cost, corruption and nil recovery of investment, time has come to involve beneficiaries on one hand and unemployed technical graduates on the other hand. These classes can afford tractors and various other mechanical tools at cost to take up entrepreneurial activities relating to soil conservation. They can charge for their service and even take up backward and forward linked programme like plantation of both commercial and non-commercial crops, and horticulture, forest linked activities.

Privatisation of drinking water system envisages on the one hand involvement of local people and traditional storage system and on the other the modern technological inputs available for locating new sources of water. Here also the plethora of Government Departments working in the field of making water supply often indulges in exploitation over spending and mis-utilisation of resources. If we go into the statistical jugglery and cost involved, we find tremendous duplication both in effort and showing results. Villages may be earmarked for local initiative to come forward and take up responsibility for making water available.

Education

Apart from higher and secondary education even primary education in rural areas has already been privatised. The fact is whether we like it or not, majority of teachers in rural areas do not take their job seriously and either compel the children to have tuition or appoint a low paid teacher on their behalf to teach in rural areas. While politics has become the major deviation, many others utilise time, energy for private business including agriculture. The other class is of the many poor women in village who make higher payment of tuition fees for their children. Hence the time has come to take privatisation even in primary school education field.

If we accept rural development as a central theme, encompassing all the activities which have taken up in the rural areas, then we have also to accept that for rural employment as the central theme there are more activities which have to be clearly understood. The following chart makes this concept very clear.

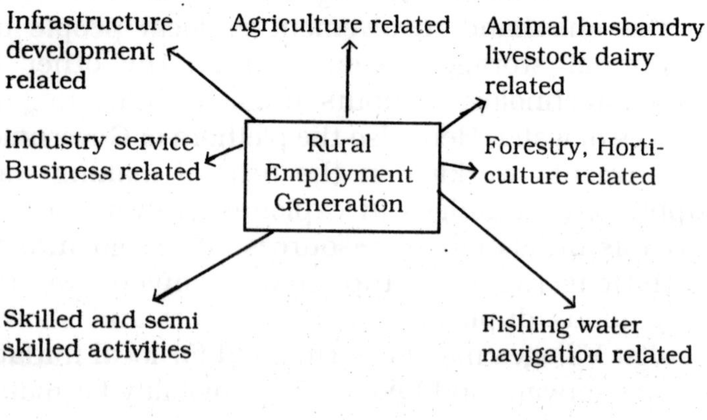

The above are only some of the broad expressions of feeling, based on the analysis of experience and observation. The 20-point programme caters basically for rural development in totality. If the progress achieved in the successful 20-point programme is examined, the urgency for privatisation would emerge clearly. Instead of paying attention to regulatory activities, district administration, policy planners, policy makers and implementors have undoubtedly got involved so much in other activities of the society for initiating steps for internal resource generation which has suffered heavily. How this process will be reversed is also becoming abundantly clear. A beginning has to be made by encouraging private initiatives and sustained costing of each facility. From roads to sanitation, energy conservation and various activities relating to rural development will need proper appreciation in terms of costing and long term holistic impacts.

Action Plan for Employment Generation

1. Employment must be generated in rural areas.
2. Employment must be on self supporting, replicable basis which means it should not be on charity, grant and repaid subsidy basis.
3. Employment may not be through Government or semi-government programme. But ultimately must support this either through institution or individual efforts.
4. Employment must result ultimately not only in giving him sustained source of surplus but also capacity to develop his full potential without exploiting others. This means loan regulation, value system implementation, policies—all must support honest growth with sustenance.
5. Aggressive export will have to be the theme of any future employment generation programme.
6. Experience of all stages and programme will have to be kept in mind whether it is employment

guarantee scheme of Maharashtra of Jawahar Rojgar Yojana or Labour Department programme or KVI sector or organised or unorganised sector, ISBD sector, manufacturing sector, farm or non-farm sector linkages and monitoring system will have to be developed at low cost high impact basis.

7. Future employment will have to be on decentralised basis rather than organised factory urban area basis.

39

Working for Reform (WFR)

We are living in a situation where all efforts in the direction of reform are not succeeding even after 50 years of independence. There are problems. Many feel that the problems are increasing.

It is important to understand the working strategy, tactics, definitions, directions by taking up a systematic, scientific study. The following areas bring out with reference to strength, weaknesses opportunities and threat of India, some points for understanding in the working for reforms. The idea is to examine areawise, productwise, activitywise, certain issues in reforms and how by neglecting the holistic analysis lot of harm has been done. Along with working for reforms some other areas of pertinence also need understanding like places of arbitrariness, thought sharing and essential for success of the programme also need attention. Hence these are only some areas for consideration.

1. Analysis of problem

Levels of Attention (LoA)

1. Expanded role of Bureaucracy
2. Top, middle, lower Bureaucracy
3. Points of interaction
4. Work culture
5. Resource of Resentment
6. GRS impact

7. Recruitment — landing at a place — choice to shift — Jt. Secretary, Engineer, Doctor, File Pushing man.
8. Role of Top — Test of academic excellence — good

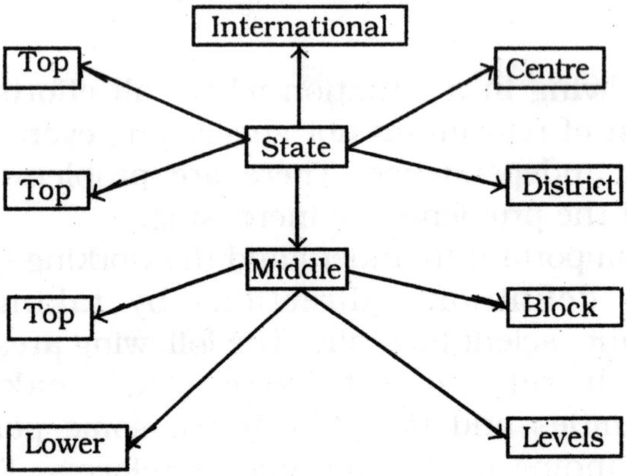

2. Case Study: Areas — We must learn from past experience. Case study method gives us an opportunity to re-examine the lessons. The present need not be the same as future. Hence blending with reference to present condition is must.
3. Reforms necessary — See in totality
4. Glamourisation of Bureaucracy — Power and money — Patwari to power
5. Socialist assumptions — feudal elements got all support 'Government of feudal' and hence 'feudal structure' got reinforced.
6. Replace of Baniya by baboo — "Problem of Mutuality"

Role of civil society vis-a-vis Government Problems analysis from experience vis-a-vis-Right questions not asked Hypocracy and its related problems — Vested interest of keeping 'people ignorant'

7. Lessons of history — How do State become rich
8. Human behaviour patterns
9. Industrial development scenario — Gradual changes
10. Captive market — Institution, market, human societies have always existed well.
11. Interactive and inter linked processes
12. Analysing need of reforms—
    1. Structural reform
    2. Financial reform
    3. Attitudinal reforms
    4. Sensibility of reforms and timings
    5. Reforms for reforms
    6. Sustainability of reforms
       How it comes — spreads — parameters
    7. Post-retirement reforms
       Why not during service?
13. Decolonisation leading to colonisation —
    - Devices to perpetuate exploitation
    - Eco-edu-cultural subjugation
    - Statement by Gandhiji
    - British gave identity (English, Judicial, Administrative, Legislative system)
    - Lost cultural, spiritual moorings speeding away under the ground
14. "Disowning own" — Pride in being citizen of that country.
15. - Why poor self-image?
    - What is own?
    - How to relocate?
    - Where to locate?
    - How to analyse utility and relevance

India

SWOT - Strengths
Directionless
Cultural heritage
No bottom limits
How do they manage

Highly differentiated middle class need to pool individual activities into group as the known and unknown

Underutilised infrastructure

Political consciousness

Political freedom

Press freedom

Realisation of awareness

Diversity

NGOs and their problems and potential

16. Unfed democracy
    Continuation of British style minus impartiality - Bureaucracy politicised -
17. Awareness but helplessness
    Learning from life | Implications
    Learning from Book |
18. Caste system — organic linkages
19. Forum saying — who says rather than what he says?
    Individual saying
20. Individual achievement
21. After mid 70: perversion — Orissa boys to Delhi because of regionalism — Bihar, Orissa maximum boys coming to Delhi and now they are everywhere. This sizeable cumulative achievement will give 'pride' — linkages
    Going America — best of work — same way villages are neglected
22. Perverted materialism —
    We live in past or future

Present is always costly casualty
India a wounded civilisation
India many mutinies now
India a valley of darkness
Indians with symbols — announcements —
Where is coordination
Individualistic hypocratic, selfish visions

23. Hope signals
    How prestige come
    Never reform in isolation — totality is must
    Creation of condition — enablers role
    Intellectual rather than financial corruption
    Individual v/s party corruption
    Maslow's hierarchy — entertainment
    Non-realisable — non-sustainable objectives
24. What is development
    Changing concepts - 1940
    1960
    1980
    1990
    2000
25. Understanding nature of state —
    Role
    Factors affecting it
    IFS v/s IAS organised and unorganised
    Tensions — social, economic, political, criminal—
26. Understanding how 'systems' work?
    - Getting over cynicism
    - Redefining quality of life
    - Broaden vision
    - Learn from lessons
    - Encourage of openness
    - 'Spirit' of enlightenment.

While working for reform there is no short cut. A systematic approach with open mind, transparency and vaiability is called for a sound principle. For management, observations, analysis, decision making, implementation, diversification, codification will require a systematic approach.

The above suggestions may help in understanding some issues with reference to our system. It is here that the places of arbitrariness, thoughtlessness and other essentials for the success of the programme are also considered important.

40

Job Protection *versus* Job Creation

In a recently published data, it has been mentioned that the cost of protecting the job of 1.5 lakh workers in a sick group of industries is Rs. 23,123 per worker and Rs. 13,500 every year by way of losses. If the cost of capitalised at the market rate of interest, the cost is protecting the job for each worker comes to Rs. 1,05,000 per year. It is expected that the cost of creating a job in private sector is about Rs. 40,000 while in the case of rural and tiny industries sector, this is hardly about Rs. 10,000. When the author discussed with Union leaders, political masters, bureaucrats, social workers, etc., the question of bearing the burden of sick units, he was asked the question of alternative options. While accepting the weakness of the system to take unpleasant steps, no prudent management of economy can justify the growth of sick industries without fixing responsibility. The private sector cannot exploit industries for their own gains and once going gets tough, hand over the units to State on the plea of protecting the jobs. It would be worth considering the practical aspects of need to keep industries viable and at the same time ensure responsibility of the managers. The speed with which the sickness in industry specially in large sector is going up calls for fresh thinking not only for saving depositers confidence but also to keep the liability of the State to manageable proportion. One can understand the need to look after the employees of the sick units but running these units at public cost would definitely be not the wise course.

Some measures to run the sick units may be considered. Once some workers are thrown out of the sick units, the remaining units would be more accountable and the units will be forced to ensure leakage of funds do not take place. Job insurance for the employees of sick units may be the second answer. Fixing the responsibility of the entrepreneur and forcing him to pay from their successful units would be the third alternative along with a policy to keep close watch on the siphoning of funds. Keeping in mind the problems of cities, —urbanisation, dwelling places, drinking water and transportation, — the role of village and tiny industries would have to be revised. Their economics of scale would have to be justified by giving them the benefit of social cost. The scientists, research institutions, policy experts and environmentalists would have to give the break up of advantages if industries can be started in rural and tiny sector. Their problems relating to quality, costing, packing, storage, transportation and marketing would be suitably looked after by low-cost appropriate technology and continuous research and extension would be necessary. Here the role of delivery system will have to be examined and low-cost system capable of understanding the philosophy and heart of self-employed rural and tiny entrepreneur would have to be pressed upon. This is a difficult proposition and, hence, successful rural entrepreneurs and voluntary organizations capable of giving umbrella cover would have to be involved. Marketing would be the ultimate deciding factor and if more jobs have to be created, they would have to be in the non-farm sector in rural areas. Special incentives to rural entrepreneurs who through their untiring zeal and innovative organizational capacity can set the change for rural industries must be given all support. The organizations working in the sector would have to be manned by people who have the experience of self-employment. In an interview in U.P. Khadi and Village Industries Board, not even a single candidate was willing to become a self-entrepreneur. They all wanted Government jobs.

While discussing job creation, capacity to accept challenges and take calculated risk would have to be developed in the managers responsible for the implementation of job creation in non-farm and self-employment programmes. Our experience in this sector has been quite innovative but keeping in mind the need to solve the massive problem of unemployment, we have to try again and with better planning and optimism.

41

A Letter

I remember long ago a letter was sent by one of the readers of *The Times of India* addressed to the then Prime Minister of India, Mrs. Indira Gandhi, asking her to act and translate her speeches into realities. In a very prominent coverage, the Editor, *The Times of India* had published that letter with the comment that normally letters of this nature would not have been found place but for the relevance, pertinence and importance of the letter, the Editor wanted it to be printed in full. What was printed in that letter at that time becomes very important now as things have definitely deteriorated for the worst.

Taking inspiration from that letter, one would like to mention few points which can help concretising ideas into plan of action. With every change of time, new aspirations do come up. The problems are reprioritised depending on the pressure, they go up and down. In today's circumstance, of mounting import bill, unemployment, loss of confidence in the system, all-round uncertainty in every field has become the major concern areas. As inflation increases, demand by organised groups to safeguard their present level of living becomes first consideration. In all these, worst sufferers are those unorganised wherever they may be. The inspiration of common man suffers badly and loss of confidence takes over. The euphoria which normally flows with new government has been lost of.

It is nothing but frustration and cynicism. Howsoever, good ideas and pious wish one may extend, they have to be reflected in plan of action. They can be reflected and be visible in price control, disposal of papers and people's perception of them, improvement in the work culture and all-round cleanliness and increase in desire by motivation and self-conviction to do something. In a country where hypocracy and ambitions seem widespread, can mere change of type of leaders bring the perceived improvements? The answer must, with all humility, be positively no. Arun Shuorie has written somewhere that precaution must be taken by the people who work. Work has its own risk. The biggest antipathy is shown by those who are made to work. They may be your own friends and colleagues around. But then how electricity, transport, punctuality, discipline can improve unless the workers, the men behind everything, feel an urge to move. We are in a vicious circle and earlier we accept the responsibility of each one of us, the better it is. Only the change in top civil servant or top political masters cannot *ipso facto* usher in the change and we have to accept it. Unless basic milieu affecting the work culture, the holidays, undergo radical change, how can we expect the system to move. We are all part of a system and nobody can reduce the importance of driver. But each nut and screw need proper oiling, maintenance and replacement wherever necessary. The engine cannot be replaced and so it has to be made more efficient. Nobody can dispute the role of Manager and specially top Manager. But how can we say that others have no role at all. Let us not be diffident. Some action plan has to be thought of to move the system. Hence we may first of all analyse the reasons why the system should be made efficient. Hence we may pray that:

Before hope turns into despair,
Before mass support getting disillusioned
Before your own people start taxing
Before groups and castes start asserting
Before you also become diffident and start
Blaming the people and contemplate punishing

Then further, let us accept the change if possible. Induction of change is a very scientific process and with proper homogeneity, clarity, team work, organisations can be revamped in the same way systems can be made to perform.

Let us realise the SWOT of this country. This is not a country which has been discovered before 3 or 4 centuries. It has strong root and like an old baniyan tree, it can still give life through new roots. This sub-continent had its own culture, system affecting the entire eco-system over a period of time. This may have outlived their pristine glory. But changes based on those realisation will easily be pushable rather than display alien concept. The time test has a very important role to play for the continuity of various practices or malpractices. Hence it is from here that we have to take the next step of learning from our experience in this century. While we are in the last decade, this decade has been of science, mass awakening, education — a century age offers maximum capacity to utilise one's potential. At the same time dichotomies in their absolute sense have been noticed. This is a century when massive developmental in terms of material progress activities have taken place. This is a century when maximum countries got their independence and were replaced by country rulers. The alien concepts, language, systems of medicines, administration, education have continued with all the evils. The countries of origin might have discarded them once they became redundant. But due to attitudinal blockade and the need to continue vested interest those model practices continue. This century also saw before 50s in all walks of life mass leaders of dedication and gradual fall of them and rise of bogie in all walks of life. While the Ganges and other rivers were the most purer form when this century came, probably it is in the worst dirty carrying mission this time. But the worst thing is not the realisation but the thing that all efforts to purify the Ganga and with all its massive financial expenditure have remained total failure. This is what should cause concern. Who have been spending this money? Who have been making the Plan? Who have been monitoring them? Unless these issues are attended to any talk of improvement is bound to fail. Politics have permeated all walks of life, but it was always so. The administrative efficiency and linking up with intensive monitoring system along with proper backward forward linkages and corrective steps at the right time would have definitely helped in better performance. Hypocracy along with capacity to save wrong doers and the collapse of various institutions is another area requiring attention. How this can be revitalised needs very simple analysis and study of those organisations which are turning from despondency to hope. There are success models available. The greatest requirement is that of attitudinal acceptance.

The first step which need attention will be the role of officers, their selection, knowledge, integrity commitment, will to change, experience, skills and capacity. Secondly, duties and responsibilities and performance would be the other areas which should guide in the selection of Advisers. Thirdly, the system of bringing people on contract, nor necessarily to spoil system, may have to be tried. The fourth area is the acceptance and identification of need to change.

If senior managers are reluctant to change, then it is better they are allowed to find some better jobs for themselves. Normally these people have political, financial, judicial and even press facilities available to them. One has to only open the films of totally corrupt ill-repute officials to see and realise how they could manage support from various pillars of democracy. They even normally go scot free. A well meaning conscious officer dare not touch them. It is here we have lot to learn from Mahatma Gandhi. Well meaning people will have to do some time what the ill-meaning always does. One should not be cowed down by character assassination, pamphlets and even *gheraos*. Then this needs an organisation of like minded people who will sustain the will to improve.

Another area requiring attention will be started with the possible and not with impossibilities. While individuals and their organisations must aim higher, they should start with possibles. Paper work in itself is not the end. But a proper planning on paper after discussing with the like-minded people will go a long way to ensure confidence retaining. Encouraging even little good work may widen the circle of well meanings. Enthusiasm, innovation and initiative will go a long way to kill vested interests and encouraging inefficiency. This also means never issue highly expensive issue, pay and other promotion. It is only the organised who make the best use of them and hence it is better more incentives offered through outputs rather than fixed incomes. This also calls for institutional of various activities which Government Departments have proved incapable of performing. We have experience on this decade to help us in understanding relations of world history and the problems which we are facing today have not come to the world for the first time our generation might be facing them. But any historian will be able to give innumerable instances when the world has seen the worst corruption, treachery, nepotism, heartlessness. Today machines and science have made the exploitation in the worst form which is not the failure of machines and science, but that of human beings' greedy nature. But again as any historian will bring out, human beings whether of 10 thousand years old or of today is hounded by some greed selfishness and desire to rule. This probably is one single factor in human being which has not changed. Since the capacity or to resist has increased, the equity based on humanity and *adyatma* will probably need better synthesis. It is here one might agree with the concept of trusteeship or low cost high impact activities or replicable self-supporting, sustainable developmental models. But there is a growing feeling of their relevance. Hence the policy planners, implementors, educators must take today a holistic view of things and the extra specialisation which has been bane of this century will have to be turned into holistic wider perspective use.

While identifying areas for analysing the maximum, one would like to break this activity into Central and State activity. Improvement of Central Government will be reflected in terms of better performance, cost reduction of railways, post and telegraph, income tax, banks and insurance and passport offices, the common man would judge the performance of State in terms of road transport, revenue, police, sales tax, regional transport offices, electricity, tourism, road maintenance and other services and commercial oriented departments. He will also like to watch the recommendation makers not able to get their jobs done. He would like to see the culprit being booked by the police and not allowed to go scot free. The judge may need the help from evidence. The people residing in the area know very well who the culprit is. Satisfying factor that they also know how this conduct has been the development of system which permits the relief to the scoundrels. Hence the regulatory, developmental and commercial activities will have to prove the confidence which were reposed only by the State. This means State cannot function as the monopoly of only the larger occupiers. It is here institutionalisation of various activities out of government sector would open up vistas for employment and need to work will find relevance. Job protection does not mean no work. It also does not mean overloading job doer at public exchequer's cost. The role of organised unions has to be made more positive and result oriented which again means competition among the class.

I and we concepts have great relevance in our administration. The leadership contentment to results will need substitution of I by we. Role of leaders in all fields of activities need reexamination. Utter apathy and carelessness to public property and spending of public funds must be got over and marketing concept with its linkages must come to fore-front. Not only products but concepts, skills, attitudes, personalities, ideas must be marketed properly and it is this radical change which will help in forcing each individual and organisation to rise from inertia to movement.

Another area is the acceptance of some harsh realities in the sense that English has come to stay, parliamentary, administrative, judicial and educational system led by Britishers have to be the basis model for our future. Tinkering with them on massive scale would lead to catastrophic results. Hence answer is to suitably modify them so that they become effective tools of achieving the objectives and for that enough experiences are available today right from lowest level to the highest level for immediate implementation. It is here computerised monitoring system wherein data will come directly from field level would be of great help.

The sacrifice should not go unrewarded. Organised groups have to make sacrifices. While one need not be in haste for results, one must remember that in the supersonic age of today it is quite necessary that we realise the SWOT each individual activity, organisation and follow an agreed path and allowing non-functioning by the vested interested group. How good schemes are made to fail is well-known. The wisdom lies in ensuring preparations to see that schemes do succeed. Here the role of key personnel or change agents has to be perceived. The more problem is with unorganised sector, since change induction and monitoring does create a lot of problems in this area. Hence while vested interest must be identified, the players both at national and local level, their perceptions, goals and their future has to be properly codified. Their liabilities also need codification and decentralised centralisation will, probably, be the important for the change agents to be effective.

The above are only some of the points which come to lay man's mind. They may offer some solution, not all. The wisdom will have to be scaled down to accepted level for induction of systematic change for both long-term and short-term. Their output will have to be constantly monitored and confidence will have to be build up, sustained and allowed to grow both in youth and aged. There are no short cuts. But change induction can definitely be improved up and ensured.

BIBLIOGRAPHY

Acharya, Sarthi, *et al.*, *Employment and Mobility: A Study among workers of Low Income Household in Bombay city*, ARTEP/ILO.

Akolkar, V.V., *Special Psychology*, Asia Publishing House.

Amjad, Rashid, *Human Resource Planning*. The Asian Experience, Asian Regional Team for Employment Promotion for International Labour Organisation.

Ananda, "Men and Institutions", *Bhavan Journal*, Vol. 36, No. 15 to 20, March 15, 1990 to May 31, 1990.

Arun, Ghosh, "From the Ivory Tower", *Economic and Political Weekly*, November 11, 1989.

Azad, Nandini, Empowering Women Workers, Working Women's Forum, Madras.

Bajaj, Rahul, *Management Challenges for the 90s*, Forum of Free Enterprise, Bombay.

Bakshi, S.R., *Gandhi and Ideology Swadeshi.*

— —, *Gandhi and Status of Women*, Griterion Publications.

Baragava, Rajeev, "Continuing Relevance of Socialism" *Economic and Political Weekly*, October 3, 1992.

Bijlani, K., *What does GATT Mean for Indian*, Doaba House, Delhi.

Blackwell, Jonathan M., *et al*, *Environment and Development in Africa*, World Bank.

Bose, Amitava, "Liberalisation Debate: Some Careless Mistakes", *Economic and Political Weekly*, July 31, 1993.

Brown, Judith M., *Gandhi*, Oxford University Press.

Brunton, Paul, *A Search in Secret India*, B.I. Publications Pvt. Limited.

Chakravarti, M., *Gandhian Humanism.*

Chandrashekhar, C.P., "An Asian Perspective on the Human Development Report", 1993.

Chaturvedi, T.N. (ed), *The Indian Journal of Public Administration*, October-December, 1994.

Chengappa, Raj, "How the World sees India", *India Today*, October 15, 1991.

Cohen, G.A., "Amartya Sen's Unequal World", *Economic and Political Weekly*, October 2, 1993.

Dantwala, M.C., *Asian Seminar on Rural Development : The Indian Experience*, Oxford & IBH Publishing Co. Pvt. Ltd., Delhi.

Dantwala, M.L., "Trusteeship-An Alternative Ideology", Indian Association of Social Science Institutions, New Delhi.

Das, Arvind, "Radicalised and Globalised". Hypotheses on Indian Society, *The Times of India*, Bombay, January 1, 1994.

Dasgupta, A. and Sengupta, N.K., *Government and Business*, Vikas Publishing House.

de Soto, Hernando, *The Order Path*, Harper & Row.

De'Silva, Vincent, "Attitudes and Skills", *The Times of India.*

Deshmukh, B.G., "Forum of Free Enterprise", *Can Bureaucracy Meeet the Challenge of Liberalisation?*

Dey, S.K., *Panchayati Raj*, Asia Publishing House.

Dharmadhikari, Dada, *Philosophy of Total Revolution*, Sarva Seva Sangh Prakashan, Varanasi.

Dhawan, Sunil K., "Steps to improve organisational effectiveness", *Financial Express*, Bombay, December 10, 1993.

Drucker, P.F., *The Frontiers of Management*, Truman Talley Books, New York.

Fischer, Louis, *The Life of M.G.*, Harper & Row Publishers, New York.

Frost, M. Gilbert, *Management*, The English Universities Press Ltd. London.

Gaikwad, V.R., *Application of Science and Technology for Integrated Agricultural and Rural Development.*

Ganapathy, R.S. *et al*, *Public Policy and Policy Analysis in India*, Sage Publication, New Delhi.

Ganguli, H.C., *Structure and Processes of Organization*, Asia Publishing House.

Ghosh, S.K., *Social Order in India*, Ashish Publishing House, New Delhi.

— —, *The Indian Mafia*, Ashish Publishing House, New Delhi.

Gooneratne, W., (ed.), *Labour Absorption in Rice Based*

Agriculture, Asian Employment Programme & ARTEP.

Gore, M.S., "Change and Turbulence in Indian Society. *Economic and Political Weekly*, 26 March, 1994.

Goyal, S.K., *et al.*, *Small Scale Sector and Big Business*, February, 1984.

Gupta, Devendra B., *Upgrading of Technology in Rural Industries in India: A Review of Experience*, Asian Regional Team for Employment Promotion and International Labour Organisation.

Gupta, S.P. and A.K. Sarkar, "Fiscal Correction and Human Resource Development Expenditure at Central and State Levels." *Economic and Political Weekly*, 26 March, 1994.

Haeckel, Stephen H. and Richard L. Nolan, "Managing by Wire", *The Economic Times*, Bombay, January 3, 1994.

Hancock, Graham, *Lords of Poverty*, The Atlantic Monthly Press, New York.

Harper, Malcolm, *Empowerment through Enterprise*, Oxford & IBH Publishing Co. Pvt. Ltd.

Islam Rizwanul, "Growth of Rural Industries in Post-Reforms China: Patterns, Determinants and Consequences", Asian Regional Team for Employment Promotion and International Labour Organisation.

— — (ed.), *Rural Industrialisation and Employment in Asia*, ILO-ARTEP.

Jose, A.V., (ed.) *Limited Options. Women Workers in Rural India*, Asian Regional Team for Employment Promotion.

Kamal Taori and Prof. Surendrayati. *Rural Industrialisation Planning for Future*, Vikas Publication.

Kamal Taori, "Changes in the system-Around us", (IAS Training Course, 6-10 January, 1992, Tata Institute of Social Sciences, Bombay).

— —, "Effectiveness of KVIC as an organisation in various terms in servicing", Khadi and Village Industries. Report to ILO ARTE (1994).

— —, *Gram Yojana*.

— —, "Organisers Training for Employment through Rural Industries Cluster." *Jagriti*, December 1, 1991.

— —, "*Rural Development and Privatisation*".

— —, "*Working for Reform (WFR).*

— —, *Beekeeping in India-Role of KVIC.*

— —, *Enterpreneurship in the Decentralised Sector*, Regency Publication, Delhi.

— —, *et al.*, "Project TBCHs—An Alternative for U.P. NTC Mills"

— —, *Five Powers for Today.*

— —, *Institutions of Wardha.*

— —, *Issues of Reawakening*, S.I.R.D.

— —, *Khadi Gramodyog, Journal of Rural Economy*. 6 March, 1992.

— —, *Khadi Gramodyog, Journal of Rural Economy*, 2 November, 1993.

— —, *Mahatma Gandhi and Peaceful World Order.*

— —, *Need to Free Village Industries.*

— —, *Religion Work.*

— —, Social Objective of Economic, Legislation, Generation of Employment and Income, Alleviation of Poverty and Enhancement of Quality of Life.

— —, *Sustainable Development-Real Issues.*

— —, *Unemployment and Poverty Issues Relating to Rural Industry Expansion.*

— —, Unemployment and poverty issues relating to rural industry expansion.

— —, *Green and Grameen—The Erofriendly Handmade Paper Industry*, Regency Publication, Delhi.

— —, *Marketing of Unorganised sector*, Regency Publication, Delhi.

Kamlani, Ajit D., *et al.*, *How to Response to Petroleum Crisis in India*, Forum of Free Enterprises, Bombay.

Karunakaran, K.P., *Gandhi Interpretations*, Gitanjali Publishing house, New Delhi.

Kaul, Inge and Saraswati Menon, "Human Development from Concept to Action, A 10-point Agenda". A report of Human Development Report Office Occasional Papers published by UNDP.

Khan, Azizur Rahman and Eddy Lee, *Poverty in Rural Asia*, Asian Regional Team for Employment Promotion for International Labour Organisation.

— —, *Poverty in Rural Asia*, ARTEP (Bangkok).

Klitgaard, Robert, Adjusting to Reality Beyond "State versus Market" in *Economic Development*, International Center for Economic Growth Publication.

Lawania, V.K., *Socio Economic Development in India.*

Lee, Eddy, *Export-Led Industrialisation and Development*, ILO.

Li, K.T., *Taiwan: A Case Study in Rapid Economic Growth*, Forum of Free Enterprise, Bombay.

Mahalingam, N., On the Road to Prosperity. *Kisan World*, March, 1994.

Maqtada, M. and A. Hildeman, *Labour Markets and Human Resource Planning in Asia*, ARTEP.

Meenakshi, R., "Dynamism—A Sword in the Manager's sheath".

Mehta, Fredie A., *Is There a Middle Way?* Forum of Free Enterprises, Bombay.

Misra, Baidyanath (ed.), *Poverty, Unemployment and Rural Development*, Ashish Publishing House, New Delhi.

Mukhi, M.D., "Power of Communication", *Financial Express*, Bombay, September 14, 1993.

Muqtada, M. and A. Hildeman, *Labour Markets and Human Resource Planning in Asia*, UNDP and ARTEP.

— —, *The Elusive Target*, ARTEP.

Murphy, G. Campbell, *Community Organization Practice*, Houghton Mifflin company, San Francisco

Nanda, B.R., *Gandhiji and His Critics*, Oxford University Press.

Nelson, Robert E., *Country Studies Entrepreneurship and Self-Employment Training*, Asian Development Bank, Philippines.

Nicolo, N.M., *The World Conspiracy*, PO Box 784, Portland 97207.

Nolan, Brian and Vincent Turbat, *Cost Recovery in Public Health Services in Sub-Saharan Africa*, World Bank.

Pal, Jalandhar, *The Moral Philosophy of Gandhi*, Gyan Publishing House, New Delhi.

Panday, Janardan, *Gandhiji And 21 Century*, Concept Publishing Company, New Delhi, 1998.

Patel, Amri and Praful Pandya, "Action Plan for Promoting Village Industries".

Patwardhan, M.S., *Economic Development and Deregulation; The Role of Industry*, Forum of Free Enterprise, Bombay.

Paul, A.P., Nutrition and Productivity in India (A preliminary study), ILO.

Raghavan, V., *The Indian Heritage*. The Indian Institute of World Culture.

Ramachandran, G., *Non-violent Revaluation*, August 1993.

Ramanujam, M.S. *et al.*, *Employment in the Informal Sector*, Agricole Publishing Academy.

Ranina, H.P., "Subsidy As Incentive", *Financial Express*, Bombay, September 13, 1993.

Romijn, Henny B., *Dynamism in the Informal Sector in a Fast Growing Economic: The Case of Bangkok*, Asian Regional Team for Employment Promotion and International Labour Organisation.

Ross, Murray, G., *Community Organization : Theory and Principles*.

Saha, Anamitra, and Madhura Swaminathan, "Agricultural Growth in West Bengal in the 1980s. A disaggregation by Districts and Crops." *Economic and Political Weekly*, March 26, 1994.

Sanderson, D. and Robert A. Polson, *Rural Community Organisation*, John Willy & Sons Inc. London.

Saragi, P.K., "Et Esquire" *The Economic Times*, 24 September, 1993.

Sarma, A.V.K., *Self-Employment Programmes: Retrospect and Prospect*, SEDME, Vol. XVII.

Saroja, S., "*Privatisation or Liberalisation—Strategic Options for LDCs*".

Schumacher, E.F., *A Guide for the Perplexed*, ABACUS

Sedmal, S., *Nature's Ecofriendly Economical Miracle*.

Sen, Amartya, *Public Action to Remedy Hunger*, Forum of Free Enterprise, Bombay.

Sharma, K.N., *Institutions, Networks and Social Change*, Indian Institute of Advanced Study, Simla

Singh, Coomi, A study of women's participation in Programme implemented by Employers' Organisation in South Asia: Promotional Action to facilitate Greater involvement of women in mainstream economic activities and development, ILO.

Singh, P.N., "Career objectives and academic courses, *The Times of India*, Bombay, October 16, 1993.

Srinivasan, M.S., *India's Maladies and Remedies*, First Public Protection Trust, Madras.

Subramaniam, K., "Science and Ethics Decision-Making. Case of Big Dams, *Economic and Political Weekly*, April 2, 1994.

Taylor, Eric, *How to Look Younger*, Sudha Publications Pvt. Ltd.

Ul Haq, Mahbub, *New Imperatives of Human Security*, Rajiv Gandhi Institute for Contemporary Studies.

Valadez, Joseph and Michael Bamberger (ed.), *Monitoring and Evaluating Social Programme in Developing Countries*, World Bank.

Vierira, W., *Pride and Style in Selling, Ideas, Services and Products*, India Book House Pvt. Ltd. Bombay.

Vohra, B.B., *When 'Minor' Become "Major" Some problems of Ground Water Management.*

Wallace, R.K., "Neurophysiology of Enlightenment" Paper presented on 26th International Congress of Physiological Sciences at New Delhi in October 1974.

Walsh, James, Where Have all the Leaders Gone. *Time International*, 12 July, 1993.

Wilde, Chris, *Community Centered Approach to Rural Development Association for Sarva Seva Farms*, Foster Plan International, New Delhi.

Winterburn, Roy, *Case Study Method in Management Development.*

Yugandhar, B.N. and Amita Mukherji, *Reading in Decentraliged Planning*, Concept Publishing Company.

INDEX